A Portrait of Egypt

A PORTRAIT
OF EGYPT

A Journey Through the
World of Militant Islam

M A R Y   A N N E   W E A V E R

Farrar, Straus and Giroux
New York

Farrar, Straus and Giroux
19 Union Square West, New York 10003

Distributed in Canada by Douglas & McIntyre Ltd.
Printed in the United States of America
Designed by Lisa Stokes
First edition, 1999

Some of the material in Chapters 4, 5, 6, and 7 first appeared, in a different form, in
The New Yorker.

Library of Congress Cataloging-in-Publication Data
Weaver, Mary Anne.
    A portrait of Egypt : a journey through the world of militant
Islam / Mary Anne Weaver.
        p.   cm.
    ISBN 0-374-23542-2 (alk. paper)
    1. Islam and politics—Egypt. 2. Egypt—Politics and
government—20th century. I. Title.
BP64.E3W43   1998
297.2'72'0962—dc21   98-26375

For Daddy and Mother
and, as always, for Dean

ACKNOWLEDGMENTS

THIS BOOK IS THE RESULT OF A JOURNEY OF MORE THAN ten years, and in the process I became deeply indebted to many friends, whom I can only begin to acknowledge here. But it could never have been written, or even conceptualized, without the unflagging support of so many Egyptians, some of whom have shared my journey since my student days, and some of whom I have met much more recently. Many are named in these pages, and I thank them now. Any errors in fact or judgment are mine, not theirs. Equally important are the many Egyptians whose voices, although not their identities, are part of this book. Their reluctance to be quoted is both prudent and understandable.

Some of the material in these pages first appeared, in different form, in *The New Yorker* and *The Atlantic Monthly* magazines. To my editors there, John Bennet, Klara Glowczewska, and Jack Beatty: I salute you all.

I would also like to pay special thanks to Ahmad Sattar, my patient and unwavering interpreter, and an aide to Sheikh Omar Abdel-Rahman. He was always there for me, as was his wife, Lisa, when I was in New York, too far from Egypt to understand the nuances of certain events. I also owe a special debt to my friend Virginia Sherry, the associate director of Human Rights Watch for the Middle East. We first met in the office of an Islamist lawyer in Cairo, in 1993, and since then she has shared much of this journey with me.

I had hoped to receive a grant for the writing of this book but, unfortunately, did not. Therefore it would have been impossible to have put it all together without the invaluable help of a number of friends at *The New Yorker* who took charge of the production phase: in particular, Liza Goodwin, Harold Ambler, and Justine Cook. Many thanks. I also owe a special debt to my intrepid fact-checking team at the magazine—Nandi Rodrigo, Anne Stringfield, and John Dorfman—who saved me from acute embarrassment. Any remaining gremlins are mine, not theirs.

My editor at Farrar, Straus and Giroux, John A. Glusman, was more than gracious from beginning to end, remaining of good cheer through lapsed deadlines, and as he attempted to reconstruct and comprehend what surely was the longest sentence ever written by anyone, anywhere. My agent, Sarah Chalfant, and the team at the Wylie Agency were as involved in this project as I was. On more than one occasion, Sarah was even more involved in this endeavor than I was.

This book is dedicated to the memory of my father, Clay N. Weaver, to my mother, Barbara, and to my husband, Dean Brelis, and it is to the three of them that I owe the most. Without their constant commitment to this book, it would never have been finished, or even embarked upon.

Mary Anne Weaver
New York City
September 1998

A PORTRAIT OF EGYPT

I FIRST ARRIVED IN EGYPT MORE THAN TWENTY YEARS
ago, my curiosity my only companion and guide. A cub
reporter for UPI and a stringer for *The Washington
Post*, I was about to enroll at the American University
of Cairo as a graduate student in Arab affairs. I carried
no erudition with me, no Middle Eastern ancestry, no
preconceptions, not even a muse.

It was June 1977, an insufferably hot early night,
when, along with my husband, Dean Brelis, the newly
appointed Middle Eastern bureau chief of *Time* magazine, I struggled out of the cabin of the TWA plane to
be enveloped at once by a blinding Saharan sandstorm
that obscured all outlines and forms. Twinkling lights
in the distance spoke of the Cairo airport terminal beyond. We walked slowly toward it, buffeted by sand
and dust. Against the flat emptiness of the desert, the
terminal buildings, as they came into hazy focus, suggested a gathering of giant dinosaurs. Feet shuffling
around us were the only sounds. Then, from somewhere
in the far distance, I heard the mournful chants of a
mullah summoning the faithful to evening prayers from
atop a mosque. The sun was just beginning to set, and
the sky turned a dusty violet-pink. All around us, the
silent desert stretched endlessly.

There was something about that moment, at once
elusive, then filled with magic, then with wrath, that
would return to haunt me over the next three years. For
it was a moment, I would later learn, that was not unlike Egypt itself: strangely fascinating, enigmatic, and
contradictory, filled with evasion and surprise.

Looking back on those early years, which lasted until the end of 1979, I find it nearly impossible to recall anything—beyond the most tiresome domestic details—that *was* predictable. I began to wonder whether anomalies weren't the rule. I covered food riots, in which the rioters took breaks for lunch and prayers. I dined in elegant splendor in turn-of-the-century mansions with large sprawling lawns, as incongruous as a sudden burst of color in the desert as they lofted from the midst of dismal slums. I found mirth and laughter in the City of the Dead among the hundreds of thousands of Cairenes who lived within the medieval mausoleums and tombs, performing their rites of passage with the same rhythmic precision that a Pharaonic priestess might have done. Even poverty in Egypt has a splendid kind of opulence.

I met bank clerks and civil servants—in one case, even an agronomist—who were cautious, often tedious men: gray, one-dimensional figures, almost smaller than life. Then, one Friday evening, I went to a neighborhood mosque and noticed some of their faces in the crowd. Dressed in the long, flowing robes and the white crocheted prayer caps of Islam, they each, in turn—impassioned and charismatic—addressed the crowd on the revolution that was yet to come.

It was the unexpected paradoxes of Egypt that beguiled me the most.

There were shouts, screams, and pandemonium coexisting, almost as though by design, with the ageless grace of feluccas gliding effortlessly down the Nile, their lateen sails reaching for heaven, as they have done since Cleopatra's time. There were monumental astonishments and monumental confusions, contention, anarchy, and change, as forty million Egyptians grappled with modern times, and with one another, in their ancient land. Their colonial past and the worlds that it embraced were being vanquished as their Pharaonic tombs and monuments were being preserved. In between, there was a disquieting lack of equilibrium where Egypt occupied the Middle Ages and the twentieth century at once: it has research institutions for space rockets and for bullock carts. One of my most abiding images from those early days was of a SAM-7 missile being ferried to a military parade atop a donkey cart.

This book grew out of those early years and my curiosity about all the paradoxical forces that shape Egyptian life. I was determined then, as I was in later years, to get through to the Egyptians and to try to see them as they see themselves—to tell their stories in their own voices and through their own eyes. It also grew out of that distant Friday evening twenty years ago when I first visited my neighborhood mosque and began my own personal journey through the world of militant Islam. It was a strange, always human, sometimes violent, unpredictable road that I traveled for more than ten years from Egypt to Israel, the occupied West Bank and Gaza Strip, and then to Pakistan and Afghanistan. But it was to Egypt that I always returned in an attempt to trap the spirit of place that had haunted me while I was there.

I also kept returning, most intensely over the last five years, in order to understand the dynamics of a movement to which I was introduced during my student days but which had, since then, assumed so many different faces and forms. Was it possible, I wondered, that Egypt—now with over sixty million people, one-third of the Arab world—could lose its struggle against militant Islam? And, in the event that that occurred in the Arab world's most populous and most important state, what would it mean for Sunni Islam in general, and in particular for American foreign policy in the Middle East?

We all had a tendency—journalists, diplomats, government officials, Egyptians, Israelis, Americans alike—to paint the 1970s in Egypt and the Middle East upon a monumental tapestry of bold color and design. There were remembrances of grand battles fought and grand illusions shattered during the 1973 October War. There were massive projects, such as the Aswan High Dam, and the arrival in Egypt of nearly twenty thousand Soviets, who arrived as quickly as they would later disappear. There was extraordinary wealth and undreamed-of profits that accompanied OPEC's rise. And there were the events of 1979: Egypt and Israel signed their peace treaty; the Soviet Union invaded Afghanistan; and the Iranian revolution occurred. Visionaries and showmen pranced across the world's stage; terrorists, nihilists, anarchists, rogues, and mystics came and went, accommodated by the season, as whimsical as the sandstorms blown by the Sahara's wind. President Anwar Sadat presided over Egypt and he consumed our nights and days, for the years we lived in Cairo were the years of the first Arab-Israeli peace.

Six months after our arrival, to the astonishment of many and the sheer incredulity of most, Sadat traveled to Jerusalem on his "sacred mission" to speak directly to the people of Israel about Middle Eastern peace. Never before had an Arab leader visited the Jewish state—it was one of the most improbable moments in modern Arab-Israeli history. One year later, he retreated to Camp David, in the Maryland hills, with President Jimmy Carter and Israeli Prime Minister Menachem Begin for often painful, sometimes furious, secret talks that would ultimately lead to transforming his intentions into reality.

As Sadat flew out of Cairo on Egyptian Air Force One, student union elections were being held at Alexandria University, elections that would prove to be a turning point. Islamist associations swept the boards, taking control of the prestigious faculties of medicine, engineering, pharmacy, and law, where they immediately began to impose their will: forcibly preventing the teaching of Darwin and forbidding the celebration of secular national holidays. (Mother's Day was deemed to be an "atheistical feast.") It was the first time that Egypt's Islamist movement, in its present form, had expressed itself so forcefully in the north. Previously, it appeared to have been confined to the villages and towns of Upper and Middle Egypt, especially in and around the University of Asyut, where for a number of years the Islamists, with growing vigor, had been gaining valued ground as they intensified their activities against the Middle East peace process in general and, in particular, against Sadat's secular regime. Their campaign was being led by a blind cleric, then little known outside Upper Egypt. His name was Sheikh Omar Abdel-Rahman.

But despite the Islamists' cries of protest—protests that began to sweep across the Islamic world—in March 1979, on the White House lawn, the Camp David peace treaty between Egypt and Israel became a reality.

By that time I had completed my graduate studies at the American University of Cairo and returned to journalism full-time. I spent endless hours in those same government offices which I had earlier, and assiduously, shunned, having preferred instead the university's wonderfully rich libraries and its well-manicured lawns, and the coffeehouses favored by students, strung like lanterns along the Nile. It was a rarefied life of academe. During that time my only "political" contacts were, in the vaguest way, with one little-known government official—who was, in fact, Hosni Mubarak, the then little-known Vice President, whose wife, Suzanne, was a classmate of mine—and with a handful of fellow students, who became my friends: wealthy, sophisticated, chic Cairenes who, for reasons that I was then unable to fully comprehend, spent their summers in military training in remote desert camps.

This book is about our shared journey: theirs, Mubarak's, Sheikh Omar's, and mine, and that of the people I met along the way—intellectuals and slum dwellers; Marxists and sheikhs; belly dancers and drummers; mothers whose sons have disappeared, on both sides, in an increasingly vengeful war between Mubarak's security forces and Sheikh Omar's Islamic militants. It is not meant to be an academic or a definitive account. It is simply one woman's journey through the world of militant Islam.

الإخوان المسلمون
وأعدّوا

THE BEGINNING

*T*HE STREETS OF CAIRO ARE LIKE NO OTHER STREETS IN THE world. Every corner, every crevice, every alleyway seems to be inhabited. Crowds of pedestrians and traffic jostle for space, and noise is everywhere—a pervasive din of car horns tooting, street vendors hawking their wares, and muezzins, their voices shrilly amplified, calling the faithful to prayers. I imagine that there was a time when the streets of every great city resounded with hawkers' cries, but now they are to be found only in cities such as this. Here in Cairo, in the centuries-old Khan el-Khalili Bazaar, there are still itinerant sellers of roasted nuts, of discarded metal, of baskets and paraffin, of shawls, of trinkets, and of ornaments. The calls that have vanished from other great cities still echo here. This is one of my most vivid impressions of that first day, a bright June morning in 1977, when I first ventured into Cairo's alleyways. In dark basements, old men were ironing old clothes. In dark alleys, young men dressed in Islamic robes were selling cassettes of sermons delivered at "popular"—as opposed to official government—mosques. Yet it is perhaps a shy little boy from that first day in Cairo whom I remember the most.

I met him by chance in a corner coffeehouse, inside a covered market at the edge of the bazaar. It was, in fact, a rather strange coffeehouse, as I remember it now, with photographs of the Ayatollah Khomeini (who was still in exile near Paris) and PLO chairman Yasir Arafat competing for attention on its greasy walls. The smells were of freshly ground coffee, garlic, and dung; the loudest sound, coming through an open window, was the chant of a mullah—or interpreter of Islamic religious law—amplified by a loudspeaker attached to a nearby mosque. As I got up to leave, the little boy attached himself to me and offered to show me around. He wore a flat woolen cap of a style favored by Afghanistan's Pashtun tribe, and a black-and-white Palestinian kaffiyeh hung from his small shoulders like a shawl: it looked as though he were attempting to blend all the world's militant Islamic movements into one.

As we began walking through the narrow alleys, shambolic with their stalls, shallow recesses, and small dark shops, the colors were of yellow, gray, and ocher—the colors of dust. Cairo's alleys, along with its temples, its mosques and pyramids, continue to awe, as they have awed adventurers from Caesar to Napoleon, and have been immortalized by Flaubert and Melville, Florence Nightingale and Naguib Mahfouz. Various different pasts intruded into our present as we walked: Roman aqueducts, medieval mosques, and the famed al-Fishawi's, a Napoleonic-era coffeehouse. Fragments of old buildings poked out of the rubble, and we peered at them: wooden-latticed balconies, arabesque inscriptions, and gingerbread grilles. Cairo, more than any other capital city I have ever known, is overwhelmingly linked to its past.

It is difficult to be neutral about Cairo; at least, it has always been difficult for me. It is so old, so steeped in history, so diversified that when we lived there I always thought of it as four or five different places at once—a great, infuriating, ramshackle, remarkable city, set superbly on the Nile. For centuries, it had been the citadel of Islamic learning and thought—enlightened, civilized, yet secular and chic. It is also violent, vigorous, and vivid. It assaults you every day.

Egyptians love to talk about Egypt, and they confess that they often find it baffling themselves. It is a place where the Eastern, as well as the Western, mind frequently has to adjust. The paradoxes are palpable, like the poverty, the indifference and squalor, and the grotesque displays of wealth; the impression of a country with a civilization going back five thousand years but inchoate, formless, built insecurely upon the ruins of its past. Yet there is something immutable about it which is difficult to trap—that spirit of place which haunted me while I was there. I often asked Egyptian friends how they would explain that elusive yet seductive appeal which overshadows broken pavements, air filled with dust, poverty as debilitating as Calcutta's. It announced its presence in abundant form; its definition, however, proved far more inscrutable. Various answers have been attached to my question over the years, none particularly edifying, but then, Egypt has always been a place that provoked more questions than answers. That is part of its appeal.

I often wonder if anyone has ever been fully able to comprehend the enigmatic smiles of the Pharaonic sculptures, the colossal effigies of the tombs of Upper Egypt, which have always filled me with a sense of foreboding and unease. Or the spirit that is somehow entrapped in the feluccas, as they glide serenely down the Nile, as flirtatious as a courtesan in Cleopatra's time? How does one explain the magic of those moments that confront you in the desert, always at one's elbow here, as the sun is just beginning to rise or just beginning to set, or in the hundreds of villages and towns that stand in muted form, encased in a patina carried by the desert's wind?

Modern Cairo was built in the early twentieth century to house three million people; by 1977 it was bursting with more than five million exuberant Cairenes. Brightly painted carts of garbage collectors, herds of goats and sheep competed with the city's 250,000 private cars. Even then Cairo—the Islamic world's largest city—was one of the most congested in the Middle East, perhaps in the world. I was told that it was a difficult, if not impossible, place in which to live. There were recurrent power failures; food shortages were sometimes acute. I could often find imported cheese and caviar in the market, but not flour or local soap. It was often impossible to telephone an apartment downstairs. Cairo specializes in a state of total pandemonium.

Yet on the tony island of Zamalek, where we lived, there was a sense of the world that came before—old Edwardian mansions, now mostly in disrepair, and large, untended lawns shaded by cypresses and eucalyptus; broad avenues spoke of being traversed by carriage and horse. Life remained gracious on this side of the Nile. There were hostesses and soirees, afternoon teas, poetry readings. The conversation was often of politics, of Voltaire and Kant. There was the feeling that Egypt was drifting—no one knew where.

I remember those early evenings, when we sat on well-appointed terraces overhanging the Nile, and looked across the water at the slum of Imbaba; we speculated on *its* lifestyle. Its population density was 105,000 people per 2.2 square miles; an average of 3.7 people lived in every room. On our side of the Nile, the level of literacy was among the highest in the world; in Imbaba, the average income was thirty dollars a month. Here, four languages were normally spoken at dinner parties, served by candlelight; rooms were filled with books. There, hidden away in the alleys, far from our understanding or view, sheep, goats, and children drank from open sewers, and, after dark, some neighborhoods yielded to packs of wild dogs. I remember one evening in particular as I watched with friends the flickering lights of a funeral procession passing through Imbaba. The next morning, we read in the newspaper that two children had been eaten alive by rats.

What I had only begun to glimpse during those early years was that the real Egypt was two Egypts—at least two. There was our world in Zamalek and theirs in Imbaba, separated by the serpentine Nile. There was Upper Egypt and the Nile Delta hugging the Mediterranean Sea. There was the present and there was the past, but the future was indefinite and ill defined.

In much of the Middle East, the future has been buried by the past. Today's Egypt is a monument and also a hostage to its ancient past. It gave the world the Pharaonic dynasties, the Gezira Sporting Club, and the Pyramids, those most magnificent of all monuments. But it has a darker side as well, in which not only does its present battle its past but secularists battle Islamists, and Islamists battle Christian Copts; astonishing poverty coalesces uneasily with astonishing wealth. Egyptians—unlike Westerners, who sometimes romanticize their ancient land—are their own fiercest critics, railing against their repression and corruption, their apartheids, their lack of democracy, their prisons filled with forgotten men, and their barriers between their own people as unrelenting as India's system of caste.

Every morning, just after nine o'clock, Miss Pennypecker used to take her morning walk. She began rather slowly and a bit stiffly because of arthritis in her leg, but by the time she reached the Nile her gait had hastened and her dignity had swelled, since she had survived, miraculously, I always thought, the school buses that rattled down the narrow streets and the speeding cars, the hucksters selling fruits and vegetables, exotic essences of perfumes, hot cereals and cheeses and flat *baladi* bread. She clearly relished the high-speed game of defying the oncoming buses and cars and, at the same time, springing free of the morning merchants, dark-eyed women and men dressed in long, flowing galabiyas, who sat cross-legged on the sidewalks or squatted on the curbs. They fused with the traffic on both sides of the road.

Miss Pennypecker, in a sense, was my introduction to Cairo. Before I saw her, I heard her voice on an otherwise uneventful morning shortly after dawn. It was a high-pitched voice, not entirely on key, yet not altogether off, that was rising and falling to "God Save the King" outside our bedroom door. I stumbled out of bed and to the door and there she was, ironing linens in the narrow hallway of Saint Miriam's. It was a small Coptic monastery set in the heart of Zamalek, which rented out four or five rooms—a sober yet tasteful place, with high lofted ceilings, a flagstone courtyard, and windows framed by arabesque tiles. We lived there for a week or so after our arrival while our apartment was being prepared; Miss Pennypecker lived there because she had nowhere else to go.

She had spent fifty-three of her seventy-five years in Egypt, having "come out," as she said, as a missionary on a tramp steamer from England in 1924. She was tall and lanky and always reminded me a bit of a stork. She had sharp, well-chiseled features, a prominent beaklike nose, and spindly legs. Tufts of frizzy gray hair framed her aquiline face, and rimless spectacles balanced precariously on her nose. She was a no-nonsense woman who was governed by a few simple rules: a morning walk to assist her constitution; common sense to confront the unsettling changes in her life; and, above all, an abiding loyalty to the Crown. She believed that the British had behaved abominably when they quit Egypt and left another part of the Empire behind, including her.

But she was neither self-pitying nor self-indulgent about her fate. Miss Pennypecker was nothing if not matter-of-fact.

One morning as she loped alongside the Nile and I struggled behind, I asked her what the high point of her years in Egypt had been.

"The Revolution of 1919," she replied.

"But you weren't yet here."

She then taught me a lesson that I would not forget.

Imagination, she told me, was demanded here.

She went on to say that the "Revolution"—not a stunning revolution, as revolutions go—was, in a way, still going on. For although the original might have been ambivalent and highly flawed —and consisted largely of a series of anti-British demonstrations, which were provoked by Britain's refusal to negotiate Egypt's independence after World War I—it had ushered in the Liberal Age, as it is called. "So, you see," she said with emphatic dismissal, "it *was* a revolution, after all."

After spending nearly ten years coming to and going from Egypt, I would eventually agree. Then, however, I was not at all convinced, and I persisted with Miss Pennypecker, with as much persistence as good manners would permit.

She looked at me with exasperation, as I remember a favored grammar-school teacher once had done, and finally replied, "It was a revolution because, for the first time in two thousand three hundred years, the Egyptians finally said, 'We want to rule ourselves.' "

I was startled but, as always, Miss Pennypecker was right. For 2,284 years, to be precise—from the arrival of Alexander the Great, in 332 B.C., until the abdication of King Farouk, in 1952—Egyptians, in spite of their deep-seated sense of nationhood, had been ruled, without interruption, by foreigners.

"What was it like when the British left?" I asked Miss Pennypecker as we settled into wicker chairs at an elevated tea shop that overhung the Nile. Before responding, she pulled out a set of diaries, which she had squirreled away in the recesses of a large straw hand-bag, a product, like Miss Pennypecker, of an earlier age.

"Ignominious," she answered, and her voice trailed off as she seemed to be studying life on the Nile. Boats skirted across the wa-ter: speedboats; paddleboats; boats filled with produce, straining un-der its weight; boats filled with tourists, some bikini-clad. And, as always, the feluccas were there. Just beyond them, on the other side of the Nile, downtown Cairo continued to define itself: a hazy sky-line of five-star hotels, soaring apartment buildings, squat mustard-colored villas and other forgotten nineteenth-century forms; bridges and flyovers; sulfurous smog, and the towering domes and minarets of a dozen or so mosques.

Miss Pennypecker finally turned back to me and said, "But the departure of the English was long overdue. Such innocents abroad we were: clumsy, noisy, waving the Union Jack. If I were a gambler, I would wager to say that not more than a handful of our colonial officials even spoke Arabic." Miss Pennypecker, needless to say, spoke it flawlessly.

Nostalgia seemed to guide her as she leafed through a diary, now yellowed with age, until she found the entry from June 1956. She had taken the train from Upper Egypt to Port Said to attend the final Trooping of the Colors, when the last of the Empire's eighty thousand troops, who had been guarding the Suez Canal zone, left. She was wearing—as she was wearing now—a wide-brimmed straw hat and a long cotton dress. She also wore the silver cross that al-ways hung from her neck. Inside her picnic hamper, a touch ro-mantic, she said, among the bottles of water, bread, and cheese, she had packed a small Union Jack. The two-day train trip had been arduous: sweltering hot, the second-class compartment was rancid with cigarette smoke, and grit, and squalls of dust. But it would be worth it in the end, so Miss Pennypecker endured, frequently wet-ting a lace handkerchief and holding it to her head. She arrived in Port Said around lunchtime, she recalled, and immediately went in search of the honor guard, the bagpipes and brass bands. She antic-ipated that moment in history when, after seventy-four years, the red, white, and black colors of Egypt would replace the Union Jack.

It was the first time she had felt betrayed by Empire and Crown. For there would be no Trooping of the Colors, no bagpipes or brass bands. The Second Battalion of the Grenadier Guards and the D Squadron of the Life Guards had departed quietly before dawn. No confetti, no streamers, nothing was left behind.

Standing alone on the empty dock, Miss Pennypecker called out, "Where are the English?"

"They left early," an old man who now approached her replied. "They didn't want an Egyptian brass band seeing them off."

Miss Pennypecker took her Union Jack out of her picnic hamper and dropped it into the sea. As she watched it float away, she realized how much she didn't understand.

I wondered how much the British understood, or the Americans now, who had begun to arrive in Cairo in early 1979, scores and scores of them, like an army of ants. They had come to shore up Anwar Sadat and his authoritarian regime, a reward of sorts for Sadat's bold initiative in securing Middle Eastern—or at least an Egyptian-Israeli—peace. By the time of our arrival, Egypt was assuming immense strategic importance to U.S. interests in the Middle East; by the time of our departure, at the end of 1979, it had been transformed into the hub of Washington's Middle Eastern policy. The United States has an enormous stake in its Army-backed regime.

Our looming presence is perhaps best symbolized by the U.S. Embassy, or "Fortress America," as it is referred to derisively by many Cairenes. I've always thought of it as a battleship of vast iron plates, soaring off a central square: a tower surrounded by a block-long wall. Its very architecture seems to express the fear of what might happen next in Egypt; and here, unlike Tehran and Beirut, Washington was determined to be prepared. U.S. Ambassador Hermann Eilts, it was often said, had argued against making our presence too big or too obvious; but little heed was paid to his cautionary words. The embassy continued to grow, and by the time we left Cairo, it was Washington's largest diplomatic mission in the world—and the largest in U.S. history after Vietnam.

But the Americans—apart from a handful of Arabists—always seemed to me to be not unlike Miss Pennypecker's subalterns: part of the chattering classes, rarely venturing outside their fortress walls, tourists, all noise and adolescence; innocents abroad. I puzzled over what they'd read and wondered if Herodotus was on their list. He had written some twenty-five hundred years ago that Egypt was the "gift of the river" Nile. As I traveled around the country, I realized that it still is.

Looked at on a map, Egypt is large: 386,900 square miles, about the size of Spain and France combined. But if you look again, it's a very different image when you distinguish between the desert and the arable land. Viewed from a plane, flying south to north, the real Egypt—the land on which man can live—is small and lotus-shaped. A thin, two-to-eighteen-mile-wide strip of green, the flower's stem, follows the Nile north from Egypt's border with Sudan; then, near Cairo and on to the Mediterranean Sea, comes the Nile Delta, the blossom, as the river flows unhurriedly down to the sea. In that narrow strip of 13,800 square miles, about the size of Taiwan, over sixty million people now live. Ninety-five percent of Egypt's population lives on less than 5 percent of its land. The rest of the country is desert, brutal and unchanged, scarcely touched since Pharaonic times.

It is easy to understand why the Nile has molded Egypt's character as well as its geography. Men needed to organize to cope with its fickle ebbs and floods; thus civilization emerged. They required means of surveying their tiny plots of irrigated land; thus geometry emerged. Protected in their green river valley by the barriers the desert imposed, the ancient Egyptians constructed perdurable institutions, like the Pyramids and the effigies of Upper Egypt—cocoons to their immortality. With scarcely an interruption, Pharaoh succeeded Pharaoh and dynasty followed dynasty for nearly three thousand years before Christ, a continuity of government unmatched by any in the world.

Both history and the river have set Egypt apart.

The Persians broke the Pharaonic line and, for nearly twenty-three hundred years, Egypt was little more than a province of foreign conquerors: Greeks, Romans, Arabs, Mamluks, Turks, and French, and finally the British, until Egypt, forty-six years ago, reclaimed its past. Yet, through the centuries, the Nile flowed on, and the Egyptian determined his life by the rise and fall of its waters, rather than by a foreign master's whims.

The Arabs arrived with Koran and sword in the seventh century, and their conquest of Egypt made the Egyptians Muslim; whether it made them Arab, however, is far more debatable. The early Arab dynasties did impose their language, which replaced the widely spoken Greek and the old Pharaonic tongue; but after three hundred years of Arab rule Egypt fell, first to the Fatimids (who founded Cairo and al-Azhar, the oldest university in the world), then to the Ayyubids, the Mamluks, and the Ottomans—all of them Islamic but none of them Arab. History, like the river, again set Egypt apart.

A Hamitic strain prevails in the blood of its river people; by contrast, the desert Arabs are Semites. An Egyptian's physiognomy is different; his Arabic is different, peppered with odd words, some Pharaonic, others borrowed from European conquerors. His customs are different from those of the desert Arabs: his tombs; his veneration of saints; and his elaborate burials. His poetry is different, as is his literature. And although Arab by definition now, Egyptians—by emotion and inclination—still consider themselves Egyptians first.

I once met a man at a dinner party, a small, sparrowlike man, who told me that he had spent two days inside the Mugamma—the headquarters of Egypt's nightmarish bureaucracy—in order to get a much-needed stamp affixed to a document. He was slightly claustrophobic and hated crowds, he said. Inside the Mugamma, he had been terrified. One of the cardinal rules of Egyptian life is that you do not queue. Rather, you are somehow swept along by the sheer gravity of a crowd. And that is precisely what happened to this tiny, bespectacled man. "No left turns were permitted," he recalled of those two days, during which he was engulfed by "miles of people," he said, shuffling, pushing, and shoving as they moved, in disorderly cadence, from room to room. At each stop, they each secured yet another form. Finally, the sparrowlike man reached the coveted door of the only bureaucrat who possessed the stamp for which he had come in search. He was totally devastated when he was told that the bureaucrat had died two weeks before. No successor had yet been named. And the stamp? It was probably secreted away in a locked drawer, along with the personal papers of the dead man.

I was duly impressed with his apocryphal tale, and not at all prepared for the little man's bemusement or pride when he made his final point: Egypt's bureaucracy was the oldest in the world and had spun red tape for at least three thousand years before the Arabs arrived.

This was Egypt, with all of its curious juxtapositions and charms. The unexpected was always there, just around a corner or down an alleyway, and, even during those early years, it had begun to announce itself in our upper-class neighborhood of Zamalek, where, tucked away from public view, there were a growing number of unofficial, or storefront, mosques. I remarked on them to Miss Pennypecker as we passed one on a morning walk. "They do no harm," she said. "They're merely another way of worship; we all worship the same God."

Over the years I've often wondered whether or not Miss Pennypecker had lived long enough to see the rise of militant Islam. In the late 1970s, it had begun to express itself only in a tentative way—apart from the Iranian revolution, but that was Shi'ite (a minority branch of Islam), and it didn't occur until 1979. Yet it was easy to find it in Egypt in any of the thirty thousand or so unofficial, or "popular," mosques, as they are called, which are often little more than a room in an apartment building, or above a garage, or behind a grocery shop. They are recognizable by the pro-Islamist slogans scrawled defiantly across their walls.

The first one I visited, with a classmate named Nadine, a not at all conventional upper-class Cairene, was in an unpaved alley just off one of Zamalek's fashionable shopping streets, on the ground floor of a dun-colored apartment building, with latticed windows and chocolate doors. Tattered streamers of yellow, red, and green flew above the doors, somehow defiant, yet faded and torn. As we waited for permission to enter the mosque, I watched a group of men transform a small adjacent empty square, spreading out straw mats for Friday evening prayers. The few women in evidence were shrouded in black abayas, covered from head to toe; anonymous forms, they glided in and out of storefront shops. The sounds, from amplified systems or from radios, were those of the Koran. The smells were of open sewers, wet wool, and mud.

A friend of Nadine's appeared and led us into the women's section of the mosque. I covered my head, as I had been instructed to do, and removed my shoes, before entering a damp, bare, and drafty room. In a far corner—which was difficult to see, since in the women's section we were hidden from the main prayer area by an improvised white sheet that fell from the ceiling beams—I was able to glimpse a high-backed wooden chair, which had been elevated slightly on a cluster of cement blocks. A single bare lightbulb was the only source of light except for tiny shafts that filtered through the room's dirty windows and its open doors. It seemed an unlikely setting for a powerful spiritual voice.

There was a stir as the "popular" Sheikh of Zamalek entered the room, wearing traditional Islamic dress—a long white robe and a tiny white crocheted prayer cap. He was a fiery speaker, whose views carried great weight, Nadine said. There was utter silence while he climbed into the high-backed wooden chair. I peeked out from behind the sheeting and was astonished by what I saw. For the "popular" Sheikh of Zamalek was a man whom I recognized at once: a polite and rather boring—or so I had thought—lecturer at the university. An agronomist! Yet when he began to speak, he was transformed. In amazement, I watched his flailing arms and heard his voice begin to rise as he admonished the crowd: "Islam is the solution!" He had begun to shout.

I glanced around our area, hidden behind the sheet, where all the women wore head scarves, or *hijabs;* a few wore veils. Some of them held their children by the hand. No one in our area appeared to be poor. The women stood and listened to the sheikh in silence, in crisply aligned rows.

A muezzin began chanting, his melancholy voice piped by a loudspeaker to the overflow crowd outside. The men in the prayer room began to chant, *"Allahu akbar!"*—"God is most great!" Behind the sheeting, the women did the same.

Seemingly on cue, the "popular" Sheikh of Zamalek became vehement, and his voice rose to an even higher pitch.

"Dictators will go to hell!" he shouted. "Power goes to their heads!" He then spoke elliptically of chaos and betrayal. He never mentioned President Sadat by name, but everyone knew whom he meant.

I was struck by the realization, as I listened to the powerful voice of the sheikh—whom I had known before, albeit somewhat vaguely, as a timid professor dressed in button-down shirts and outrageously outdated ties—that so much of Egypt wore a mask, including Zamalek itself. And the deeper into its alleys I went, the more they became an expression of Islam.

Nadine was the one who taught me that. We met at the American University of Cairo (or AUC) in 1978. She was a graduate student in sociology, I in Arab affairs, and it was Nadine who introduced me to the tumultuous world of campus politics. We were mostly removed from it at AUC, which was a rarefied kind of place, whose students were largely drawn from Egypt's upper class. Yet even there I was becoming increasingly conspicuous in my jeans and Western dress.

"How *can* you not see what's happening?" Nadine used to rail, and her eyes would flash. She was one of the most spirited women that I have ever met. Tall and elegant, with large, luminous, kohl-rimmed dark eyes and a swanlike neck, she had once worn blue jeans, studied American literature, and painted her nails. But on a late October morning in 1978, she had stood, along with three other young women, before the faculty of Cairo University's medical school, hooded and shrouded, in a faceless, Iranian-style black chador. She had joined the others, all medical students, including a sister of hers, as a member of a national university council, which had been elected that spring, in elections in which the Islamists had captured more than 60 percent of the seats. She invited me to come along that morning, and I did. Standing outside the classroom, I watched a group of professors pass. As they glimpsed the young women through the open door, they were clearly aghast. Melodic in their chants praising Allah, graceful in their flowing robes, the women were nevertheless didactic in their demands: they refused to dissect male corpses; to be integrated academically with men; and they demanded that a dual curriculum be established, as well as university centers for prayer.

Nadine was then in her early twenties, a daughter of Zamalek's immensely wealthy upper class. And if it was a paradox for the daughter of a patrician family to be preaching Islamist politics, then she failed to grasp it. It was just one of the anomalies of her life. She was an Eastern fatalist by birth, a Western liberal by education, a feminist who donned Islamic robes and maintained an abiding fascination with designer clothes.

I asked her later that afternoon, while we lolled on the grass of AUC—where, in deference to university regulations, she had abandoned her austere chador and was dressed instead in a long white robe—whether her recently acquired Islamic attire was a sign of protest, as it was increasingly becoming for young coeds in Iran. "It's more a matter of identity than of protest," she replied. "If you dress and behave Western, then you are compelled to *be* Western. Islam gives you yourself."

I glanced around the campus, and even here, it seemed to me, a growing number of women had begun to cover their heads in the Islamic fashion, and a growing number of men now sported full Islamic beards.

Students came and went as we continued to chat, and, in retrospect, our conversations seem to have always been the same: eyewitness accounts of clashes in Upper Egypt between Islamists and Christian Copts; vicious underground fights, often with knives flashing, both in Upper Egypt and at northern universities. Figures were not being officially released, but scores had been wounded. People had died. Egypt's 360-member rubber-stamp parliament had begun to debate a return to Shariah, or Islamic law; a rampant consumerism, bred in large part by the peace policies of President Sadat, had drawn poignant distinction between Cairo's haves and have-nots. Certainly Egypt was becoming increasingly tied to Washington as a result of the Camp David Accords. It stood dangerously isolated in the Arab world.

That summer, much to the distress of her mother, and to the astonishment of some of her friends, Nadine left Cairo for military training, in a remote Islamist desert camp. She gave me a hug when we said our goodbyes. Then, hidden behind her enveloping black chador, she boarded the train for Upper Egypt, and was gone.

As I left the train station and walked through Cairo's fashionable streets with their handsomely stocked shops, I first sensed that growing tension between Western values and the currents of Islam.

The Islamic revival movement at Egypt's thirteen universities had clearly baffled university authorities. Hundreds of young women less committed than Nadine were "taking the veil," as it is called; others were demanding classes separate from men. Still others were covering themselves in robes from head to foot—to the dismay of most of their mothers, who had fought for the freedom to unveil their faces and to wear short skirts. What was perhaps even more unsettling, however, was the fact that the Islamists had begun to infiltrate university faculties and had set up clandestine campus cells. They were demanding the abrogation of all Western influence in the schools and had begun publishing a large number of newspapers and tracts. Their funding came largely from the conservative, oil-rich kingdoms and sheikhdoms of the Persian Gulf—most significantly from Saudi Arabia, with the encouragement of Anwar Sadat.

With strongholds at Alexandria University, the University of Asyut, Cairo University's medical and scientific schools, and the Technical Military Academy, the Islamists had backgrounds as eclectic as their accents were diverse. Some were of peasant stock, from the villages of Upper Egypt; others were the sons and daughters of the merchant or the civil-servant class; still others, like Nadine, were the children of Egypt's most privileged class. Their common denominator was discontent. They bonded on their strict adherence to Islam and on their intellect. They were generally high achievers scholastically, and they were largely drawn from Egypt's most demanding university faculties. They defied stereotyping, I quickly learned, and could not be called reactionary, as some were very progressive in thought; others wanted a return to a seventh-century caliphate, and to Shariah law; still others propagated violence, as a means of "expurgating sin." They were a fusion of all Egyptian trends.

Nadine had told me (and I later confirmed) that the activists among them probably numbered no more than twenty thousand, but that they could draw on the support of a million or so sympathizers, or perhaps more. Western diplomats worried that, after the military, they were Egypt's best-organized social force.

One morning shortly after Nadine had left, I went in search of Dr. Sa'ad el-Din Ibrahim, a professor of sociology at AUC who had studied the Islamist movement more than many at the time, and found him at his desk, which was covered with piles of paper and with half-finished cups of tea. He told me that the reappearance of the movement was predictable in the context of the history of the Arab world—a history in which revival movements have appeared in the aftermath of what was perceived to be a great failure of existing regimes. The present cycle began in 1974 and 1975, he said, when disillusionment replaced the early euphoria of Arab victories in the 1973 October War. "Students looked with alarm at the apparent rapprochement with Israel, and generally with the West. They disdained the emphasis on a consumer society, and the corruption that it was seen to breed. There was also the socioeconomic dislocation of society," he went on, "the frustrations of the lower and middle class. In the January 1977 riots, we saw a massive symbol of floating discontent."

I remember what it had been like then.

For forty-eight hours, hundreds of thousands of outraged workers and students, slum dwellers, and government bureaucrats poured into Cairo's streets, rioted, burned, and looted when food subsidies—which benefit all Egyptians—were cut. Thousands more cheered them on from rooftops. The shadow of revolution seemed to loom over Egypt during those two days. And what the mobs attacked was as revealing as what they did not. They tried to burn government buildings (and sometimes succeeded); they gutted buses and trams and ripped up railroad tracks, a protest against the appalling system of public transport. But they directed most of their anger toward symbols of luxury and wealth. (They did not attack foreigners or embassies, nor did they paint anti-American slogans, although that was considered quite fashionable at the time.)

On the second morning of the riots, I watched a group of mullahs surging through the streets—bearded men, in large turbans, brandishing Korans. They were visible only sporadically, engulfed in the swelling crowd. Yet later that afternoon, as I looked down at the demonstrators from a balcony on Pyramid Road—a strip of sometimes stylish, often seedy, nightclubs and bars—they seemed a sea of flowing white prayer robes and caps as they flailed bamboo clubs, iron pipes, and machetes in the air. The Venus Club, where visiting Saudi Arabian businessmen drank twenty-five-dollar bottles of whiskey, was sacked and burned. Mercedeses and other imported cars were gleefully smashed. Chants of "Sadat, O Sadat, you dress in the latest fashion, while we sleep twelve to a room" reverberated through the crowd and were picked up by its supporters on the rooftops.

Stunned by the depth of the rioters' passion—and by the 120 buses and hundreds of buildings that had been burned in Cairo alone—the government reversed its earlier decree that would have increased the cost of such basic necessities as bread, rice, and bottled gas by between 12 and 45 percent. The increases had shown a barely credible governmental insensitivity to a population where a worker's monthly pay was three times less than a bottle of imported French wine.

By the evening of the second day a reluctant Army was patrolling Cairo's streets. Camouflaged army trucks, their occupants in battle dress, guarded its bridges. Along the Nile, steel-helmeted troops manned barricades, which had been assembled hastily, mile after mile. Flames licked at overturned buses and cars, and in central Tahrir Square the loudest sound was the pop-pop-pop of exploding tear gas. The weight of the military had driven the mobs back to their dark streets. At least 160 people had died. Over a thousand were wounded; another two thousand were arrested, as a consequence of what the government announced, with an astonishing lack of reticence, was a "major Communist plot." Few Cairenes—including some within the government—took the allegations seriously. Yet even though the riots were generally considered to be a spontaneous outburst of rage, there certainly was some organization in some parts of town, where men could be seen directing the crowds and telling them which way to march.

I thought of all the flowing white prayer robes and caps I had seen on Pyramid Road. And I remembered what someone had told me earlier. Islam is the world's only major faith that can truly be defined as political.

Islam's militant revivalist movement was born in Egypt seventy years ago, when a schoolteacher named Hassan al-Banna founded the Muslim Brotherhood—or al-Ikhwan al-Muslimun—to protest Britain's colonial rule over Egypt following the First World War. A bit of a mystic and an adherent of the Sufi'i school of Islam, al-Banna was inspired in part by Rashid Rida, an Islamic modernist and reformer of the late nineteenth and early twentieth centuries, and his movement quickly spread—from fewer than a hundred adherents in 1929 to more than half a million in 1949. It was Islam's Reformation, in a sense.

Spiritually, it was grounded on the Five Pillars of Islam, the world's youngest and—with over a billion adherents—second-largest universal faith. Seven words in Arabic perhaps best summarize its central belief: "There is no god but God, and Muhammad is the Messenger of God." Five times a day, across the Muslim world, this Shahadah (or profession of faith) is recited by the devout as muezzins summon them to worship God. To give charitably is another spiritual duty of Islam, as is fasting during the daylight hours of the lunar month of Ramadan. The fifth, and last, pillar is to make the hajj, or pilgrimage to Mecca, the holiest city of Islam, at least once, provided that you are financially and physically able to do so.

Politically, Hassan al-Banna's doctrine provoked considerably more debate. It recognized no separation between church and state, and, as a consequence, it rejected secularism, as well as Westernization, and any colonial influences perceived to exacerbate economic and social ills. Calling for the abolition of Egypt's Napoleonic legal code, it was based instead on a return to the principles of Shariah law—a code of honor, a system of jurisprudence, and an all-encompassing way of life. Yet in any discussion of Shariah law one has to ask: Which school of jurisprudence? Which body of law? For, over the centuries, the Muslim world has been consumed by an intense and often angry debate on the use and abuse of Islamic law.

The Koran itself does not provide a legal code per se, and includes only eighty verses that can be thought of as "laws." Thus four major schools of Islamic thought—the Hanafite, the Malikite, the Shafi'ite, and the Hanbalite—had evolved by the ninth century. Their various interpretations of the Koran, and of Islam's other holy texts—the Hadith and the Sunnah, the sayings and the deeds of the Prophet Muhammad—have produced both rationalist theologians and rigid ideologues.

Over the years, I've asked several Islamic scholars, "Is polygamy sanctioned by Islam? Should the hand of a thief be severed?" I have received as many responses as there are schools of Islamic thought. Islam does allow a man to take four wives but, according to the Koran, he must treat them equally. When I asked one recently divorced, and formerly polygamous, sheikh if this was possible, he responded: "Absolutely not!"

As to the harsh punishment of having a hand cut off, according to all four schools of classical Islamic thought, a thief should be forgiven if he has stolen out of need; amputation for theft, according to many modern Islamic thinkers, is justified only in a totally egalitarian society.

Like Christianity and Judaism, Islam has continued to evolve over the centuries.

When I visited the offices of the Muslim Brotherhood in the early months of 1998, Mamoun al-Hudaibi, the movement's deputy leader, told me that today's harsh practices of, for example, Afghanistan's ruling Taliban—which have forced women out of the workplace, closed girls' schools, banned music and television, and stoned adulterers to death—were an egregious distortion of Islam.

They were as much anathema to him as they would have been, I'm sure, to Hassan al-Banna and the other founders of the Muslim Brotherhood.

For it was not only al-Banna's personal magnetism and his charisma that commanded fierce loyalty, it was his doctrine of reclaiming Islam's manifest destiny: an empire, founded in the seventh century, that reached from Spain to Indonesia and whose accomplishments—in philosophical thought, linguistics, algebra, early medicine, and chemistry—would shine for a thousand years. The Muslim Brotherhood's doctrine aimed at recapturing this.

During the Second World War, the movement turned militant. A secret organization within the Brotherhood called the Special Order was formed. Its recruits swore allegiance to Islam on a revolver and a Koran.

Among the many drawn to the Brotherhood during these early years were Gamal Abdel Nasser and Anwar Sadat, obscure young officers at the time, who met with members of underground Brotherhood cells to plan attacks against British installations and troops. When Hassan al-Banna was imprisoned by the British during the Second World War for making contact with agents of Nazi Germany, another "radical" also caught up in the roundup was Anwar Sadat.

When the war ended, the Brotherhood stepped up its campaign, attacking British billets and blowing up cinemas showing Western films. When the first Arab-Israeli war occurred in Palestine in 1948, it—unlike most Arab governments—sent a company of well-armed commandos to fight on the Palestinian side. By the following year, however, as the Brotherhood's strength and influence continued to grow, the monarchy in Cairo grew alarmed. King Farouk and his government cracked down. Hassan al-Banna was shot to death in the streets of Cairo, and thousands of his followers were rounded up and deported to the Western Desert, where they languished in harsh concentration camps.

But by 1952 the Brothers were back on the streets, aiding and abetting the anti-government efforts of the Free Officers group, which was led by a colonel whom the Brotherhood knew well:

Gamal Abdel Nasser, who was assisted by Captain Anwar Sadat. When the Free Officers seized power in July 1952—forcing Britain's final departure and the abdication of King Farouk—a honeymoon ensued between the new Army-backed government and the Muslim Brotherhood. But the Brotherhood continued to agitate for an Islamic government, and the honeymoon was short-lived. In 1954, having been held responsible for an attempt on Nasser's life, the Brotherhood was suppressed: its leaders were executed or tortured, the organization was banned, and it went underground. Over four thousand of its members were returned to the concentration camps —a pattern that would be repeated in 1965 and 1966, with more executions and more arrests, when the Brotherhood was accused of conspiracy in an ill-defined plot against Nasser's regime. After Nasser's death in September 1970, however, the Brotherhood received yet another new lease on life.

On coming to power, Anwar Sadat almost immediately began to reverse many of Nasser's policies. Nasserites and Communists were officially branded as enemies of the regime; thousands of Brothers still in prison were hastily released. Since Sadat had no power base of his own other than the Army, the decision was made to cultivate the political right—particularly the religious right. Thus, in 1971, with Sadat's encouragement, King Faisal of Saudi Arabia —in what amounted to a unique treaty between a state and a foreign religious institution—offered the rector of al-Azhar (which is considered to be the Oxford of Islamic learning and thought) $100 million for a campaign against Communism and atheism, and for the triumph of Islam. Among the campaign's most zealous supporters were members of the Muslim Brotherhood.

Yet on university campuses, after Nasser's death, another organization began to dominate the Islamic trend—the Gama'a al-Islamiya, or Islamic Group, generally known as Gama'a. Its spiritual mentor was Sheikh Omar Abdel-Rahman. With the encouragement of Sadat, who was far more fearful of leftists than of Islamists, other groups—increasingly militant—expanded or sprang up. Among these was al-Jihad, whose military wing later organized the assassination of Sadat.

Huge sums of money, from both home and abroad, transformed the Islamist groups, whose influence began to spread outside the universities, into the "popular" neighborhoods, as the inner city and the slum areas are called, and into some of Cairo's largest and most influential mosques. According to the Egyptian writer Mohamed Hassanein Heikal, not only was money being funneled to the Islamists by the state but Sadat encouraged contributions from some of his closest friends, including a millionaire contractor named Osman Ahmed Osman, who supported several of the groups, providing them with uniforms, money, and arms.

Today's militant Islamic movement consists of essentially these same groups (now some forty-four in all), which came of age on university campuses during the 1970s—encouraged, armed, and trained by Anwar Sadat himself.

الإخوان المسلمون
وأعدّوا

PEACE

LATE ONE EVENING IN 1978, HASAN TUHAMY STOOD ALONE in the corridor of the Abdin presidential palace, saluting the darkened halls. When interrupted by a group of passing Egyptian officials and asked what he had seen, the Deputy Prime Minister whispered that a ghost was passing—that of the legendary twelfth-century military hero Salah al-Din. Mystic and clairvoyant (or so it was believed) and the interpreter of presidential dreams, Tuhamy was the symbol and, some concerned Egyptians believed, the Rasputin-like source of an often inexplicable side of President Mohammed Anwar al-Sadat.

Sadat was a loner who was deeply religious, unpredictable, and withdrawn. He predicated his years in power on showing an extraordinary flair for finding the right moment and seizing the initiative. He so changed events and circumstances that he was largely exonerated from the past. His advisers applauded his purpose and vision; his critics charged that he was a showman, so dazzled by immediate success that he deemed it unnecessary to consider the consequences, paying little heed to what came next. He was undoubtedly a man of exceptional courage who had taken immeasurable risks. But while he gambled heavily in the international arena, Sadat evinced little interest in Egypt's domestic affairs.

As he was catapulted onto the international stage—at the age of fifty-four—as the Arab who showed that Israel was not invincible during the 1973 October War, the rate of population growth in Egypt climbed to 2½ percent. Four years later, as he journeyed to the Israeli Knesset in November 1977 on his "sacred mission" for peace, he carried memories of the food riots in January of that year, the greatest challenge to his presidency. And as he signed the Egyptian-Israeli peace treaty in March 1979 on the White House lawn, the Islamist groups in Egypt, which he had largely spawned, seemed to be veering dangerously beyond his control.

He should not have been surprised. All the signs were there, as early as April 1974.

The day was not a particularly eventful one, Egyptians now recall, until midafternoon, when a young Palestinian doctor of philosophy named Saleh Sarrieh led a small group of men—mostly students who were members of the Islamic Liberation Organization's military wing, Muhammad's Youth—in an abortive mutiny at the Technical Military Academy, which was a stronghold of the Islamists even then. There Sarrieh collected arms and volunteers and proceeded to march to the headquarters of the governing Arab Socialist Union with the intent of assassinating its leadership, including Sadat. It was a hopeless venture, quickly crushed. But eleven people died. Saleh Sarrieh was later hanged. Yet Sadat appeared to regard the affair as little more than an isolated incident—as he would regard a series of attacks later that year against Islamic shrines and mosques by a strange extremist Muslim sect whose white-robed, bearded, desert-dwelling teenagers and young men believed in retreat from the evils of the modern world and repentance for sin. They had vowed to redress Egypt's "godless" society. They called themselves the Society for Repentance and Retreat—or the Gama'a al-Takfir wal-Hijra—and they seemed to blend the terrorist tactics of West Germany's Baader-Meinhof gang with something akin to the actions of Charles Manson and his acolytes.

Three years later, in July 1977, while Sadat was planning his pilgrimage to Jerusalem, al-Takfir kidnapped and killed Sheikh Mohammed Hussein Dhahabi, a distinguished Islamic scholar and Egypt's former Minister of Religious Endowments. Dhahabi was tortured, strangled, and shot through the eye for alleged apostasy.

The real reason for his execution, however, was that Sadat refused to pay a $300,000 ransom or to release sixty al-Takfir members from jail. Al-Takfir's self-styled Commander of the Faithful, a wild-eyed thirty-four-year-old agronomist named Shukri Ahmed Mustafa, and four of his lieutenants were hanged. But once again Sadat and his advisers preferred to regard the affair as just another isolated incident.

As I wandered around Cairo on the day that Sadat's peace treaty with Israel was signed—talking to old men in favored colonial-era coffeehouses in the Khan el-Khalili Bazaar; watching young men, largely civil servants, labor furiously to plant shrubs and flowers (even trees) along the route from the airport that Sadat's motorcade would pass; meeting friends at Cairo University, where thousands of students sat on the grass and glowered out at the street, patrolled by truckloads of uniformed police—I found few discernible signs of jubilation at what was happening in Washington, half a world away.

Yet, two days later, when Sadat returned, a crowd estimated by the Egyptian police to number two million lined the route of his motorcade from the airport to one of his official residences, fifteen miles away. All over Cairo there were white doves of peace: doves on billboards; doves on floats; stuffed doves and live doves, soaring and dipping and dropping their droppings over the crowds. Pictures of Sadat—in full face and in profile; smiling and brooding; as a young man and as an older one; as a stern leader of the revolution, in full military dress; as the benevolent father of the nation, in a dark business suit; as a son of the soil of the Nile Delta, in an open-necked safari suit—were all over town. Various bands in the procession and along the route played a new national anthem extolling peace, written by a well-known composer, Mohammed Abdel-Wahab, on whom the President had conferred the rank of honorary general somewhat inexplicably.

But for all of the thousands—or perhaps a million—references to peace we saw as we followed the motorcade, there was one conspicuous absence. Nowhere did I see a reference to peace with whom. There was not one mention of Israel.

Yet in the months and the years ahead, Israel and the war effort could no longer be blamed for Egypt's food shortages, or its hundreds of thousands of unemployed; martial law could no longer explain away political restrictions and the lack of democracy.

Looking back on that late March afternoon, I remember one billboard in particular along Sadat's route. It stood across from the Sheraton Hotel, only a few hundred yards from Sadat's favored official residence, and I imagine that he could have seen it from his drawing room. In bold green lettering the billboard asked: "Why Peace?" And then the reply: "Well, What Has War Done for Us?" I wondered then if Sadat would continue to gamble. He did.

In hindsight, his approach to domestic issues seems fairly simplistic: any voice not firmly behind him was judged to be a foe. Any potential challenge, any potential threat—except for the Islamists—was neutralized before it developed, as Sadat consolidated his own position in advance. For despite his early opening to democracy—his dismantling of Nasser's police apparatus and his closing of the concentration camps; his permitting Egyptians to travel; and his giving limited freedom to political parties and the press—Sadat, having doled out certain freedoms, began reining them in.

Four times during the years we lived in Cairo, he reverted to "popular referendums" to override his own Constitution and laws; each time he received a barely credible mandate of support of more than 98 percent. His referendums sanctioned life imprisonment for anyone organizing demonstrations or strikes. They precluded any public discussion of the peace treaty with Israel, and they barred nearly the entire political spectrum from parliamentary life.

By the time I finished my studies, in early 1979, Egypt's officially sanctioned political parties bore little resemblance to the country's political trends. Some fifty underground groups had begun operating, from the extreme right to the extreme left, and a growing number of Islamist students spent their summer vacations in military training at remote desert camps.

Yet Sadat remained seemingly unconcerned by the potential Islamist threat to his regime, and during those years he proved to be a quintessential survivalist.

Sadat is a difficult man to describe. Each time I saw him he looked markedly different, depending upon whom he was seeing, where he was, and the mood in which he had dressed that day. One of his ministers told me, "He's a chameleon. He can be anything." Twice imprisoned by the British—first for his flirtation with Nazi agents during the Second World War, then for his role in the assassination of one of King Farouk's ministers—Sadat had developed a lifelong antipathy for colonial rule; yet he nevertheless appeared at times to be fashioning himself, if not on the Pharaohs, on Britain's royal vassal King Farouk. Although austere in his personal habits— he ate only one meal a day and fasted assiduously during religious holidays—he relished his opulent life, helicoptering between one or another of King Farouk's ten palaces, many of which he had reopened for the first time since 1952, when the Free Officers deposed Farouk. The palaces, the cabinet meetings, and Sadat's summer homes all embraced the atmosphere of a royal court. And, like the King, Sadat deified himself on billboards and marquees, and he thrived on his exposure abroad. He truly seemed to believe that he was the only man who could rule Egypt, and he amassed nearly total power in his hands.

Rising from the ranks of the Army out of poverty, Sadat had entered the prestigious Military Academy in 1936, when its doors were opened to all Egyptians for the first time. He was one of only fifty-two commoners to be admitted to the school; another was Gamal Abdel Nasser, whom Sadat later served as a rather lackluster aide. Nasser had considered him a pliable, self-effacing choice when he elevated him to Vice President in 1969—a pattern that Sadat would repeat in 1975 when he chose the rather lackluster Hosni Mubarak, his pliable and self-effacing (or so he thought) commander of the Egyptian Air Force to be his Vice President. But, unlike Nasser, who relegated scant power to Sadat, Sadat would mold Mubarak in his own image over the years, for the stocky, taciturn Air Force man—who, at forty-seven, was a decade younger than Sadat —fulfilled two of Sadat's chief hopes: to see his policies continued and, one day, to bequeath power to a member of the "October Generation," the men in uniform who helped regain Egypt's self-esteem by their initial victories in the 1973 October War.

For years Mubarak sat in obscurity at Sadat's side, quietly taking notes. Henry Kissinger once assumed he was a junior aide, only to learn later that he was Egypt's Vice President.

As the years went on, Sadat became increasingly isolated and bizarre. He tolerated corruption among his closest advisers and friends, and he surrounded himself largely with sycophants. A Western ambassador told me one morning, when I called on him, that Sadat was creating "a highly dangerous state of mind." He then went on to explain that at a ministerial dinner he had attended a few nights before, some of Sadat's closest advisers spent much of the night openly discussing the best black-market rate. The ambassador was startled, and appalled. He warned me, "This is a serious element of instability, which will come back to haunt them one day."

I thought of what he'd said as I spent a morning sifting through old files. One that I found was a 1976 study by the Egyptian Ministry of Planning, according to which, 321 families in Egypt had incomes the equivalent of more than $1.5 million a year; 4.5 million families had incomes of less than $180 a year. A hundred thousand private cars then served some two hundred thousand Cairenes; twelve hundred buses served three million Cairenes.

Sadat continued to gamble, even while the stakes grew considerably higher and the problems more acute. At a time of domestic economic chaos, he had isolated Egypt from its traditional patrons in the oil-rich Arab world.

Dr. Boutros Boutros-Ghali, according to his account, had what was probably Egypt's most difficult job. As Minister of State for Foreign Affairs from 1977 to 1991, he was charged with damage control in easing Egypt's relations with the European Community and the nonaligned world following the signing of the Egyptian-Israeli peace accord. In his memoir *Egypt's Road to Jerusalem*, the aristocratic Copt (who would later serve as Secretary General of the UN) recalls his appointment only three weeks before Sadat made his "sacred pilgrimage" to Jerusalem—an appointment that was the direct result of the resignations of both his predecessor and Egypt's Minister of Foreign Affairs, highly skilled and respected diplomats, who had refused to countenance Sadat's Jerusalem trip. (A second Egyptian foreign minister would resign at Camp David itself, moments before the official treaty signing on the White House lawn, adding to the collective bewilderment of the world's press, none of us being able, from one moment to the next, to fully comprehend who, in fact, was managing Egypt's foreign affairs.)

Two years later, in September 1979, a stressed Boutros-Ghali was summoned by Sadat to one of his presidential retreats, in Ismailia, overlooking the Suez Canal. The Minister of State had just returned to Egypt after having had a most unpleasant time touring Europe and the nonaligned world. Arab kings and sultans, Arab socialists and sheikhs had been making the same diplomatic rounds, and they possessed the "oil weapon," as they had already clearly shown when they threatened to hold the world hostage to an oil embargo after the October War. Boutros Ghali fretted to Sadat: The Egyptian-Israeli treaty was considered little more than a separate peace; Egypt was dangerously isolated; the peace treaty was doomed.

"I want you to move your chair," Sadat told his minister, who quickly complied, although he was not at all certain what was on the President's mind.

"Now," said Sadat—looking out through a bay window no longer obstructed by his minister's slouching frame, and with a clear view of the Suez Canal and the Sinai Desert, which he was about to reclaim—"I do not wish to underestimate the magnitude of the problems and worries that Egyptian diplomacy is facing [now], but all these problems and worries pale in comparison with this land we have regained. They [the Arabs] are not worth one square meter of this land, which we have regained without spilling the blood of my children . . . I am not afraid of condemnations. I am not afraid of countries severing diplomatic relations with us. And I am not afraid of the provocation and trivia of the Arab world."*

---

*Boutros Boutros-Ghali, *Egypt's Road to Jerusalem* (New York: Random House, 1997).

Egypt was to regret that erroneous assumption for nearly a decade.

There was a special vanity about Sadat, and to a great extent he personalized his quarrel with the Arab world, constantly taunting, constantly irritating its leadership. It was as though this always frustrating, bewildering man—part cunning peasant, part statesman, part thespian and charlatan—had once again reinvented himself.

"It is simply impossible for Egypt to isolate itself from the Arab world," the former foreign minister Ismail Fahmy, one of those who resigned to protest Sadat's Jerusalem trip, told me one morning in 1979 when I called on him. He had submitted his resignation primarily because Sadat had not consulted other Arab leaders about the trip, nor had the President consulted him. "We never had a chance to oppose him," Fahmy said. "He dramatized events to make it seem that there was a black-and-white choice between peace and war. It was peace by circus—a separate peace which has done little to alleviate the problems of the Middle East."

For, despite the fact that after four wars in thirty years, the guns had fallen silent along the Egyptian-Israeli frontier, effectively reducing—if not eliminating—the possibility of any combination of Arab power being able to threaten war against the Jewish state, the belligerency between Egypt and Israel had never been the core of the conflict in the Middle East. The fulcrum of that conflict has always been Israel's seizure and occupation of Palestinian land. And an appendage to the Camp David treaty, calling for Palestinian autonomy talks—an appendage negotiated almost as an afterthought—was not really taken seriously by anyone at the time, not by Sadat, not by the United States, and most certainly not by the nearly four million Palestinians. Protests swept through the Palestinian refugee camps, and across the Arab and the Islamic world. But Sadat appeared inured to the Palestinian outcry, even though he was ostensibly negotiating in the Palestinians' name.

"Yasir Arafat has never been in control," Sadat told one interviewer in discussing the chairman of the Palestine Liberation Organization (PLO). "He can't make decisions; he has no authority."

"The psychology of the Palestinian diaspora and of the Arab-

Israeli conflict never interested Sadat," Mohamed Sid-Ahmed, a seminal columnist and writer, told me at the time. One of Egypt's leading political thinkers, who is loosely aligned with the Nasserites and leftists who dominate the country's intellectual life, Sid-Ahmed had in 1975 published a breakthrough book, *When the Guns Fall Silent*, advocating détente with Israel. After the Camp David peace treaty, he quickly changed his mind. Sitting in his book-lined study, he complained bitterly to me of the hazards of Sadat's "separate peace," which not only did nothing to address Palestinian concerns but was, in his view, little more than a "Pax Americana"—a view that Sid-Ahmed continues to hold. He also worried, as did most Egyptian intellectuals of both the right and the left, along with much of the country's educated middle class, about Sadat's constant irritation of the Arab world at a time when Egypt's economic statistics ran on an ascending scale, in the words of one American diplomat, "from worthless to bad."

The country's gross national product was roughly $14 billion, a substantial amount of which came, in one form or another, from its patrons in the oil-rich Arab states. It was always an uneasy relationship between provider and ward. The providers, mainly Saudi Arabia and Kuwait during those years, resented cosmopolitan Cairo's interpretation of the world, and its leadership over their more insular and puritanical world. The proud Egyptians, for their part, inhabited the region's sole exception to an artificial nation-state; they had a history going back thousands of years; and they weren't *really* Arabs. Their present nomenclature, in their minds, was merely an accident of geography. They were galled, and they were embarrassed, to have to wait, like beggars on their own streets, for handouts from the desert sheikhs. But despite their history, the reality was that Egypt in the late 1970s was a supplicant, technically bankrupt.

It was kept alive only by massive handouts and loans from abroad. Its largest single source of foreign currency—a billion and a half dollars a year—came in remittances from the roughly million and a half Egyptians working in the Persian Gulf. Tourism, which included a substantial number of Arab visitors, came next and accounted for some $686 million a year. Economic aid from Saudi Arabia alone totaled another $5 billion annually—$2 billion in direct bilateral payments, $2 billion into the coffers of regional organizations for Egypt's development, and $1 billion paid externally against Egypt's massive foreign debt. By cutting all aid after the peace treaty was signed, Saudi Arabia's feudal, pro-Western monarchy placed the burden of Egypt's economic survival squarely on the shoulders of the United States.

It was certainly one of the most astonishing by-products of peace.

"One thing that Sadat did not take into account was that the Saudi monarchy would risk antagonizing Washington," one Arab League official told me at the time. "But Saudi priorities have clearly changed. What is happening now between Egypt and the Kingdom is secondary to what is really at stake—and that is a redefinition of the U.S.-Saudi relationship. Until that is reconciled to Riyadh's satisfaction, Sadat, I'm afraid, will become more isolated every day. The Saudis have looked with alarm at the political upheaval in Iran, and are angered by Washington's failure to assist the Shah; they are obsessed with what they perceive to be American indecision and weakness in the region in containing the Soviet threat. Until these matters are resolved, Sadat will continue to be a scapegoat in a sense."

And that is precisely what happened in the early years of peace.

At the urging of Saudi Arabia—most particularly the Saudi Foreign Minister, Prince Saud al-Faisal, who was one of the Kingdom's most resolute opponents of the peace accord—and those Arab countries lined up against the agreement in the rejectionist front, eighteen of the Arab League's twenty-two member states imposed sanctions against Cairo: they withdrew their bank deposits, closed their embassies, and flew home. One afternoon, driving through the diplomatic enclave, I watched a small man, with a large white kaffiyeh twirled around his head, shutter the windows of the Saudi Embassy and padlock its doors. Farther along, I noticed that the Iraqi Embassy now flew the Yugoslavian flag. And as Israeli vessels began to steam through the Suez Canal, Egyptian vessels were blacklisted at the prestigious shipyard in Bahrain.

Attempting to sketch a profile of the Middle Eastern groups from which Egypt was expelled was to paint a vibrant canvas of a regional Who's Who. The headquarters of the Arab League moved from Cairo to Tunis; the Arab world's only arms industry—the Arab Organization for Industrialization—which was based in Cairo, was dissolved; the Arab Tourist Organization moved its headquarters from Cairo to Amman. The Gulf Organization for the Development of Egypt—a $2 billion regional organization that had assisted Egypt in securing international funding and serviced its foreign debt—froze its remaining assets. And although Egypt is an oil exporter (it then produced 500,000 barrels a day), it needed to import $150 million in refined products each year to meet domestic needs. OPEC's oil exporters in the Persian Gulf embargoed the deliveries. They also expelled Egypt, a conservative country whose thirty-four million Muslims were largely devout, from the Conference of Islamic States. But it was the affront to Sadat's only power base—the Armed Forces—that nettled the most. One of Saudi Arabia's most unpardonable acts, in the eyes of Sadat, was its withdrawal of payment for over $500 million worth of American F-5 warplanes sold to Egypt by the United States on the understanding that Riyadh would pay the bill. The standoff between the desert sheikhs and the peasant-soldier had become highly personal.

Sadat was privately outraged, one of his aides said to me; but he was publicly undaunted, and he continued apace.

I remember one rather remarkable press conference that he gave inside the Abdin Palace, where he sat surrounded by marble, alabaster, and gold. When asked how he was possibly going to cope with the loss of billions of dollars in Arab aid, he smiled and then referred to a Carter Plan for Egypt (rather like the Marshall Plan, it seemed), which he was confident of receiving from his "very good friends Jimmy Carter, Henry Kissinger, and American congressmen."

"How much money will be involved?" one questioner asked.

"Oh," Sadat replied, "it can be from ten to fifteen billion dollars for four or five years." He seemed to toss the figures out of nowhere, and genuinely didn't seem to think that there was much difference between ten billion and fifteen.

"What is your personal relationship with [Israeli Prime Minister] Menachem Begin?" I asked.

"An interesting question," Sadat replied; and then he went on: "I used to say that the problem between Begin and me, between Egypt and Israel, was seventy-five percent psychological. But just before signing the peace treaty, I met Begin alone for the first time. We talked for two hours, just the two of us. Now I can tell you the problem is eighty-five percent psychological."

No one in the room understood what he meant.

Sadat had sent men to war in 1973 in order to achieve peace. He glimpsed the road ahead as one of prosperity, of an ill-defined Carter Plan. But, perhaps as important as anything else, he foresaw the return of Egyptian land—the Sinai Desert that he could see through the bay window of his Ismailia presidential retreat. That land had been lost by his legendary predecessor Gamal Abdel Nasser during the June 1967 War, when Israel had decimated the Egyptian Army, and Egyptian pride, in six bloody days. It positioned its troops along the Suez Canal, only some sixty miles from downtown Cairo. The Nasser era ended, for all intents and purposes, during those few days, but in much of the Arab world Nasser was still venerated—passionately—as a modern prophet or saint. Sadat had grown weary of standing in Nasser's shadow; and he disdained the Pan-Arabism, nonalignment, Pan-Africanism, Marxism, and socialism of those days. After all, he had grown, with cunning and ease, from a "simple soldier"—as he often described himself during the Nasser years—into a surefooted leader.

Sadat had brought Egypt peace, and he was not frightened of the bogeyman of a separate peace.

A plume of smoke drifted out from the village of Abu Siar to a field of sorghum just beyond, where I spotted Mohammed Abdel-Karim working his water buffalo. Where I stood, the fields were green and lush. But only a mile or so beyond them, the desert began to define itself: alien and monotonous at first glance, then holding its own secrets and charms, playfully changing its color, its texture and contour as the dust blew in. Its silence was broken only by the wind. I tried to imagine all of the conquerors who had swept across it from the north, but here no traces remained: no monuments or mausoleums; no Doric temples or Roman colonnades. Egypt has done little to preserve its colonial past.

The sun had not yet begun to set, and the sky was a cloudless blue. All around us, the flat emptiness of the desert stretched endlessly. Here and there, scattered about, were black slate formations that resembled giant marshmallows burned in a bonfire. Other than that there was little that distinguished itself; only a scattering of shrubs, bushes, and a gray veneer of vegetation waiting for the rains. Nestled among them was a cluster of shabby army tents, which were little more than telephone outposts. On the horizon was a sizable army camp.

I puzzled over what the Army thought of the peace accord. Its officers tended to be prudent men and, like army officers around the Arab world, they tended to shun the cocktail party circuit and foreign diplomats; and they most emphatically tended to shun the press. What we did know, however, was that between the Arab-Israeli wars of 1967 and 1973 two million young men had passed through the Army's ranks; most of them had undergone rigorous training programs that included survival techniques, commando methods, and the use of the most sophisticated weaponry. When they returned to their villages and towns, after the last war, large quantities of weapons found their way from the battlefields into private hands all over Egypt. But their largest concentration was at the universities. And it was also there, on campuses from Cairo to Alexandria, and to Middle and Upper Egypt in the south, that Islamist students— who by now were in control of the most prestigious faculties—were in the forefront of those challenging Sadat, his peace treaty, his support of the Shah of Iran, and his very legitimacy. We began to hear the names of Mohammed al-Islambouli, Talat Qasim, Isam al-Ariyan—student leaders of the Islamic Group, which closed down universities across the south to protest the peace accord, denouncing it as an "Islamic sin." But more often than not, we heard the name of their spiritual leader, the blind cleric Sheikh Omar Abdel-Rahman.

I had come to the village of Abu Siar late one afternoon in 1979, shortly after the peace treaty was signed, and I hoped to get a sense of how it was received in this Bedouin village, just beyond the Pyramids, on the Sahara's edge. Abu Siar is only an hour's drive from Cairo, but it is a journey backward in time. Single-story mud houses line a thin canal, where women squatted in tidy rows washing the family clothes; in the water, children frolicked, bathed, and defecated, and washed water buffalo. Bedouins—now peasants—returned from the fields for their evening meal, hinging their donkeys and camels outside their front doors. Goats scavenged in a nearby rubbish bin as buffalo lumbered by them on their way home from the sorghum field.

Mohammed Abdel-Karim walked slowly toward me from across the field, giving me a slightly mischievous glance. By way of introduction he smiled: "Are you an Israeli?" he asked. The question was not put with suspicion, or with animosity, but with that barely concealed delight which Egyptians reserve for anything new, or unusual, or rare. Then he stood and waited, his eyes fixed on me, like a mad ornithologist hunting an extinct bird, to see if he really had discovered a live Israeli in his midst.

"No, I'm an American," I replied.

He shrugged. "It's all the same."

That was the way many of my conversations went during the early days of peace. For the Camp David treaty was already being described, not only by leftists like Mohamed Sid-Ahmed but by Islamists as well, as an understanding not between Israel and Egypt but between Egypt and the United States. It was the only common ground that the Islamists and the Marxists shared; at least, it was the only common ground that they shared then.

Mohammed Abdel-Karim continued to stare at me with unembarrassed curiosity. He was a small, wiry man with a jolly face and a mouth shaped by yellowed teeth. He could have been fifty or seventy. He wore a tattered galabiya topped by a brown waistcoat. An astonishingly large turban of soiled white cloth swathed his tiny head. With the help of various interpreters who had gathered around, he told me that he had sixteen children and two wives; his eldest son, Tariq, to whom he introduced me, was studying engineering in Upper Egypt, at the University of Asyut. Mohammed had moved his family from the desert—where only the Bedouin survive —to Abu Siar a few years before. He was thus officially now a peasant, since he no longer roamed the desert with his flocks. But basically, he told me, he was still a Bedouin at heart.

After our exchange of pleasantries, Mohammed suggested that we walk through the town. Town was little more than a few dusty streets leading to a soccer field and an elaborately inlaid arabesque mosque. Outside tea stalls, men sat cross-legged on roped beds, smoking hashish and water pipes. A line of silent women walked home from the well, balancing earthen jugs of water on their heads. They were indistinguishable behind colorful ankle-length veils, which were handsomely decorated with gold, silver, and copper coins, a testament to the dowries they had brought to married life.

A group of students joined us; some talked of the Prophet Muhammad and some of Marx. A wizened mullah joined us, and he talked of the Koran. There were no paved roads in the village, but I spotted a number of Japanese motorbikes; there were no schools —illiteracy here was 85 percent—but everyone seemed to have a radio and, as in the most isolated villages, Egyptians were agile in discussing world affairs. Undeveloped, Egyptian villages certainly were; backward, they were not.

We stopped to greet Mohammed's camel, which sat under a tree outside his one-room home, chewing on some grass, its eyes half closed. "Camels!" Mohammed's son Tariq was clearly outraged. "We still ride camels in the twentieth century. And it will become even worse now that the Arabs have cut off their aid. We need electricity, water, hospitals, roads, and schools."

"What we need is a revolution," said his friend Abdou.

I glanced at Mohammed, who ventured no opinion. And then he smiled.

"Do you miss the desert?" I asked him.

His eyes told me that his mind was going back. He then talked about his boyhood years when water was rationed, available only once a day. "Water"—he said the word in broken English—was always mysterious to him. Now he drew water from the Nile, via an irrigation canal. For Mohammed, a man unreconciled to the new peace, the Nile still ruled. As he continued talking, I realized that a peasant from Pharaonic times would find life little changed along much of its riverbank today. Mohammed's three buffalo, as buffalo have done for thousands of years, raised the precious water from the irrigation canal by turning a crude wooden lift, balanced by a weight of mud. They were blindfolded now, as they were blindfolded then.

Mohammed caught my eye as I watched his buffalo go round and round. "My camel is even more important," he announced. "In fact, she does almost everything: she works in the fields and she carries loads; when I have no work for her, I rent her out. When she's no longer useful, I will slaughter her and eat her meat; one of my wives will cure her skin, and we will make it into a hassock and jackets for the kids"—precisely what Bedouins have been doing with their camels for more than fifteen hundred years.

We had reached the end of the village, began retracing our steps through Abu Siar's dusty streets, and came upon the mosque, one of three in the village or on its outskirts, built with money from Saudi Arabia. Mohammed wondered aloud if such private Saudi funding would now stop.

Arab Islamic history began in Saudi Arabia, for that was the birthplace of the Prophet Muhammad, and of Islam. But it was in Cairo, more than anyplace else, that Islam fashioned a civilization, where it outwitted and outwaited conquerors. And if Saudi Arabia was the custodian of Islam's holiest shrines, Cairo was home to the Islamic world's oldest and most prestigious university, and to its pre-eminent press. Political dissidents, since the days of the Ottoman Empire, had sought refuge here. Foreign students flocked to its universities. Publishing, intellectual debate, and, later, cinema formed its core. Cairo—unlike the instant satellite cities of Saudi Arabia—was a unique, authentic capital, fashioned after nothing that came before.

It was also in Egypt that modern Arab nationalism came of age and the Muslim Brotherhood was born. Any political or cultural unity that the Arabs possessed was largely the work of Egyptians: in recent history, primarily Nasser and, after him, to a lesser extent,

Sadat. But the relationship between the puritanism and tradition of the desert and the cosmopolitanism of Cairo had always been an uneasy one, so Sadat was undeterred. As he dismissed the desert sheikhs and their economic sanctions, so he dismissed the protests against his peace treaty that were sweeping across Egyptian campuses and across much of the Arab and the Islamic world. He proved to be quintessentially Sadat, and he treated both the protests and the sanctions as just another minor irritant.

"Are you religious?" I asked Mohammed when we paused outside the mosque.

"Goodness, yes," he replied. "I live the way the Prophet Muhammad said that we should live." He thought for a moment, and then added, "The Prophet Muhammad was also a Bedouin."

I thought of Sadat, the peasant-soldier, sitting at the bay window of his Ismailia retreat, looking out at his land. And I was struck by the realization, as we stood outside the mosque and I watched a swirl of dust blow in from the desert just beyond, that land was one of two constant themes of Egyptian village life. The other, in the tens of thousands of villages, hamlets, and towns where more than 55 percent of Egyptians lived, was religion. And, as Mohammed said, the Prophet himself was a Bedouin.

It has only been in recent years that the Bedouin of Egypt, Syria, and Jordan, and now the administrative authority of Palestine, have begun leaving the deserts, largely as a result, beginning in 1948, of the Arab-Israeli wars. When the generals expanded their fronts into the deserts, the Bedouins found themselves under siege. They were incapable of defending themselves against warplanes and tanks, and their migration began. They came to places like Abu Siar, at the desert's edge. When I visited the village, there was no electricity, though I imagine that has now changed; there were no movie houses, no generators, and no cars. But from time to time during our walk, we were interrupted by a long-haired young man whizzing by us on a Japanese motorbike, challenging all in his path, as though he were leading a charge against a soon-to-be-plundered desert caravan.

However, it is perhaps that evening, by a campfire, that I remember most.

Mohammed had insisted that we share a meal with him, his

friends, and his family before we left. Sitting around the campfire, we could have been in *The Thousand and One Nights.* A brilliant sunset hung over the desert, and the air was clear. Beyond us, a fire was being laid in a pit dug in the sand. Women wearing silver necklaces and bracelets of ivory and gold began preparing food and large cisterns of thick, sugary tea. They scooped dough out of elaborately painted earthenware bowls and laid it on the coals, while others served us dates, mashed eggs in olive oil, and pungent goat's cheese; we scooped the food into our mouths with large lumps of bread, eating the meal with our hands. In the far distance the twinkling lights of Cairo began to come on. But no one at the campfire was tempted by the city or its life, and they sat around the embers of the wood fire as of old. They recited ancient poetry—poetry of war and of revenge—or satiric verse about an unpopular moneylender or an unpopular king.

They complained about their wives, about their neighbors, about the local authorities. They complained about the irrigation officials, and about the tax men. They complained, in effect, about the running themes of Egyptian life.

As I listened to them, I couldn't help but recall *The Complaints of the Peasant*, written some four thousand years ago. The peasant, Khunanup, had complained about precisely the same things to his Pharaoh, Nebkaure, who was so entranced by the peasant's eloquence that ruler and ruled commenced a correspondence lasting several years.

A few days later, I remarked on this to Dr. Sa'ad el-Din Ibrahim, the professor of sociology at AUC. "Egyptians were fascinated by that book," he said, "for they realized that their own complaints were four to five thousand years old."

He then went on to tell me that, some twenty years ago, a distinguished Egyptian sociologist named Sayyid Uways wrote a book about going to the post office one Friday afternoon.* No clerks were

---

*Dr. Uways's book, *A Message to Imam al-Shafi'i*, was published in 1978 in Cairo.

around, for it was the Sabbath, but, peering through a window, Dr. Uways saw a postal worker about to set fire to a heap of letters in the postal courtyard.

Pounding on the window, Dr. Uways began to shout, "It's a crime to burn the mail!"

Impatiently, the young postal worker cried back, "These are letters with no addresses, neither to nor from; or they have a fantastical address. They are letters sent to God."

The elderly sociologist cajoled the young postal worker out and onto the street, along with his heaps of mail, and pleaded with him to give him the letters. The postal worker did. Many were addressed to saints, to the Virgin Mary, to the Prophet Muhammad, to God. Sifting through them, the sociologist was amazed. For the complaints and the rumors were precisely the same as those voiced four thousand years ago by the eloquent peasant when he wrote to his Pharaoh.

Dr. Ibrahim leaned back in his chair and lit his pipe. "So, you see," he said, "from the letters of the peasant, which were almost like a prayer, to the letters in the post office, to the Bedouins you met, you get an idea of what has been here from time immemorial: the continuity of Egyptian society."

I asked him how, in his view, its centers of power have changed since that time, some four thousand years ago, when the eloquent peasant wrote to his Pharaoh.

He smiled at me from across his desk. "They haven't," he said.

He explained that in a hydraulic society, which depended upon a great river to survive, there was always a disproportionate regulation of power in order to protect the river; for whoever controlled the river controlled society. "And in order to do this," he went on, "a Pharaoh had to rely on coercion and persuasion, and he did so through three critical arms: his security apparatus; his civil bureaucracy; and his religious establishment. Through his security forces, the Pharaoh's message was clear: he wanted his people to always remember that he was there—that was the coercion side; through his civil bureaucracy, he collected taxes, but he gave his people public works—that was the persuasive part. And what he could not accomplish through these two he internalized; and that internal control was done by religion, and by the religious establishment, so that his subjects would obey out of conviction."

He paused for a moment, and then he said, "That's why Egypt perfected the first doctrine of the God-King."

I thought of what he said as I left his office at AUC and walked out onto the street, past government ministries, past the Egyptian Museum, and past the Saiyida Nafissa Mosque. When Upper and Lower Egypt were first unified around 3200 B.C. under the Pharaoh Menes, who founded the First Dynasty, the divinity of Pharaohs was proclaimed. A thousand years later, at about the time that the eloquent peasant spoke, the Pharaohs began to claim immortality.

I stopped to watch a security detail in crisply starched uniforms, take up its position in Tahrir Square, to wait for Anwar Sadat's motorcade, which in a few hours was scheduled to pass. I listened to a muezzin whose melancholy voice floated across rooftops as he called the faithful to prayer. And I was struck by the realization that not so much *has* changed since the Pharaonic years. For Egypt, despite its many layers—some distinct, some jumbled—was now, as then, dominated by the holy trinity of king, army, and church.

By December 1979, against the odds, Sadat had managed to survive the singular weaknesses and vulnerabilities of his peace accord and a succession of political crises, conspiracies, and attempts on his life. He had consolidated his power in the decade he had ruled, retired potential rivals, and, by conscientiously honoring the status quo, managed to retain the loyalty of his 300,000-man army, whose leaders are the arbiters of power in Egypt, and have been for more than forty-five years. The relationship between the President and the Army had always been taken for granted, in one sense, because Sadat's regime, through that of Gamal Abdel Nasser, had sprung from a military coup, or from the Revolution of 1952. The overthrow of King Farouk by an obscure group of young Egyptian officers was a seminal event in modern Middle Eastern history. It was not only a milestone in the long history of Egypt—"the most important country," in Napoleon's words—but it profoundly influenced other Arab and Islamic states. Proximity and experience had proven to them that Egypt—the region's most powerful and most advanced state—was often a bellwether of what lay ahead.

The ascent of the Free Officers to power, without firing a shot, was arguably a revolution; it was also arguably a coup. Some historians have written that the Egyptians, by instinct and by temperament, are not a revolutionary people, attested to by the fact that only two regimes have governed modern Egypt over the last two centuries: the dynasty of an Albanian freebooter named Mohammed Ali—a grand modernizer who emerged in the chaos that followed Napoleon's conquest of Egypt in 1798—whose last scion was King Farouk; and then the Free Officers of 1952. The mathematical equation is accurate, of course, but it seems to me that the far greater significance of the events of July 1952 was that the Egyptians, for the first time in 2,284 years, had finally begun to rule themselves.

Their nominal head of government in the early years was a fifty-year-old general named Mohammed Naguib, but it was the charismatic Nasser who wielded power behind the scenes, and, as his successor, Sadat, would do, he wielded power with absolute control. Two modern Pharaohs—Colonel Gamal Abdel Nasser and Captain Anwar Sadat—would, between them, rule Egypt for nearly thirty years. Artfully embellishing Pharaonic traditions that emphasized loyalty to the leader, *al Rais*, they had at their disposal an abundance of means for isolating, ridiculing, dividing, and, if necessary, crushing any opposition to their rule. And, like the Pharaohs before them, they relied on the unassailable triad of king, army, and church.

Nasser moved quickly to bring the ancient educational and religious institution of al-Azhar under state control. He appointed its sheikhs and its teachers, its administrators and its imams. He also, as the inheritors of his revolution—Sadat and now Hosni Mubarak—would do, began his presidency by making alliances with the Islamists, particularly the Muslim Brotherhood, for his own purposes. And then, after a time, when he recognized the dangers that the Islamists posed to his regime, he turned fiercely and suddenly against them, especially against their militant undergrounds. (It was a pattern to be repeated by Sadat during the last year of his rule; and a pattern being repeated by Hosni Mubarak now.)

But in the early years of Nasser's rule a honeymoon had ensued between the Free Officers and the Muslim Brotherhood. Few Egyptians had regarded the Army as a candidate for power when the secret association of junior officers took control. The country had not been ruled by the military since the Mamluks in the sixteenth century. Shaped by nearly a century of a monarchic-parliamentary regime, most Egyptians believed that if there was an alternative to colonial rule, it appeared to come from the forces of traditional Islam. For it was the Muslim Brotherhood that had been in the forefront of the anti-British campaign for almost a quarter of a century, a campaign that had resulted, only six months before, in the burning of the center of Cairo—an attack in direct response to the massacre of some fifty Egyptian policemen by the British on the banks of the Suez Canal. Nasser and his Free Officers decided that their time had come.

The leaders of the Brotherhood were not unknown to them, for the agendas of the young army officers and the Islamists had been mutually reinforcing for more than ten years. The two groups had been drawn together by their shared antipathy toward colonial rule, and it was during the anti-British riots, bombings, and strikes—and on the battlefields of the first Arab-Israeli war, in 1948—that the Free Officers and the Muslim Brothers first embraced.

Their backgrounds and their loyalties were not that dissimilar, in fact, for both Egypt's Army and its religious establishment largely drew their ranks from the more than 55 percent of Egyptians who live in the countryside. The soldier and the preacher is a recurrent theme of Egyptian village life. Nasser's roots, like those of nearly all the Free Officers, sprang from Egypt's villages and towns, and from the lower middle class, and, perhaps more than anything else, this would mold him for the rest of his life. For although he was a passionate reader of history and political biography, Nasser, like his colleagues in the Free Officers group, came to power with no distinctive political ideology. Theirs was a revolution built solely on the desire to expel Britain, to overthrow King Farouk, and to eliminate the power of the quasi-feudal landowning class.

A few of the Free Officers leaned toward Marxism; others, including Sadat, leaned toward the Islamic reformism of the Muslim

Brotherhood. The institutions of king, army, and church worked compatibly. Each may have had internal dissensions, and each had rivalries. But an intelligent Pharaoh—like Nasser and the heirs to his realm—made certain that his religious establishment and his army were under his control.

Like nearly all previous Egyptian leaders, whether Pharaonic or foreign, republican or royal, the inheritors of the Revolution of 1952 ruled by colonizing the institutions under their control. They appointed men wholly loyal to them as their Vice Presidents, their Prime Ministers, their Ministers of the Interior and Defense, the commanders of their Army, and the Grand Sheikh of al-Azhar and the Coptic Pope of their religious establishments. All the regional governors were creations of theirs, as were editors, university rectors, and the chairmen of all public-sector boards. It was an octopodian structure fashioned with precision on what had come before.

Yet even in the early years of Nasser's rule, one element of the trinity began to elude his control. The Muslim Brothers continued to agitate for an Islamic government, and their honeymoon with the Army was short-lived. They had gone beyond the tacit limits of their power, in the Free Officers' view. Thus, in October 1954, when they were held responsible for an attempt on Nasser's life, his Army-backed regime moved against them with brutal force: the organization was banned; its leaders were executed and tortured; and over four thousand of its members were returned to the concentration camps. (Ironically, one of the officers who sat on the military tribunals that condemned the Muslim Brothers to death was the young Anwar Sadat, who, two decades later, would preside as the Islamic phoenix rose from its ashes yet another time.)

Meanwhile Nasser, who had come to power with only a remote interest in Arab nationalism and no political philosophy of his own, had begun to evolve into a leader who would leave an indelible mark, not only on Egypt but on the larger Arab-Islamic world. If there was one single event that guided him in the creation of his regime, it was his experience in the disastrous Arab campaign against Israel in 1948. From the day he seized power, the defeat would dominate his domestic and foreign policies. In a sense, everything else sprang from it: his determination to break the economic and political power of the former ruling class; his reorientation of Egypt's foreign policy and his drastic reduction in the influence of the West; his reliance on the Soviet Union for military aid; and his almost obsessive desire to capture and control an elusive Arab unity, whatever the cost.

I've often asked Egyptian friends how they would define the legacy that Nasser bequeathed to his heirs. Perhaps not surprisingly, the responses have been as diverse, and as contradictory, as the man. A product of the 1950s, Nasser was a pillar of the nonaligned world who played the Americans off against the Soviets, and favored the Chinese. He was a nationalist, a socialist, a Pan-Arabist, a man of considerable vanity. A charismatic populist, he assured with his sweeping land reforms that every peasant received at least one small plot of land; the urban poor received free education and free health care; rents and food were subsidized. State jobs were guaranteed to all university graduates. Almost the entire economy—a step that later proved disastrous—was nationalized. But Nasser, like his inheritors, also had a darker side. With a strong arm and the Army at his command, he curtailed the appreciable measure of intellectual and political liberty that had previously prevailed. He abolished political parties—except for his own—and established concentration camps, where thousands of prisoners languished at any given time. Many had been given no trial, nor been charged with any crime. Some, whom I met later, to this day do not know why they had been arrested.

Nasser was as anomalous as Egypt itself.

Living in the shadow of the ancient Pyramids, he crafted monumental edifices of his own, such as the Aswan High Dam. He also presided over the arrival in Egypt of nearly twenty thousand Soviets, who arrived as quickly as, under Sadat, they would disappear. In July 1956, he nationalized the Suez Canal, which provoked an invasion by Israeli, British, and French troops. President Dwight D. Eisenhower reversed the results when he forced a cease-fire. It was perhaps Washington's greatest moment in the eyes of the Arab world.

The forced departure of the tripartite invasion force also consolidated Nasser's leadership over that world. But his overreaching in the 1960s was paving the way for what would be prophetic military defeats—in Yemen, in the Congo, and in Sinai. His ultimate humiliation, and that of the Army he controlled, was Egypt's devastating defeat by Israel during the June 1967 War. Nasser's era ended, for all intents and purposes, during those six days, as yet another arm of his holy trinity was decimated, as it had never—in thousands of years of history—been decimated before.

The shame and the humiliation of that defeat was brought home to me thirty years later, graphically. When I visited Cairo in June 1997, on the anniversary of the war, the mourning was almost palpable and the wounds remained profound. As I read the Egyptian papers on the morning of June 5, I was astonished to find that they were recounting the 1967 war as though it had happened yesterday.

The Islamist revival in Egypt quickened after that war, fed by the humiliation of Egypt's defeat and the Arab loss of Jerusalem, and radical underground groups sprang up—such as the Islamic Liberation Organization and the Gama'a al-Takfir wal-Hijra—groups that in the 1970s would challenge with deadly effect the inheritors of Nasser's legacy.

For its part, the Muslim Brotherhood—which, over the next decade, would establish branches in nearly every Muslim state—intensified its campaign to export its revolution abroad, particularly to those areas occupied by Israel during the Six-Day War. A key figure in this effort was Sheikh Ahmed Yassin, a charismatic Palestinian cleric who had received a Ph.D. from the University of al-Azhar and, while in Cairo, had become a member of the secret leadership of the Brotherhood. On his return to the occupied Gaza Strip, the sheikh became the Islamists' leading political voice. Ironically, not unlike Sadat, who had encouraged, armed, and trained Egypt's Islamists as a counterpoint to the left, the Israelis encouraged Sheikh Yassin—who would later found Hamas—and not only allowed his Islamic movement to flourish but even covertly supported it. Far more fearful of the secular PLO, the Israelis saw the Islamists as a perfect

instrument for their policy of divide and rule. They regret—as Anwar Sadat would regret—that erroneous assumption now.

By the time we left Egypt, at the end of 1979, Sadat had grown
increasingly alarmed over the dangers that the Islamists posed to his
regime. The Muslim Brotherhood, over whose rehabilitation he had
presided a decade earlier, had been evolving into the mainstream of
political life, and it was no longer the loyal opposition he had en-
visaged in his efforts to undermine the left. It was becoming *the*
opposition and Egypt's strongest, and best-organized, political force.
Its rejection of the Egyptian-Israeli peace treaty was no less forceful
than was its bitter denunciation of Israel and the United States. Like
the Islamist student groups, which Sadat had largely spawned, the
Brotherhood, too, was veering beyond his control.

But as it gained respectability, its more militant youthful members began to slip away. During my last months in Cairo, I was
fascinated yet bewildered to watch its highly organized Islamic
structure beginning to yield to a plethora of amorphous Islamist or
"neo-Islamist" groups, which were becoming as numerous as their
memberships were diverse. In their view, the Brotherhood had become bourgeois—so bourgeois, in fact, that some of its members
were now drawn from the Armed Forces, including at least one of
the Army's most elite groups.

Yet far more worrisome to Sadat, and to Western diplomats,
was the discovery, earlier that year, that a handful of officers and
soldiers were members of the clandestine Gama'a al-Takfir wal-
Hijra, the nihilist Muslim sect that had kidnapped and killed Sadat's
former Minister of Religious Endowments as the President was planning his "sacred pilgrimage" to Jerusalem. On university campuses,
the Gama'a al-Islamiya—the Islamic Group—continued to augment
its strength; at the same time, the cadet-survivors of the Islamic Liberation Organization who had staged the abortive mutiny at the
Technical Military Academy in 1974 had regrouped as the militant
underground organization al-Jihad. And neither it nor the Gama'a
now drew its membership exclusively from students like Nadine and
members of university faculties, but recruited from the ranks of gov-

ernment civil servants, employees of state-controlled television and radio, members of military intelligence and the Presidential Guard. The church and the Army appeared to be bonding once more. And even if small in number—it was impossible to know—the Army's membership in the militant Islamist underground was significant because it meant that the Islamists had penetrated the sole bastion of Sadat's political strength.

The greatest challenge to his presidency had been the food riots of 1977, but in a curious way, they had been both his lowest and his highest point. For the Army had stood behind him and, although with great reluctance, had positioned its troops on Cairo's streets in order to safeguard Sadat's presidency. It was one of only two times in modern Egyptian history—the other occurred a decade later, in 1986, during bloody riots by police recruits—that the commander of the Egyptian Army agreed to deploy his troops against the civilian population, in contravention of a pledge given to the Army following the 1973 October War by its President. Sadat always knew, one of his advisers told me at the time, that the food riots would come to represent the first crack in his legitimacy.

But 1979 would be the most prophetic year for him, for it was then that the tapestry of the Islamic world was inexorably redesigned.

As Sadat basked in the attention given him and his peace treaty by the United States, in nearby Iran a twenty-five-hundred-year-old monarchy, backed by the most powerful military force in the Middle East and a surfeit of oil wealth, was staggered by a loosely organized, unarmed opposition led by militant Islamic clergymen. In mid-January, the dynasty of Shah Mohammed Riza Pahlavi collapsed after his army withdrew its support of him. On February 1 the militant cleric Ayatollah Ruhollah Khomeini, who had been in exile near Paris, was tumultuously welcomed home. It was a turning point in the history of the modern Islamic world.

For although the ayatollahs were Shi'ites—a minority, and largely Persian, branch of Islam, concentrated in Iraq and Iran, which had split with the majority Sunnis over the questions of the rightful successor to the Prophet Muhammad and the interpretation of Shariah (Islamic religious law)—the impact of their revolution was profound. It was Islam's most stunning political triumph in centuries.

Thus, at least for the moment, Sunni-Shi'ite differences over the question of the Prophet's rightful heir—whether in line of direct descent through Ali, his first cousin and son-in-law, as the Shi'ites believe; or through a caliphate, based on election and consensus of the elders of the community, as the Sunnis (and the traditions of the desert) hold—were not argued with their usual force. Frenzied crowds danced in the streets of Cairo and other capitals of the Islamic world. Perhaps no one was as badly shaken as Anwar Sadat.

There was an intoxication, and, in retrospect, it is impossible to know whether the triumph of the clerics would have been as profound if it had not fortuitously moved in tandem with other upheavals in the larger Islamic world. For as the Ayatollah Khomeini was just beginning to savor the spoils of power in Tehran, in December 1979 the Soviet Union invaded neighboring Afghanistan to prop up its pro-Communist regime.

Startled American policy makers were ill prepared for either event, and they responded in often paradoxical, always shortsighted, ways. The zeal of the Reagan Administration to "bleed" the Soviet Union at a time when it was perceived to be overextended and potentially vulnerable led to its support of a fractious alliance of Afghan resistance groups, known as the mujahideen. The United States, over the coming years, intentionally or not, would launch Pan-Islam's first holy war in eight centuries.

In so doing, Washington received crucial support from neighboring Pakistan, whose military ruler, General Mohammed Zia ul-Haq, had two passions: Afghanistan and Islam. And the actions they moved him to take had powerful effects: he divided his country by his imposition of the harsher aspects of Islamic law and his agreement to provide the Afghan resistance armies with ever-increasing shipments of arms supplied by the CIA—an undertaking that was supported no less enthusiastically by Anwar Sadat than by Egypt's various branches of militant Islam. By the early 1980s armies in

Afghanistan, Pakistan, and Iran were all ruling—or fighting—in the name of Islam.

According to the Koran, a reform movement arises within the Muslim world once each century to rekindle the torch of Islam. And by the time we left Egypt, nearly all Islamic scholars believed that that moment had come. From North Africa and the Middle East to Central and Southeast Asia, the winds of a religious revival were sweeping, with various degrees of force, through nearly every country of the Islamic world. Regimes both conservative and radical appeared vulnerable as the resurgent Islamist movement took special aim at the alleged excesses of Western influence, and at Marxism, to a lesser degree. For Islam—which means "submission"—is by nature a conservative force, with a strict, tradition-bound behavioral code, both public as well as personal. Thus any social change comes as a challenge to the faith itself. Of all the world's great religions, Islam is the most cohesive one, and the only one that can be defined as political.

Throughout Egypt, by the end of 1979, there was a feeling of irresolution and drift, and the popularity of Sadat would dip to its lowest ebb over the next two years. Normally a politician of extraordinary skill, he had gambled his future on the United States and on his peace accord. At least for the moment, he appeared to have lost. Thus, as he had done so many times before, Sadat retreated behind his enigmatic veil. There was anger and incomprehension among many Egyptians, and there was also the tangible fear of what lay ahead. At the very time that Egypt was being swept by a resurgence of Islam, Sadat, whether through his peace treaty or in Afghanistan, would become inexorably linked to the policies of the United States. Washington, for its part, seemed oblivious to the winds of Islamic change and, having lost the critical support of the Shah of Iran, had come to rely increasingly on Sadat, on Pakistan's General Zia, and on the feudal Saudi Arabian throne. It was another trinity, in a sense, but one that would later prove disastrous for all of them.

A reasonably stable Egypt was essential to peace, and there was still stability in late 1979, but economic expectations ran unrealistically high. The Arab world was in a state of turmoil, and Egypt was threatened by potential divisions—the same kind of political, social, and economic discord that had gripped Iran before the Shah was deposed.

Our bags were packed for the journey out of Egypt, and I barely remembered the chaos and pandemonium, the daily hassles, the stickiness of the flies. Instead, I always came back to certain moments: the feel of the desert wind; the Nile and its fickle currents; a civilization magnificent and indestructible over thousands of years.

Yet there was also something very different from the time that we arrived. *"Allahu akbar!"*—"God is most great!"—was first uttered at the time of the Prophet Muhammad thirteen and a half centuries ago. This ancient Arabic prayer was now a call to arms. It was the cry that accompanied the seizure of the American Embassy in Tehran just before we left, a seizure that resulted in the hostage-taking of more than fifty U.S. diplomats. It was the cry of a group of well-armed and well-trained Saudi dissidents who seized the Great Mosque in Mecca, one of Islam's holiest shrines. It was a cry of defiance against unpopular regimes. In Cairo, during our last months, *"Allahu akbar!"* resounded increasingly from darkened rooftops.

"MY SONS"

*T*HE ANNIVERSARY OF EGYPT'S RECAPTURE FROM ISRAEL OF A salient of land in the Sinai Peninsula during the 1973 war was always celebrated with special pomp, for it was when Egyptian troops crossed the Suez Canal and broke through Israel's Bar-Lev Line that Anwar Sadat cemented his authority. The crossing of the canal was for Sadat what its nationalization had been for Gamal Abdel Nasser: it afforded his regime supreme legitimacy.

Sadat, who was under mounting criticism at home, was particularly ebullient as he greeted foreign guests on their arrival at the reviewing stand for the celebration's military parade on a beautiful fall day in October 1981. He was dressed in an immaculately tailored Prussian-style uniform, which had arrived only a few days before from his tailor in London. With more than average vanity, Sadat had chosen not to wear his bulletproof waistcoat, explaining to his wife (according to the Egyptian writer Mohamed Hassanein Heikal) that it would ruin the lines. Few of those present paid more than passing heed to Hosni Mubarak, Egypt's unassuming Vice President, who stood next to Sadat. Even fewer had ever heard of the obscure Islamic scholar Sheikh Omar Abdel-Rahman.

Mubarak, one of his friends told me later, had urged Sadat not to attend the parade. The President had been complaining of fatigue and of dizzy spells. He had also been warned by Mubarak, over the previous months, of military intelligence reports of assassination plots. Mubarak had admonished Sadat to crack down on his more visceral foes, particularly the militant Islamist underground, advice with which Sadat had complied, in a manner of speaking. The previous month he had launched the greatest repression of his presidency, and rounded up more than fifteen hundred of Egypt's brightest and most politically prominent. Former ministers, professors, lawyers, and journalists; rightists and leftists; Islamists and Copts; men and women were summarily sent off to the most notorious prisons in Greater Cairo.

But on Mubarak's suggestion that he not attend the parade, Sadat was adamant. October 6 was his favorite holiday, and he loved the pageantry of a military parade. He was also so certain of the loyalty of his troops that on parade days he most often rode in an open car—a black Cadillac convertible on this particular day. He often told his security guards, "Please go away—I am with my sons."

The eighth-anniversary parade was an extravagant military show, and it was also something of a milestone, since, for the first time, it would display as much Western military equipment as Soviet; there would be American Phantom jet fighters and Chinook helicopters and French Mirage fighter aircraft.

The air show was to be the parade's crowning event, and therefore most of the dignitaries in the reviewing stand chatted among themselves obliviously as phalanxes of ZIL trucks towing 130 mm Russian field guns passed in front of them. In the open back of each truck were six helmeted gunners, holding their weapons between their knees. When one of the trucks veered off and stopped in front of the reviewing stand, the few who happened to notice assumed that it had broken down. A stocky, broad-shouldered man in a peaked cap, followed by three others, leaped out.

Sadat rose from his throne-like chair, in the front row of the reviewing stand, expecting a salute. Instead, two of the soldiers lobbed grenades directly at him. Then automatic machine-gun fire began. Lieutenant Khaled Shawky al-Islambouli, the officer in the peaked cap, fired for forty-five seconds into the crumpled body of Sadat before the President's seemingly paralyzed security guard began to return fire. Sadat and seven others died on the spot.

The young leader of the assassins cried out, "I am Khaled Islambouli. I have killed Pharaoh, and I do not fear death."

There was shock in Cairo, but little more: few Egyptians went to the streets to mourn the passing of Sadat.

Eight days later, Hosni Mubarak, then fifty-three, a cautious, self-effacing man, a former fighter pilot and commander of the Egyptian Air Force, was sworn in as only the fourth President in Egypt's history. It was a job that he had never aspired to, and never really wanted, he told friends.

One month later, Lieutenant Islambouli sat in the front row, on a wooden bench, inside a giant metal cage that had been set up—in a special military court—for the trial of twenty-four men accused of complicity in the assassination of Sadat. Next to him, dressed in a long brown clerical robe and a red fez-like cap with a wide white band—the badge of al-Azhar—sat the man who would assume a commanding voice in the Islamist revolution that, a decade later, threatened to tear Egypt apart: the then forty-three-year-old cleric Sheikh Omar Abdel-Rahman.

Sadat's assassins were part of an underground army cell of al-Jihad, whose leader, Colonel Abbud al-Zumur, a military intelligence officer, had disappeared from his post a few months before. According to government prosecutors, the group's spiritual mentor was Sheikh Omar. He now stood accused of having issued a fatwa, or religious opinion, that justified the assassination of Sadat.

During a good part of the three-month-long trial, which ended in March 1982, Sheikh Omar talked in whispers to Lieutenant Islambouli, who sat to his right (and who, along with four others, including the champion marksman of the Army, was executed after the trial). Sheikh Omar was one of only two defendants acquitted by Mubarak's court.

To the best of the sheikh's knowledge, he had never met Hosni Mubarak—nor had the Egyptian President, as he told me later, ever heard of the sheikh—although both of them were born in tiny villages only some seventy miles apart in the Nile Delta, and into poverty. And not unlike other young men from such villages, both the President and the sheikh chose one of two traditional routes of upward mobility: the elder became a soldier, the younger a priest.

They seemed an odd coupling, the President and the sheikh. But

I would discover, over the years, that they had far more in common than it might appear.

Their lives were joined, in a sense, by Khaled al-Islambouli, the fresh-faced, twenty-four-year-old lieutenant who had commanded an artillery battery on the eighth anniversary of the October War. And Islambouli, in a curious way, was nothing more or less than the young Anwar Sadat some forty years on.

Rereading Sadat's autobiography, *In Search of Identity*, I was stopped abruptly by one paragraph:

> *According to plan, Tewfik was waiting for him at the door of the building. As Osman was about to take the elevator, Tewfik called out, "Pasha! Pasha!" When he turned round to answer the caller Tewfik fired his pistol at him. Tewfik, in calling him, applied the rule that forbade the shooting of a man in the back.* *

The passage related to the part that Sadat had played in the assassination, in January 1946, of the intensely pro-British Amin Osman Pasha, King Farouk's Minister of Finance. I couldn't help but recall how Islambouli had shouted out, "Pharaoh! Pharaoh!" before emptying his automatic weapon into the body of Sadat.

Born in Upper Egypt in 1957, the year after Nasser's triumphant nationalization of the Suez Canal—and named after Nasser's eldest son—Khaled al-Islambouli was ten years old when Egypt suffered its devastating defeat by Israel during the Six-Day War. A son of Nasser's revolution, he was, in nearly every sense, a mirror of its highs and lows. For most of his life he was not particularly religious, although his family was. His father was a lawyer; his mother was protective; and his elder brother, Mohammed, whom the young Khaled adored, was a student leader of the Islamic Group. The family, by the standards of Upper Egypt—the poorest part of the country, ignored and largely forgotten over time—was of a prominent class; its members were patriotic and, like Nasser, were nationalists.

---

*Anwar el-Sadat, *In Search of Identity* (New York: Harper & Row, 1977).

Khaled's dream was to become an air force pilot—as Hosni Mubarak had—but when that dream was thwarted by his failure to pass the exam for admission to the Air Force Academy, he chose the Army's School of Artillery, from which he graduated with honors in 1978. It was only during the last year of his life that the future assassin of Sadat joined the militant Islamist underground. His reasons for so doing died with him before a firing squad.

Perhaps he was influenced by his brother Mohammed, who was by then the leading figure of Gama'a in the faculty of commerce at the University of Asyut, and a protégé and pupil of Sheikh Omar Abdel-Rahman. (According to Khaled's mother, he was deeply upset when she told him of Mohammed's arrest in September 1981, during the massive roundup of Sadat's perceived political foes.)

Or perhaps Khaled was recruited in his barracks by another officer, or by an army sheikh. He was, it is now known, an enthusiastic participant in the increasingly popular Islamic study groups held weekly at army bases for officers and troops.

Unfortunately, one can only speculate now. The assassination trial was held in camera, except for three days, and military prosecutors concentrated on the single point of exactly how the actual act of assassination was carried out. The far more significant questions of the extent of the conspiracy, when and by whom the decision to assassinate Sadat was made, and how far-reaching the structure which supported that decision was were left largely unaddressed by the military court.

"How do you get live ammunition into a parade?" one U.S. official remarked to me at the time. "How do you get into the truck closest to the reviewing stand? How do you arrive at the stand at the precise moment that jets are flying over? How do you get your own men"—two of whom were no longer in the Army—"into your truck?" He paused for a moment, and then he asked, "Do lieutenants plan these kinds of things?"

A number of years later, I asked Hosni Mubarak what he thought, and he made it immediately clear that the assassination of Sadat was something he steadfastly refused to discuss publicly.

Mubarak had stood next to Sadat as his President died, having risen with him as Sadat saw Khaled al-Islambouli approach the reviewing stand. According to one of Islambouli's fellow assassins, in testimony given at the trial, he had spared Mubarak's life. "He was there in front of me, and I told him to step aside because I wanted that dog" (Sadat), Abdel-Hamid Abdel-A'al, a former army officer, testified. A request by Abdel-A'al's lawyer to summon Mubarak as a defense witness was flatly rejected by Mubarak's three-man military bench, as was a request by Islambouli's lawyer to call Sadat's two former Ministers of Foreign Affairs who had resigned to protest the Camp David peace accords or the President's "sacred pilgrimage" to Jerusalem.

The court's rejection of the two requests was no less forceful than was its rejection of any testimony—by either the military prosecutors or the defense—that exceeded the court's exceedingly narrow writ. Mubarak and his Army wished to keep the trial of army officers and NCOs as far as possible in their own hands.

Looking at news photographs, taken at the time of the trial, of the twenty-four men accused of assassinating Sadat, I was struck by the realization that the four key defendants—Colonel Abbud al-Zumur, the military leader of al-Jihad; Mohammed al-Farag, an electrical engineer who was its chief ideologue; Lieutenant Khaled al-Islambouli; and Sheikh Omar Abdel-Rahman—reflected an alliance of Egypt's military, civilian, and religious life. As they proceeded, one by one, to defend themselves before the bench, the four defendants came to represent, in the eyes of their supporters, another holy trinity in a sense.

"It's no accident that these guys who are challenging the regime call themselves the Commanders of the Caliph," remarked Dr. Sa'ad el-Din Ibrahim, my former professor at AUC, who has been studying the Islamist movement for over twenty years. "The Islamist groups have their own armies, their own military doctrine, their own vision of how to organize society and the state. Because the system is so tightly controlled from the inside, if we challenge the Pharaoh we challenge the three institutions under his control—his army, his religious establishment, and his bureaucracy. If we are calling for a new king, that means that we are also calling for a new army commander, and for a new pope. And that is precisely why the Islamists are trying to set up their own parallel system to challenge the state. And this is also why the two sides clash in such a deadly way."

Almost unnoticed on the day of Anwar Sadat's death was the timing of the bullets fired by Khaled al-Islambouli and his fellow militants. The assassination happened only six months before Israel's final withdrawal from the Sinai, and the return to Egypt—and to Sadat—of that land which he could see from the bay window of his Ismailia presidential retreat. But in return Sadat had agreed to demilitarize that land, to limit the number of Egyptian troops that could be stationed there, and to accept the presence of a U.S.-dominated United Nations peacekeeping force to monitor the demilitarization of Egyptian land. Much was said and written at the time of trouble and plots in the Army, where field-grade officers, in particular, were widely believed to be dissatisfied.

Anwar Sadat, the peasant-soldier who had sent men to war in order to achieve peace, and Lieutenant Khaled al-Islambouli, the Islamist-soldier who was appalled by the price he had paid, had both broken the unspoken covenant of the holy trinity. Within weeks of assuming his presidency, Hosni Mubarak quietly dismissed more than a hundred army officers in his first tentative step to bring one of its two arms back under presidential control.

He also declared a state of emergency—which remains in effect, and under which he has ruled the country for nearly twenty years. It permits the arrest and detention of suspects without charge, and the trial of civilians before special military courts, whose verdicts cannot be appealed.

As Islambouli stood before the court of his commanding officers in the days before he died, he was defiant and showed no remorse. "I killed Pharaoh," he repeated for the last time. Then, turning toward his mother in the shabby, makeshift court, he shouted out, brandishing a copy of the Koran, "May God join us again in paradise."

"Amen," his mother replied.

Sadat's assassination was justified under Shariah law, Islambouli and his fellow defendants testified during their trial, for the Egyptian President had deviated from Islam. Basing their case on their interpretation—a distortion, their detractors charged—of a relatively minor text of the great medieval thinker Ibn Taimiyya, they argued that Sadat was an infidel, and hence he must be killed. His greatest single infidelity, in their view, was his refusal to implement Shariah law.

By the time I returned to Egypt in 1993, twelve years after Anwar Sadat and Lieutenant Khaled al-Islambouli had died, the stakes had been perceptibly raised in an increasingly vengeful war between the inheritors of their legacies: Hosni Mubarak and Sheikh Omar Abdel-Rahman. The country's fate, it appeared, rested for the moment in the hands of these two men, along with the small circles of advisers who surrounded them and the armies that paid allegiance to them.

Both the President and the sheikh had spent the intervening years conscientiously building a power base—Mubarak moved quickly to consolidate his, while Sheikh Omar concentrated on expanding his. By retiring potential rivals and scrupulously maintaining the status quo, Mubarak had managed to stay ahead of his only real constituency—the 300,000-man Army—even as Sheikh Omar, with growing vigor, attempted to infiltrate it.

On assuming office, Mubarak had immediately reaffirmed Egypt's commitment to the peace treaty with Israel—which Sheikh Omar, ever more loudly, continued to oppose. The Arab League returned to Cairo during those years, ending Egypt's isolation in the Arab world, and both the soldier and the preacher proved adept at cultivating its leadership, most particularly the ruling dynasties of the oil-rich Persian Gulf. By the end of the 1980s, both Egypt's secular regime and its Islamist opposition were heavily subsidized—and each seemingly favored—by Saudi Arabia.

The greatest challenge to Mubarak's presidency had been in February 1986, when Central Security Forces recruits, demanding better pay, took to the streets, rioted, burned, and looted—as hundreds of thousands of other angry Egyptians had done during the food riots a decade earlier. And as had happened then, for only the second time in modern Egyptian history, a reluctant Army was dispatched to the streets in order to safeguard the Egyptian presidency.

It remains unclear to what extent the Muslim Brotherhood and Sheikh Omar's more militant Islamist underground participated in, or perhaps even provoked, the three days of rioting. What was far more discernible, then and now, is that both the moderate and the militant Islamists profited from it.

Sheikh Omar's power base continued to expand while, at the same time, his underground army began to engage in increasingly more violent acts against Mubarak's regime. In 1992, a shaken President turned fiercely and suddenly against the sheikh. Mubarak's repression was a response to the militants' accelerated assaults on Coptic Christians, intellectuals, the security forces, and the police, and their attacks on foreign tourists in an attempt to disrupt the economy and thereby bring down Mubarak's regime. The official offensive was brutal—and, in the view of many, shortsighted, since its excesses only lured more Egyptians into the Islamist fold.

In the exercise of power, the separation between the President and the sheikh was less than absolute. They were an implausible coupling at first glance: so very different yet so very much alike— the one a secularist soldier, the other an Islamist priest; both born into the Nile Delta's poverty. Both came of age at the most prestigious institutions of the holy trinity—the younger at the University of al-Azhar; the elder at the elite Air Force Academy and as a fighter pilot during the Arab-Israeli wars. Both were austere, perhaps to a fault, in their personal lives. Both were unpredictable, mystifying their closest advisers by charting one course of action and then abruptly changing their minds. Both shared the passion of the U.S.-sponsored war in Afghanistan. Both had become increasingly defiant and intransigent.

And as Egypt seemed to be sliding into an incipient guerrilla war, if neither seemed strong enough to demolish the other, neither seemed weak enough to fall.

Hosni Mubarak—like the Muslim Brotherhood—was born in 1928, in the tiny village of Kafr al-Museilha, barely a dot on the map, in the province of Menoufiya, at the cusp of the central Nile Delta, which hugs the Western Desert and is buffeted by its sands and winds. A scion of Kafr al-Museilha's large and highly structured

Mubarak clan, his father was a minor government bureaucrat (an inspector in the Ministry of Justice in the provincial capital) and a stern disciplinarian—a trait that would be inherited by his son. His mother, like the village into which the young Hosni was born, was poor, highly conservative, and highly traditional. (She produced one daughter as well as three other sons.) However, Kafr al-Museilha—like its province—prided itself on being unique: for in a country where 70 percent of the population could not then read or write, Menoufiya had a reputation for nearly complete literacy. (This curiosity was the result of the Revolution of 1919 and the role played in it by a native son, Abdel-Aziz Fahmi Pasha, who foresaw the spread of education as the only way to revolutionize Egyptian society. Menoufiya became his testing ground, and, as a consequence, it has the highest level of education in Egypt's provinces today, and its sons—"Menoufis," as they are called—dominate the Egyptian government.)

When I asked a Menoufi how he would describe the village and the province where Mubarak spent the first two decades of his life, he smiled and replied, "We have a reputation for being cunning, cautious, and stingy—all of which we are." Cunning and caution have been constants in Hosni Mubarak's life. He is also a loner, as many Menoufis are; but unlike most of them, from an early age he was assiduous about physical fitness, and he played a tough and avid game of hockey, and later squash. (Squash is one of the few apparent passions that he has carried with him throughout his life.) In one story frequently told of Mubarak's early years, he is recalled as marching through Kafr al-Museilha on his way to hockey games carrying his playing stick over his shoulder to ward off packs of dogs. But this is one of only a handful of anecdotes about his early life, for unlike Nasser and Sadat, Mubarak has an accentuated concern for privacy. Looking back now on my earlier time in Egypt, I remember all the press outings we made to Sadat's hot and dusty village of Mit Abu el-Kom, where Sadat would bask in his newly configured garden and field questions from the press, always reminding us of his peasant roots. Mubarak was sometimes present, but he never once volunteered that he was from Kafr al-Museilha, just down a dusty road.

As a child and a teenager, Mubarak attended local schools, where he was considered to be a competent student, though not a brilliant one. Then, in November 1947, at the age of nineteen, he left Menoufiya for Cairo, where he joined the prestigious Military Academy. He had no desire to follow in the footsteps of his father as a provincial bureaucrat.

The road on which he traveled was the same road that would be traveled on, a decade later, by the blind cleric from a not-so-distant village: Sheikh Omar Abdel-Rahman. And although their lives would become inexorably intertwined only decades afterward, even as young men, the two were not that dissimilar: both were from tiny, obscure places, which they left at nineteen; both had chosen one of two traditional routes of upward mobility. Both were high achievers from classes hungry for power and prestige. And although both carried the short, squat frame typical of the Nile Delta's peasants, or fellahin, once they left their villages they left their peasant roots behind. Hosni Mubarak never looked back.

Mubarak would exchange Kafr al-Museilha for nearly four decades of a comfortable middle-class military life. Following his graduation in 1949 from the Military Academy, with the rank of lieutenant, he trained as a fighter pilot at the Air Force Academy; according to one of his classmates, he was a natural. "Control and precision are two of his strongest traits," his former classmate said. "He is basically a military strategist." Over the next seven years, as an instructor at the Air Force Academy, Mubarak taught others to fly, including the man who would become the President of Syria, Hafez al-Assad. These were the happiest years of Mubarak's life. He had the reputation of being a strict disciplinarian, a tough, no-frills officer who went by the book, and who was, in every sense, uncomfortable with and scornful of politics.

Even before Nasser's Revolution of 1952—in which Mubarak had been too young to participate, if he had been so inclined—he had distinguished himself and was already on the rise. But he would profit further from the revolution, for it was his generation, those in their early twenties at the time, who experienced the greatest degree of upward military mobility occasioned, in part, by the large-scale purges of officers suspected of having close links to King

Farouk and the deposed Egyptian monarchy. It was at the behest of
Nasser that Mubarak was sent to the Soviet Union (then Egypt's
chief arms supplier), in the mid-1960s, for advanced training at
Moscow's Frunze Military Academy. "After we were nominated,
Nasser called us in," a retired general who trained with Mubarak
told me recently. "And he told us that he had only one request: he
wanted us to return home as anti-Communists." Both the general
and Mubarak did.

The young Egyptian officers disdained the obligatory history of
the Communist Party that accompanied their military course, the
heavy-handed surveillance they were subjected to, and the restriction
of movement involved. But what they most resented was the Soviet
Union's refusal to share advanced technology with them. "We were
never treated as equals; we were always patronized," the general
said. The young Captain Hosni Mubarak was enraged by this. He
has been disparaging of the former Soviet Union ever since.

(In later years, as the commander of the Air Force, he once told
Sadat that the Egyptian Air Force would not accept MiG-23 fighters
"even if the Russians give them to us free.")

By the time he trained in Moscow, Mubarak had married Suzanne Sabet, a half-Welsh, half-Egyptian woman, who has been his
wife for nearly forty years. He had been a stern taskmaster on mo-
rality, as well as discipline. "Russian girls were chasing us unbeliev-
ably," his general friend recalled. "They were all over; it was
impossible to get away. And Mubarak was the only one who told
us, even those of us who were his senior in rank, 'If you are married
and have a girlfriend, it means that you don't respect your family.' " It was a principle that would later guide Mubarak throughout
his presidency.

He was also affected by his command, in 1962, of the Egyptian
Air Force units that Nasser dispatched to fight in Yemen's civil war.
It proved to be a disastrous undertaking and the Egyptians were
accused, in their frustration, of dropping poison gas on their pro-
Saudi Royalist foes. One could say that the war in Yemen was
Egypt's Vietnam. Yet it was the Arab-Israeli wars of 1967 and 1973
that both mirrored and molded Mubarak's life.

On June 5, 1967—the day that would culminate in Egypt's humiliating defeat by Israel during the Six-Day War—Mubarak was the commander of Cairo West, the capital's main air base. Within eighty minutes on that first day of the war, nearly all of Egypt's aircraft, and its air defense systems, were destroyed. Leadership and command no longer existed once Egypt's borders were crossed, and Mubarak ordered his pilots to fly to the southern cities of Luxor and Aswan. When the war ended, his was one of only a handful of air squadrons that were left largely intact.

Further promotion followed rapidly and, months after the war, Mubarak was made director of the Air Force Academy. In June 1969, at the remarkably young age of forty-one, he was appointed by Nasser the Air Force Chief of Staff, and, in April 1972, Sadat named him its Commander in Chief. Mubarak's role in planning the 1973 October War, and in rebuilding the Egyptian Air Force from scratch, propelled him upward in the inner circle of Sadat. Then, on the morning of October 6, it was Mubarak who launched the surprise air attack against Israel, enabling Egyptian ground forces to reclaim the country's pride, as they crossed the Suez Canal and broke through Israel's Bar-Lev Line. If the 1973 war had not ended in a partial victory, Hosni Mubarak would probably have disappeared from history.

IN SEARCH OF THE SHEIKH

ON FEBRUARY 26, 1993, I WAS IN MY HOTEL ROOM IN CAIRO watching CNN when I learned of the explosion at the World Trade Center in New York. Like most people in Cairo, I was stunned by the news, but—also like most of them—I saw no reason to connect it with Egypt or, for that matter, with the larger Islamic world. I had returned to Cairo to learn more about the fiery religious leader whose name I had heard so often during my student days, Sheikh Omar Abdel-Rahman. He now lived in obscurity in the metropolitan area of New York, but in his native Egypt the frail, blind cleric, who was assisted by an international network of support, was fueling the Islamist revolution against the state he had defied for nearly thirty years.

It was only in the course of the next month, after a number of arrests were made, that I learned that the World Trade Center bombing had allegedly been carried out by followers of the sheikh. Mohammed Salameh, a member of the al-Salam Mosque in Jersey City, where Sheikh Omar preached, was the first man arrested, for his role in renting the van that carried the bomb into the parking garage of the World Trade Center. Nidal Ayyad, a chemical engineer and a regular worshipper at al-Salam, was charged with assisting in the fabrication of the bomb. Mahmud Abou-halima, who authorities said was with Salameh on the day of the bombing, had worked as an assistant and driver to Sheikh Omar. And an enigmatic stranger, known to the world as Ramzi Ahmed Yousef, had spent considerable time at al-Salam, after quietly entering the United States from Afghanistan—along with another Afghan veteran, Ahmad Moham-med Ajaj. (Ibrahim Elgabrowny, indicted on a lesser offense, was one of Sheikh Omar's closest associates in the United States.) At the time, law enforcement officers said that they had no evidence to link the sheikh to the bombing—nor would he ever be brought to trial directly for it. But it seems to me that the greater threat to the interests of the United States lies not in an act of terrorism here but, rather, in the pos-sibility of a militant Islamic government's coming to power in Egypt —a threat that could be as formidable as any we have faced from the Ayatollah Khomeini in Iran or Saddam Hussein in Iraq.

Sheikh Omar had been charged by the Immigration and Natu-ralization Service with entering this country illegally, and on Jan-uary 20, a few weeks before returning to Egypt, I went to his exclusion hearing in Newark, New Jersey, where no one I happened to talk to really believed the charges against him—certainly not his lawyers, and not any of the two hundred or so bearded young men who defiantly waved placards and signs outside the Immigration Court. Newark detectives were skeptical, too. And when, in chatting with a patrolman, I enumerated the chain of supposed mishaps that had led to the sheikh's being granted a tourist visa by the U.S. Em-bassy in the Sudan in May 1990; being granted permanent resident status and a green card by the INS in April 1991; and being allowed to reenter the country by security officials at Kennedy Airport in July 1991, his response was incredulous. "Jesus, you mean three different government agencies messed up four times?" Most of the journalists covering the hearing were skeptical as well, especially since Sheikh Omar had at one time helped United States interests by supporting the anti-Soviet mujahideen in Afghanistan. Some of us had been tracking the sheikh for weeks, on a path that often led, to our considerable surprise, to the same apartments, Levantine restau-rants, and storefront mosques that had been visited earlier by agents of the FBI. *They* had been tracking him for more than two years, and he appeared to delight in watching security officials in the Mid-dle East, Europe, and the United States attempt to link his words with others' terrorist acts.

Because the court building had been effectively sealed off by police, who had heard that Sheikh Omar's supporters would protest, I joined the sheikh's followers outside. The scene inside, in a room on the fifth floor, was described for me by witnesses afterward. The sheikh—who, because of lifelong ill health, looked considerably older than his fifty-five years—was supported by two followers as he stood before the judge wearing a long gray clerical robe and the crimson cap with white piping of al-Azhar. Unruly tufts of frizzy white hair sprouted from beneath his cap, and a full gray-white beard rested on his chest. He was not unfamiliar with court proceedings. On at least four occasions he had stood trial in Egypt, where he was widely regarded as the spiritual mentor of a network of militant underground Islamic groups, and he had spent some seven years in prison or under house arrest. He was perhaps best known as one of the key defendants in the Sadat assassination trial, and although he had been acquitted of all charges—since the prosecution was unable to prove that he had issued a fatwa declaring Sadat an infidel—the accusation had been enough to put him on this country's official terrorist list. Yet he had arrived in the United States—quietly and without attracting attention—in July 1990, via Saudi Arabia, Afghanistan, and the Sudan, on the much-disputed tourist visa issued by an undercover agent of the CIA. (State Department officials explained at the time that the visa was issued because of a "computer error" at the Khartoum Embassy, and because Sheikh Omar had used a variant of his name on his application form. I discovered later, however, that this was the sixth visa that Sheikh Omar had been issued to enter the United States.)

Now he stood somberly before immigration judge Daniel Meisner as an INS official briskly presented evidence that he had attempted to conceal his past by failing to note on his visa application that he was polygamous and that he had been convicted, in Egypt, of falsifying a check. (It was for a small sum, and the charge was later withdrawn.) Then, in a move that caught many law enforcement officials, including the sheikh's surveillants from the FBI, by surprise, the defendant requested political asylum in the United States.

At precisely two-thirty, the sheikh's supporters crossed the street in front of the court building to a parking lot. There they stood in parallel lines, facing east, and began the ritual of midday prayers. Most of them were young, but I noticed one man, with receding salt-and-pepper hair, who was older—probably in his early forties —and more distinguished-looking than the others. He was better dressed, in a fur-lined suede jacket. He also seemed to possess an air of authority. When the prayers were over, I introduced myself to him. He was Ibrahim Elgabrowny. He told me that he was a civil engineer who had come to Brooklyn from Port Said and had established a contracting business there. We soon discovered that we had both been university students in Egypt—he an engineering student at the University of Port Said—during the tumultuous 1970s, when, in their efforts to undermine the left, the governments of Egypt, Saudi Arabia, and some of the Gulf states had transformed Egypt's nascent Islamist groups into what was, after the Army, the country's best-organized social force. My mind wandered back to those earlier years, when Anwar Sadat had barred nearly the entire political spectrum from parliamentary life and some fifty underground groups had begun operating, from the extreme right to the extreme left. I wondered if Elgabrowny had been one of those Islamist students who spent their summer holidays in military training at remote desert camps.

Supporters of Sheikh Omar came and went as we talked. There was a scattering of African American Muslims, but most were Middle Eastern. Some were recently arrived immigrants and spoke no English. Others were articulate in English and well educated, among them an Egyptian lawyer who now drove a taxi and a civil engineer who had been a devout follower of Sheikh Omar for more than twenty years.

Later that afternoon, I learned that Elgabrowny was a cousin of El-Sayyid A. Nosair, a dedicated Egyptian follower of Sheikh Omar. Nosair—who had been charged with, and acquitted of, the 1990 murder of Rabbi Meir Kahane, whose rabidly anti-Arab views led him to establish the militant Jewish Defense League—was then serving a sentence of seven to twenty-two years in Attica State Prison on weapons charges relating to the crime.

Elgabrowny had been the chief fund-raiser and organizer of his cousin's defense and had made numerous trips to the Middle East —most often to Saudi Arabia—in an effort to raise money. The Saudi government agreed to help by permitting him to put collection boxes in the Kingdom's thousands of mosques. Unspecified amounts of money—"vast," according to one account—were raised. According to William Kunstler, one of the three lawyers who defended Nosair, Elgabrowny acted as a paralegal and also provided bodyguards and tight security for the lawyers, who, Kunstler maintained, were besieged by picketers and activists from the Jewish Defense League.

When the doors of the federal building in Newark opened and Sheikh Omar appeared, the scene was tumultuous. His supporters nearly toppled a hot-dog stand as they raced toward him pell-mell. Elgabrowny shouted instructions, and a tight circle of security men surrounded Sheikh Omar.

"Don't grab the sheikh!" one supporter shouted to the others. "Don't touch him! He doesn't know who you are!"

"Get those placards out of the way!" a police sergeant bellowed from his horse.

With utter calm, and an expressionless face, the man everyone had come to support plodded slowly but with determination through the crowd. He was bundled into a white Cadillac and driven off.

Over the next few days, I visited the neighborhoods in Brooklyn and Jersey City that were the strongholds of Sheikh Omar's New York support. At the time of his arrival here, he was already a powerful spiritual voice in Egypt, and—to the irritation of the region's rulers—cassettes of his fiery sermons were circulating in much of the Middle East. A controversial figure who moved with serene assurance through the worlds of militants and mullahs, he was equally at home with Islamic scholars, guerrilla leaders, such as Afghanistan's Gulbadin Hekmatyar, and chiefs of state, among them Sudan's General Omar al-Bashir and Pakistan's General Mohammed Zia ul-Haq. Perhaps as interesting as how he entered the United States is why he decided to come. His three great passions were the civil war in Afghanistan, the spread of Islam, and the overthrow of the Egyptian government. He found ready allies for all three causes along Brooklyn's Atlantic Avenue, in a neighborhood where women, their heads covered by veils or scarves, line up at the local baker's to buy pita and baklava, and where men tend to congregate around Islamic centers and mosques, which have spawned a multitude of militant groups, whose ideologies are as eclectic as the men's accents are diverse. In one corner coffee shop I found photographs of the Ayatollah Khomeini, Yasir Arafat, and Saddam Hussein competing for attention on the walls. I then visited the area's jihad office—formally, the Alkifah Refugee Center—set up in the mid-1980s by Mustafa Shalabi, an electrical contractor from Egypt, to aid the anti-Communist rebels in Afghanistan. It was here that Sheikh Omar had made his initial attempt to consolidate a power base in the United States. Shalabi had sponsored him on his arrival, found him an apartment, and provided him with a car, a driver, and a phone. The two men raised money together and recruited young men from the neighborhood, some of whom, I was reliably told, subsequently received weapons training at a site in Connecticut. More than two hundred Arabs and Arab Americans were recruited and provided with plane tickets to Pakistan, from whence they crossed the border to fight in the jihad in Afghanistan.

The jihad was an obsession with Sheikh Omar. Nonetheless, his alliance with Shalabi did not last long, and their dispute is of abiding interest to the FBI. In March 1991, Shalabi's body was found in his Brooklyn apartment with multiple stab wounds and a bullet through the head. The case remains unsolved, and while Sheikh Omar is not suspected of direct involvement in the murder, federal agents are attempting to determine whether he gave religious sanction for it. Sheikh Omar expresses outrage at that suggestion, and over the years he has steadfastly refused to discuss Shalabi, telling one interviewer, "I did not know that man," and another, "These aren't press questions—this sounds like the FBI."

At the jihad office, a Sudanese who said his name was Jalal sat behind a rickety desk in front of a tottering bookcase whose shelves held religious literature and Arabic cassettes. I asked him what had happened between Shalabi and Sheikh Omar—why their friendship had soured. (According to an acquaintance of both men, they had feuded over control of the jihad funds and over Sheikh Omar's insistence on supporting the Islamist movement in Egypt, which was battling Hosni Mubarak's government.)

"No comment," he said, and began shuffling nervously through a stack of papers on his desk.

"Why is the office still open, now that the Afghan war has ended?" I went on, attempting to keep the conversation going, such as it was.

"Bosnia."

Was Sheikh Omar recruiting fighters or attempting to raise money for that cause?

"The Muslim world is one. Wherever there is a struggle, we are ready to fight." That was all he would say.

I then went to Jersey City, where I eventually located the al-Salam Mosque. It proved to be an improvised affair on the third floor of a white brick building on Kennedy Boulevard—a cold and empty room. Tiny shafts of light filtered through its cracked windows, which had been painted blue. Plastic buckets collected rainwater from the ceiling, which was buckling and in some areas seemed dangerously close to collapse. In a far corner, a traditional high-backed wooden chair was the only furniture, and I tried to imagine Friday prayers, with Sheikh Omar perched atop the chair, suspended perhaps three feet above the worshippers sitting cross-legged on the floor. The room would hold about a hundred people, I thought. I had been told that it was always full.

I removed my shoes in the hallway and then, as judiciously as I could, avoiding the buckets scattered here and there, entered the room. Six men fingering strands of colorful prayer beads sat cross-legged on the floor. In a far corner I spotted cartons of Sony tapes, and tacked to one of the walls was a hand-scrawled sign announcing a weekend bus trip to Attica State Prison, for forty-five dollars a person, to visit "our brother" El-Sayyid A. Nosair.

"Excuse me," I said, addressing the men sitting on the floor.

For a few moments, no one turned around. Then, in unison, as though the movement had been choreographed, the six men rose.

They approached me in cadence, in two distinct lines, and asked me, in diverse Middle Eastern accents, why I'd come.

I asked them if I might hear one of Sheikh Omar's tapes, for I had been told that his sermons and lectures, calling for the overthrow of Mubarak's regime, were recorded here and smuggled into Egypt, Iran, and Lebanon by special courier.

"Are you a Muslim?" a man in a stocking cap, who identified himself as Mohammed, asked.

"No, but I'm about to travel to Egypt," I said.

No sooner had I said this than one of the men went to a corner bookshelf and returned with a stack of documents, which he handed to me. They were mostly Amnesty International reports on torture in Egypt. "Egypt is a horrible place," he said.

Suddenly a short, grim-faced man appeared. His bearded face was framed by a kaffiyeh, and he was carrying a copy of the Koran.

"We know of no tapes," he said, announcing his arrival.

Mohammed and the young man who had given me the documents discreetly walked away, and I stood alone in the middle of the mosque. The bearded man in the kaffiyeh was clearly in charge, and for a moment I felt far more estranged from his tight-knit world in Jersey City, where "foreigners" are viewed with suspicion, than I had ever felt in his homeland, some seven thousand miles away.

When I arrived in Cairo in early February 1993, an Egyptian friend told me, with considerable confidence in her voice, "It's the same Cairo you knew—it's only wearing slightly different clothes." As I strolled around the city, I wasn't sure. I was struck, more than ever before, by the contrast between the poverty that seemed to be everywhere and a world of astonishing wealth. At a downtown car dealership, I listened as two men, wearing sparkling rings, argued and gesticulated, flailing their arms, over the price—$400,000—of a new Mercedes, which had just arrived. Then I watched bands of ten-year-olds lumber by in mule-drawn carts. Their faces were pretty but filthy, and they were dressed in rags; they lived among the smoking piles in south Cairo's City of Garbage, and they survived by collecting rubbish along the streets.

I then visited a realtor in Zamalek, a large, fleshy man who told me that for $10,000 he could sell me one square meter of land; when I left him, I visited the City of the Dead, where half a million Cairenes live among mausoleums and tombs dating back to the thirteenth century. "It's called alternative housing," an architect who had come with me explained. "It's a convenient location, and, of course, there's no overhead. But the government is frightfully embarrassed by so many people living among the dead."

Since my student days in Cairo, Egypt had been receiving lavish amounts of Western aid, including some $2 billion a year from the United States. The money began arriving after the peace treaty with Israel in 1979, when Anwar Sadat embarked on policies that transformed Cairo into the hub of American policy in the Middle East. But the distribution of aid was uneven at best, and little of it filtered down. True, the telephone system was vastly improved (a decade earlier, affluent Egyptians sometimes flew to Greece or Cyprus for the day just to make telephone calls), but in the slums of Imbaba, Bulaq, and Shobra no one had a phone.

The new wealth—complemented by a dubious 1974 economic opening (known as the *infitah*) to attract private capital investment from the West—had also bred a new and ostentatious class that surrounded Sadat, as it surrounds Hosni Mubarak now. Its members thought little of spending $150,000 for a daughter's wedding at a five-star Cairo hotel, while the nation's per capita GNP remained frozen at around $700 a year. Like so much else, the *infitah*, which allowed private enterprise to flourish unchecked, did nothing to improve the economic circumstances of the common man. Few of the gains expected to accrue had materialized. Nearly all of its investments went into the nonproductive service sector, and its consequences were largely seen in the flaunting of wealth: in the importation of luxury goods, including vastly expensive cars, and in the mushrooming of five-star restaurants and nightclubs. The Egyptian writer Mohamed Hassanein Heikal, in referring to the "sordid vulgarity of its profiteers," noted that in a single Cairo supermarket no fewer than fifty-eight different brands of foreign shampoo were on sale.

Everything seemed to be swirling out of control. Corruption flourished; the population swelled; and much of the bureaucracy, which even in the best of times approached a state of ossification, seemed totally paralyzed.

But one of my most vivid impressions on this visit was of decay: of crumbling buildings seen through a patina of dust; of torn-up sidewalks and sewage in the street; of a city that was angry and was living on the edge as its population continued to grow. A thousand new residents arrived each day, in a country whose population grew by a million every ten months. And the more the city crumbled and the more its population swelled, the more eager it appeared to be to embrace a revival of Islam. Mosques were everywhere now, or so it seemed to me—more than a thousand of them, dotting the city in various shapes and forms: some of them partly ruined and others restored; some with magnificent inlaid arches of marble and gold, and others tiny, makeshift rooms in "popular" neighborhoods.

One Friday morning, just before midday prayers, I returned, with my friend Hoda, to the Khan el-Khalili Bazaar. Endless streams of people were descending on the centuries-old al-Hussein Mosque, situated nearby, as I imagine they were descending on al-Azhar, which was not too far away. The chants of a muezzin echoed through the bazaar.

On this Friday, few shops were open. "It was never like this before," Hoda remarked, irritation in her voice. "The Khan el-Khalili merchants never closed their shops for Friday prayers." The area was now swarming with people, and it was impossible to find our car, so, along with perhaps a thousand worshippers, we found ourselves being swept toward the al-Hussein Mosque.

I wondered if this was happening all over Cairo—and I discovered later that it was. The entire neighborhood, suddenly and without warning, had been transformed. Car horns were silent, and nothing moved, except the worshippers still descending upon the mosque. Many of the women were in abayas, covered from head to toe. Men bowed on the pavements, where straw prayer mats had been laid and then roofed over with dark green sheeting hung from makeshift poles. Standing outside the mosque, we listened to a sermon about giving alms to the poor, which emphasized that it was the duty of all Muslims to do charitable work. It was rather innocuous, or so it seemed to me, but then this was an official government mosque. As the sermon continued, I glanced around at the crowd. At its far edges, between buildings with peeling walls, I noticed four or five tables covered with white cloth. They were tended by tall, bearded men dressed in white crocheted prayer caps and long, flowing white robes. When the service was over, Hoda and I approached one of the tables, which was piled high with religious literature and copies of the Koran. To my surprise, I saw, at an official government mosque, cassettes of sermons by Sheikh Omar.

"Prayers are so dreary," Hoda remarked. But I had noticed that during the service, even though we were outside the mosque, she had discreetly covered her head with a scarf.

Later, when we finally found our car, Hoda said, "Now we must hear Hala." She didn't explain who Hala might be.

We drove to one of Zamalek's fashionable private clubs. Inside, some fifty upper-middle-class women, of lower-middle age, were sitting at card tables in one of the lecture halls. They sipped tea and gossiped. Then there was a hush.

A woman of rather large proportions had entered the room, her head covered by a white scarf—many yards of gauzy material, hanging to her waist. I guessed that she was in her early forties, and I later learned that she had grown up in the Imbaba slum. She was dressed in a dark crimson robe that swept the floor, and she wore no jewelry or makeup. She seemed to totter on very spindly high-heeled shoes. Taking her place at a lectern, she made a few introductory remarks and then said, "In my former life, everyone constantly stared at me. I could feel the contempt in their eyes." She paused, and broke into convulsive sobs. Some of the women at the card tables took linen handkerchiefs from their purses and dabbed at their eyes. "Then the Prophet came to me, in a dream," she went on. "He covered me, and from that moment I knew I would never feel naked again."

There was a discernible sigh of relief from the audience, and the hankies were put away. Hala Safi, one of Egypt's most successful and best-loved belly dancers, had been born again.

Later that afternoon, with another American journalist, I went in search of Abdel-Nebi Khalifa. I knew little about him except that he was the son of an upper-middle-class judge and was in Kasr al-Ayni Hospital, Room No. 34. He was a follower of Sheikh Omar and, like some eight hundred others, had slipped back into Egypt quietly after fighting in the Afghanistan war. He had been arrested ten days before. (A new law made it a capital crime to receive military training abroad, and eight Egyptians who had fought in Afghanistan had already been sentenced to death.) Khalifa, who was now in the hospital's "detention wing," had been badly tortured and was partly paralyzed, according to an Islamist lawyer. There was some question about whether he was still alive.

Kasr al-Ayni Hospital is part of Cairo University's medical school, and we entered it through an unlighted underground corridor. Only occasional shafts of light enabled us to find our way as we attempted not to attract attention but knew perfectly well that we were doing so: two foreigners wandering around in an underground tunnel looking for a secret prison ward.

A young man, clean-shaven and wearing Western clothes, approached us and told us, even before we had a chance to ask, "They've transferred the prisoners to the new annex." He led us out of the tunnel and past a complex of university classrooms, and pointed to a seven-story building. "The people from Cell 34 are on the eighth floor," he said. I looked up and saw a small rooftop extension; its windows were barred and were covered, inside the bars, by rattan shades. We entered the building and began to climb stairs.

On the seventh floor the stairs ended, and as we were deciding what to do a young woman, who was veiled, appeared. "You're looking for the political detainees" was all that she said. She then led us down a corridor to another, slightly hidden flight of stairs. Although the extension was new, the walls leading to it were filthy; excrement and discarded needles littered the narrow stairwell.

When we reached the top, we found a cream-colored iron door, bolted from the inside. Four policemen in ill-fitting black uniforms and berets were guarding the entrance, and a fifth face quickly appeared in a tiny barred window that seemed to have been chiseled into the door as an afterthought.

"We've come to see Abdel-Nebi Khalifa," my companion announced, in a voice that suggested far more confidence than he could have felt.

"Why do you want to see him?" one of the guards asked.

"We want to interview him," my companion said. "We're journalists."

To my astonishment, one of the guards opened the door. After we entered, he slammed it shut and secured it with four bolts. I had a momentary sense of claustrophobia. No one knew that we were even here. And I remembered something that a lawyer who represented scores of Islamist political detainees had told me earlier: "The most terrifying thing for the prisoners is that they could be killed in detention and no one would know, because nobody knew where they were being held."

Flanked by six policemen, three on each side, we were escorted to a tiny room a few feet beyond the door, and there we were introduced to Lieutenant Ashra Beg Hosni—at least, that was the name given to us—the officer in charge. He had a round, feminine face and white hair and wore a daunting black uniform; on his feet he had a pair of blue plastic shower thongs.

"What are you doing here?" he asked, sounding like an interrogator, which I suspected he was.

After a good deal of conversation, which seemed to lead nowhere, he told us we needed a permit from the prosecutor general, but he did confirm that Abdel-Nebi Khalifa was there.

As we left his office, I glanced down a long, empty white corridor and saw twelve bolted doors. In contrast to the bustling cacophony of the rest of the hospital, not a sound was to be heard on this floor.

Just outside the hospital, we found one of the policemen who had been guarding the entrance to the eighth floor waiting for us in the courtyard.

There were eleven detainees, all Islamists, in the prison ward, he volunteered. Most were from Cairo, but a few were from Upper Egypt. They had all been brought here from Cairo's Tora and Abu Zabal prisons and were "very sick," he said, mostly with heart or stomach ailments, but some had leg injuries and deep open wounds. When we asked him if they had been tortured, he said yes.

"Taking the veil," as it is called, had just begun to express itself when I was at AUC. Now it was the norm at universities. One afternoon I watched a group of students, all women and all veiled, as they walked across a bridge that separates the fashionable neighborhood of Giza, where Cairo University is, and the district of Bulaq, one of the city's most dismal and sprawling slums. They looked straight ahead, paying little heed to an armored personnel carrier that now guarded the bridge. Such squat gray vehicles had become a familiar sight in recent months.

In and around Zamalek, there were clusters of riot policemen, their faces partly hidden by visored helmets. They stood guard outside tourist centers, half-empty hotels, and the city's new, Japanese-built, gilded opera house. Earlier that morning, a guard had checked my parcels before I entered a boutique, and now truckloads of commandos hurtled by me along the Nile's Corniche.

During the spring of 1993, the stakes were again perceptibly raised in the shadowy war—a war in which there are no front lines—between Mubarak's security forces and Sheikh Omar's Islamic militants. Nearly every other day someone died. The militants, with a new boldness, accelerated their attacks on Coptic Christians, security forces, intellectuals, and tourist sites. The government responded brutally.

Among secular Cairenes, who seemed to have been left behind in the growing polarization of political life, there was mounting concern about the Islamist movement, which had assumed so many different faces and forms, and there was almost universal criticism of the government's response. There was also a tangible fear, which I had never known here before, that Egypt, now with over sixty million people—one-third of the Arab world—could lose its struggle against militant Islam.

Since the mid-1970s—when the Muslim Brotherhood first began

to evolve into the mainstream of political life, and the Gama'a al-Islamiya first began to dominate the Islamist trend at universities—there had been an appreciable upsurge, in both influence and profile, across Egypt of political Islam. It was easy to find it, whether in prosperous Cairo neighborhoods or in the slums, in Upper and Middle Egypt, and along the Mediterranean coast. All the various groups, militant and moderate alike, shared the ultimate goal of the establishment in Egypt of a theocratic Islamic state ruled by Shariah law. Their only difference—whether this would occur through revolutionary or evolutionary means—was in approach.

On university campuses, and in the villages and towns of Upper and Middle Egypt, near the banks of the Nile, Gama'a had established a solid base; while in the larger urban centers, and in the "popular" neighborhoods of Cairo, Alexandria, Ismailia, and Port Said, it appeared to share equal ground (sometimes cooperatively, sometimes not) with the more clandestine al-Jihad, which had regrouped—under a medical doctor named Ayman al-Zawahiri—since its assassination of Sadat. Other militant groups had formed or divided, sprung up or dispersed since my student days: some preached violence against the state; others advocated only the overthrow of the Mubarak regime; still others urged their followers to retreat from society.

But despite its divisions and new formations over the years, the present militant movement consists of essentially those same groups—some forty-four in all—that came of age on university campuses during the 1970s, under the watchful eye of Sadat. Many of them had formed a loose alliance in June 1980, the year before Sadat died, and despite differences in tactics and distinctive leaderships, they have, since then, operated from time to time under the general rubric of Gama'a and al-Jihad.

Yet for all the attention these more radical groups got, the vast majority of Islamists were engaged in a revolution by stealth to unseat the Mubarak government. And even among the militants, groups like Gama'a were armed not only with weapons but with an impressive, and continually expanding, array of charitable organizations and a network of schools, health clinics, community centers, and mosques. Some of their members—who were no longer drawn only from the universities and the "popular" neighborhoods but also from the professions, the bureaucracy, and the arts—in a now familiar pattern, had come from the Muslim Brotherhood's rank and file, who had been tortured and radicalized in prison, during the last years of Sadat.

For its part, the Brotherhood had continued to evolve in the other direction, and it now had a new lease on life: still officially banned, in reality it was tolerated by the government because it represented what had become the moderate wing of Egypt's Islamic trend. It had rebuilt its organization over twenty years, self-consciously espousing a policy of moderate reform; and as it had done with Nasser, and then with Sadat, it had worked out a modus vivendi with the Mubarak government. For although its philosophy has always carried the potential for violence, it now preached jihad in only the mildest way; the first task of its followers was to change society, through the establishment or infiltration of social structures and the control of mosques. All of this seemed quite innocuous to the Mubarak government. There was a certain irony in this, of course, since Mubarak—not unlike Nasser and Sadat—had begun his presidency by courting the Islamists, who, he hoped, could deliver to him the large constituency he needed to afford legitimacy to his regime. With time, however—as Nasser and Sadat had done—he recognized the dangers that the Islamists posed to him, and he turned quickly and brutally against them, targeting especially their militant undergrounds. Like Nasser and Sadat, Mubarak would be too late.

By the time I returned to Egypt, the Muslim Brotherhood was possessed of both substantial power and substantial wealth: the growth of Islamic banks and investment houses had been phenomenal since my student days. During the late 1980s, the Islamic movement had constructed a virtual financial state within the state. The banks and the investment houses operated without government control; they knew no regulation; and many of them dealt fast and loose, controlling sums of money estimated at between $2 and $3 billion. When the largest of them, Al-Rayyan, and some hundred others collapsed in 1988, it was the greatest financial scandal in Islamic history.

But, curiously, the partial loss of one of the movement's key financial arms did not appear to have more than a transitory effect on its otherwise expanding social and political profile. There had been a proliferation of Islamic social welfare institutions, including day-care centers, hospitals, and schools; of Islamist influence in the media, in the arts, and in the courts. The Brotherhood now controlled some of the country's most important trade unions, student bodies, and syndicates, among them the syndicates of lawyers, doctors, pharmacists, and engineers. In 1987, it had stood for parliament, under the banner of the socialist Labor Party, and even though the election was highly controlled, it emerged with nearly 20 percent of the seats, making it—until it boycotted the next elections in 1990—the leader of the parliamentary opposition to Mubarak's regime.

Nonetheless, many observers argued that the Brotherhood was losing ground to Gama'a and al-Jihad. For religious counsel and guidance, both of these militant groups, and the groups allied with them, follow the teachings of Sheikh Omar Abdel-Rahman.

The sheikh was born, in May 1938, into a poor family in the Nile Delta's Daqahliya Province. Blinded by diabetes when he was ten months old, he had few options besides Islamic studies, which were based on learning by rote. By the age of eleven, he had memorized a Braille copy of the Koran. At Cairo University's School of Theology, where he received a master's degree with distinction in 1965, he began dabbling in Islamist politics, but his activities were mild, consisting largely of writing pamphlets and lecturing on the Koran. Then, in 1967, when he had completed half the work for his Ph.D. in Islamic jurisprudence at Cairo's University of al-Azhar, the Arab world suffered its humiliating defeat by the Israeli Army in the Six-Day War. The defeat affected Abdel-Rahman's thinking profoundly. "Perhaps it was there all the time," a sheikh who was a fellow student of Sheikh Omar's and now teaches at the university told me one afternoon. "But he showed a violence of language that I had never seen before. He had always been vastly intelligent and vastly ambitious, and now he was vastly radicalized."

Sheikh Omar took a sabbatical. At the behest of al-Azhar—where, as a Ph.D. candidate, he had been elevated to the rank of sheikh (religious scholar) and imam (prayer leader)—he was posted to the obscure village of Fidimin, in the Faiyum Oasis, an hour's drive southwest of Cairo. Within two years, he had turned it—along with much of the rest of the Faiyum Oasis—into a stronghold of political Islam. He traveled from mosque to mosque, delivering sermons, considered incendiary at the time, that were targeted almost exclusively against "the Pharaoh," "the apostate," "the infidel"—who, it was clear, could be none other than Nasser. Nasser had already suppressed the Muslim Brotherhood, and he had little patience, one sheikh told me, "with this young upstart." Sheikh Omar was dismissed from his teaching position in 1969, and was arrested the following year, at the time of Nasser's death, after he traversed the villages of Faiyum admonishing people not to pray for their President. He was imprisoned, without charges, for eight months.

On his release from prison, the sheikh devoted himself to finishing his Ph.D. and to producing heirs. (He now has two wives, and one daughter and nine sons.) The year 1971, his last at al-Azhar, proved to be a turning point. Anwar Sadat had come to power, and with no political base of his own other than the Army, he had turned to the political right—particularly the religious right. The church and the Army bonded once more. Thus, in 1971, when King Faisal of Saudi Arabia, at the behest of Sadat, offered the rector of al-Azhar, Dr. Abdel-Halim Mahmoud, $100 million for the campaign against Communism and atheism, and for the triumph of Islam, the political face of Egypt was transformed. One of Sheikh Mahmoud's most promising students was Sheikh Omar. There was a lavish publicity campaign across Egypt: books were written; new mosques were built; students were recruited. Within a year, Sheikh Omar was sent back to Faiyum, then to Upper Egypt—first to al-Minya, then, in April 1973, to the University of Asyut. Here, as a professor of theology, he began adapting the absolutist teachings of the Egyptian Sayyid Qutb and the Pakistani Abul Ala el-Mawdudi, which are today revered by nearly every militant Islamic group. A member of the Muslim Brotherhood, Qutb had served as Nasser's Minister of Education but was executed in 1966 in connection with an ill-defined plot against Nasser's government. Mawdudi, the leader of a Pakistani group—the Jama'at-i-Islami—closely allied with the Brotherhood, had been sentenced to death in 1953. (He was later given a reprieve, and died in the United States in 1979.) Both are considered Islamic martyrs, or *shahids*.

Qutb, during nine years of imprisonment, had produced a seminal book, *Signposts Along the Road*, in which he argues that jihad—or struggle—should be waged not only defensively, in the protection of Muslim lands, but offensively against the enemies of Islam. Describing Nasser's regime as one of "pre-Islamic barbarism" that justified any form of resistance, Qutb's *Signposts* has been likened to Lenin's *What Is to Be Done?* in terms of its influence on today's world of militant Islam.

Sheikh Omar had been part of that revolutionary tradition since his days at al-Azhar.

(In his own most often quoted book, *A Word of Truth*, which would be published in 1987, the sheikh espouses an ideology of Pan-Islamism: of restoring the Caliphate, which was abolished in 1924 by the Turkish leader Kemal Atatürk after the dismemberment of the Ottoman Empire following the First World War; of carrying out jihad in Islam's trouble spots; and of fully implementing Shariah law. He also uncategorically rejects the Camp David peace treaty and Egypt's economic opening to the West; and he advocates instead a dependence on local resources and self-sufficiency, although he does not reject Western science and technology.)

By 1976, as Islamists in and around Asyut began to intensify their activities against Sadat's regime, Sheikh Omar no longer appeared to be the pliable, self-effacing man sent to Upper Egypt as an academic emissary of al-Azhar. His following was substantial, if a bit odd, consisting mostly of peasants, angry students, and doctors of theology. He had emerged as *the* leader of Gama'a in Upper Egypt, and although Gama'a was only a nascent, university-based Islamic activist group, which until then had been closely controlled by the government in Cairo, the regime grew alarmed. Sadat began to crack down. Rather than subject himself to repression, in 1977

Sheikh Omar, who had become the unquestionable figurehead of political Islam in Upper Egypt, left for Saudi Arabia. There he joined the faculty of the Girls' College of the Imam Muhammad Ibn Saud Islamic University of Riyadh.

Over the next three years, he traveled throughout the Middle East. With an eye to the future, he cultivated friendships that would eventually lead to the formation of an international support network for his activities—an axis that would link Afghanistan, Pakistan, and the Sudan. He also proved extraordinarily adept at exploiting political divisions within the Saudi establishment. "Charming and beguiling, dangerous and duplicitous" was the way he was described to me by an Arab diplomat who dealt with him during those years. "He had an uncanny sense of timing. He would dole out his vitriol until the Saudis reached their limit. Then, with equal ease, he was able to rein it in. The main point is that this man is a politician, not an Islamic scholar. His sermons and religious writings are really quite shallow, as far as I can tell. But he has clearly caught the imagination of the new generation. Perhaps you could best describe him as a populist."

While the sheikh was in Saudi Arabia, he met Dr. Hassan al-Turabi, the erudite leader of Sudan's National Islamic Front, who is today his country's most powerful man. (In December 1990, a rigid Islamic state took root in the Sudan, and the government is effectively controlled by the National Front.) The sheikh and Turabi had much in common, and became fast friends. They were brought even closer together by the events of 1979: the peace treaty between Egypt and Israel; the Soviet invasion of Afghanistan; and the revolution in Iran. The Arab world was in a state of turmoil, and Egypt was threatened by the same kind of potential political, social, and economic discord that had gripped Iran before the Shah was deposed. Because of its peace treaty, it stood alone in the Arab world. The next year, Sheikh Omar returned. He had amassed enough money—through what some observers refer to as "Riyalpolitik" in reference to Saudi Arabia's lavish and seemingly indiscriminate funding of disparate Islamic groups—to challenge al-Azhar and the traditional religious establishment. He made no secret of his ultimate goal: the overthrow of the Egyptian government and the establishment of a theocratic Islamic state.

It is not clear precisely where Sheikh Omar was when Anwar Sadat died. He had been arrested the previous month, during the huge security sweep in which all of Sadat's perceived critics were jailed. Then, before Sadat's assassination, under circumstances that no one could explain to me, the blind cleric escaped. Had he returned to the University of Asyut, in Upper Egypt, which remained his major power base? And was he involved in the Asyut uprising that followed Sadat's death? (The revolt, which was an exceedingly bloody affair and left more than a hundred policemen dead, was led by the Gama'a.)

In news photographs taken at the time of the trial of the twenty-four men accused of complicity in the assassination of Sadat, Sheikh Omar gave the appearance of a gentle paternal figure as he sat inside the giant metal cage that had been set up for the defendants along one wall of the court. He was easily distinguishable in his long clerical robes and his red fez-like cap with its wide white band, the badge of al-Azhar. During much of the proceedings, he talked in whispers to Lieutenant Islambouli, who sat to his right; the other defendants remained silent or, from time to time, began singing the words of the Muslims' call to prayers.

For twelve hours, Sheikh Omar, whose beard had by now become flecked with gray, testified before Hosni Mubarak's three-man military court, denying that he had issued the fatwa that resulted in the assassination of Sadat.

"Is it lawful to shed the blood of a ruler who does not rule according to God's ordinances?" one of the judges asked, as Sheikh Omar stood before the bench.

"Is this a theoretical question?" the sheikh replied.

He was told that it was, and he responded that it was lawful to shed such blood.

"What of Sadat?" the judge went on. "Had he crossed the line into infidelity?"

Sheikh Omar hesitated, and refused to respond.

And this, according to his defense lawyers, was the core of the case. Nowhere in the sheikh's reply—as was equally true with his fatwas—was there mention of any specific name. His followers applauded Sheikh Omar's shrewdness and survivability.

The sheikh was acquitted not only in the assassination trial but also in a later case, in which he stood accused, along with some three hundred others, of organizing al-Jihad, and of conspiring to overthrow the government. Nonetheless, during the 1980s he spent nearly six years in prison or under house arrest. In 1985, he made his first visit to Peshawar, the dusty Pakistani border town near the Khyber Pass that served as the staging area for the war in Afghanistan. It is easy to imagine him in Peshawar, for whenever I was there I found a constant stream of visiting clerics and mullahs, freedom fighters and spies, roaming its narrow lanes and calling, one by one, at the offices of the seven major Afghan resistance groups, which—though they had been fighting one another for years—were still, in a manner of speaking, coordinating the war effort inside Afghanistan. Sheikh Omar favored the two most stridently anti-Western and fundamentalist groups, which were led by Gulbadin Hekmatyar and Abdurrab Rasul Sayyaf; both men were heavily financed by Saudi Arabia. At the height of the war, the fanatic and ruthless Hekmatyar—whom the sheikh particularly favored, and who was also close to Pakistan's President, General Zia ul-Haq—was receiving roughly 50 percent of the arms that the CIA supplied to the Afghan jihad. All such assistance was channeled through Pakistan. In Peshawar—through Hekmatyar and Sayyaf—the sheikh was introduced to the American and Pakistani intelligence officials who were orchestrating the war.

Shobra had once been a rather elite district, I was told, where Greek, Armenian, Italian, and Coptic businessmen had settled their prosperous families. Now, as I walked through its maze of muddy lanes, nothing about it seemed to be prosperous. I had come with Mamdouah Ismail, a lawyer in his thirties, who was an articulate admirer of Sheikh Omar and had been imprisoned with him for three years, from 1981 to 1984, in the high-security wing of Cairo's

Tora Prison. He had been awaiting trial, along with three hundred others, on the charge of organizing al-Jihad. Like the sheikh, Mamdouah—and 189 of the other defendants—was acquitted by the military court. Now he represented only clients who were suspected of belonging to the Gama'a, and he worked in the Cairo office of Montasir al-Zayyat, a lawyer who had successfully defended Sheikh Omar in Egypt twice and had come to New York in 1991 to assist in the defense of El-Sayyid A. Nosair. It was al-Zayyat who had instructed Mamdouah to bring me to Shobra, to the Nasr al-Islam Mosque, which was regarded as a stronghold of Gama'a. Its sheikh, Dr. Mohammed Abdel-Maksoud, was a relentless government critic, who, as it happened, worked by day as an agricultural engineer in a government think tank.

As we carefully made our way down pitted streets, avoiding open sewers, and then along more lanes, we passed coffeehouses overflowing with idle young men (every year, Egypt produces thousands of university graduates for whom there are no jobs) and a number of Coptic Christian bookstores, many of whose owners, under recent persuasion (forcible, I was told), had removed pictures of the Virgin Mary from their walls. At one point, Mamdouah pointed out a Gama'a day-care center and, later, one of its schools. On nearly every crumbling wall we passed, and flying from balconies above, I saw the green-and-white flags and signs of the Muslim Brotherhood. "Islam is the solution," they announced. They seemed to sum up the Brotherhood's present mood of confidence.

A few days before, when I had asked a foreign diplomat how serious a threat the Islamist groups posed, he replied, "They're not regime-threatening—at least not yet—but if all the negative forces that drive this movement continue without modification for the next twelve to eighteen months I'd probably be a little less certain about that. The two key questions you have to ask are: To what extent is the Muslim Brotherhood connected to the militant underground groups? And, the real key: To what extent have the Islamists infiltrated the Armed Forces, particularly the Army? The government is worried about what is going on in the ranks, particularly below the officer level. They are newly watchful, and the watchfulness tells me there's something to be concerned about."

As Mamdouah and I approached the mosque, I asked him what he thought of the Brotherhood.

"It's old-fashioned," he replied. "Their time was the thirties, forties, and fifties. Now it's our time." He suddenly instructed me to cover my head. I did.

I glanced ahead and, even before seeing the mosque, I saw clusters of security men, who worked for the intelligence service, the *muhabarat*. They came in all shapes and sizes: some were in uniform, others in civilian clothes. Together, they formed a wide, circular phalanx on the perimeter of the Nasr al-Islam.

Their conspicuous presence seemed to have little effect on the worshippers—some seven hundred in all—who filled the mosque and spilled out into the street. They stared defiantly at the officer in charge, and he stared back. He was a rather disagreeable-looking man dressed in a black leather jacket and holding a walkie-talkie.

Mamdouah told me that most of the worshippers had been arrested and tortured and only a small fraction had ever been brought to trial. "Under our emergency law, which has been in effect for twelve years, since the assassination of Sadat, they can be held indefinitely," he said. "Many of them could be in prison for life." (At the time, over six thousand Islamist detainees were being held and Amnesty International had accused the Egyptian government of giving the police "an official license to kill with impunity" all suspected militants.)

Two weeks earlier, Mamdouah told me, some twenty armored personnel carriers and Central Security Forces troops had sealed this neighborhood off in a wide security sweep; about two hundred men had been rounded up. They included chemists and lawyers, merchants and drug dealers, and the nine-year-old son of a Gama'a suspect on the run.

Between two shabby high-rise apartment buildings, worshippers sat in neat rows; some were dressed in Western jeans and jackets, others in Islamic robes. I noticed that perhaps a dozen wore army uniforms. As the voice of the muezzin pierced the air with the call to prayer, a man in a long gray galabiya and wearing granny glasses brought us straight-backed chairs, and we sat in an alleyway on the edge of the crowd, listening to the forceful voice of Sheikh Mohammed Abdel-Maksoud, who demanded the immediate imposition of Shariah law.

"How much does an army recruit get?" I asked the man in the granny glasses.

"The equivalent of twelve dollars a month." He glanced at the recruits among the worshippers, and then he smiled.

"Dictators are infidels!" Sheikh Abdel-Maksoud shouted. "They will burn in hell!" He never mentioned Hosni Mubarak by name, but everyone knew whom he meant. "The Prophet Muhammad says that to abuse power is un-Islamic," the sheikh admonished the crowd.

"Was that a fatwa?" I asked Mamdouah.

He said he wasn't sure.

A young boy led a blind man through the crowd; he was dressed in a red-and-gray galabiya, carried a walking stick, and had white stubble on his chin. He was one of only a handful of worshippers who seemed to me to be over forty. As I glanced at the other faces, framed by beards, I wondered who belonged to Gama'a; in one fashion or another, probably all of them did. For, in the years since we had lived in Egypt, and since Sheikh Omar had led the group from the University of Asyut, it had expanded beyond university campuses and was now represented in syndicates, trade unions, hospitals, the courts, the bar. No one I spoke to was eager to speculate about the numbers involved, but the conventional assessment of Western diplomats was that Gama'a probably had between fifty thousand and a hundred thousand hard-core members and that the number of sympathizers, who provided a support system, was probably twice as large.

The more I learned about the movement, the more striking its paradoxes appeared. Egyptian officials were clearly baffled by it, and seemed at a loss about how to respond. Thus far, every effort to break it or to counter its appeal—whether by suppression or by a highly orchestrated campaign to make the government of Mubarak appear more Islamic than the Islamic activists—had failed. In fact, every recourse the government took only seemed to strengthen the Islamists' hand. A matronly Cairene woman wearing pearls told me in her study one afternoon that she considered the Gama'a rather like modern-day Robin Hoods, and that Khaled al-Islambouli had become a folk hero after he assassinated Sadat.

When the prayers were over at the Shobra mosque, about a dozen men joined us, and Mamdouah introduced me around. I asked one man why so many young people had turned to political Islam.

"Only Shariah law will rid us of corruption," he replied.

"The more the government puts pressure on young people, the more young people will rebel," another voice joined in.

"The more they put pressure on religion, the stronger we get."

As the others talked, a short, slight man stood patiently at my side. Eventually, he told me that his name was Ahmed, he was twenty-five years old, and he worked as an air-conditioning technician. He was then living underground, and his clothes—frayed black trousers and a green T-shirt—drooped on his frame. He certainly didn't look like a terrorist on the run, but he had been hardened by two years in jail and nearly twice that number underground. All he'd ever done in the beginning, he said, was to distribute pamphlets calling for women to put on the veil. "They accused me of being a ringleader," he went on. "I was tortured for four months in Tora Prison in 1988. Then they brought my mother in and tortured her in front of me."

The man in the granny glasses, who had brought us our chairs when we first arrived, had now joined us, and I asked him what he thought: Why had so many young people turned to political Islam?

"Since the 1952 Revolution, all of our leaders—Nasser, Sadat, and Mubarak—have taken us through so many twists and turns that people my age don't know if the Aswan High Dam is good or bad, if the October War was a victory or a defeat. Socialism failed us under Nasser; capitalism failed us under Sadat. Islam was the only constant—and it remains."

I thought of Miss Pennypecker, who had so often said that the Revolution of 1919 was still going on. I also thought of that distant Friday evening when I first visited my neighborhood mosque and listened to the impassioned voice of an American-educated agronomist extolling the revolution that was yet to come. The Free Officers' seizure of power in 1952 had provoked the departure of the British and the abdication of King Farouk; it had also ushered in an ambitious program of land reform. But was it a revolution, or merely a coup? The legacy it bequeathed to Egypt was one of Arab nationalism and, until 1967, one of considerable pride. But its social, economic, and political achievements were rather more debatable.

As Mamdouah chatted with his friends, I watched the last of the worshippers leave the mosque and disappear into Shobra's alleys, where the sun was just beginning to sink behind the rooftops. Once the mosque was empty, the officer in charge of the *muhabarat* spoke into his walkie-talkie; then he got into a black Mercedes and sped off. The silence of the empty square was broken only by the screeching of his tires, the chants of the muezzin, and the barking of a dog.

An old man in a soiled white robe and a white crocheted prayer cap locked the doors of the Nasr al-Islam, and as I watched him walk away, it struck me that the struggle in Egypt was not only a religious one, as some Islamists claim, but also a conflict—not unlike Lebanon's civil war—between the country's haves and its have-nots. It was as much a battle between wealth and poverty, between power held and power claimed, as it was between political or religious creeds. Islamic activism in Egypt, I am convinced, is at root a socioeconomic phenomenon, even secular in a sense. Otherwise, so many Marxists would not be embracing it.

As Mamdouah and I, joined by two of his friends, retraced our path through Shobra's narrow lanes, I remembered something that Montasir al-Zayyat had told me the night before. "The problem with the press is that every time you mention Gama'a it's in terms of an attack—an attack on a tour bus, a shoot-out with police," he said. "But this is a minuscule percentage of what the group does. What about the thousands of Islamic-funded and -controlled schools, clinics, hospitals?" Now, having visited Shobra, I saw his point. The Islamists, led by the Muslim Brotherhood, had built a social and welfare system rivaling that of the state. Parallel health, educational, and social welfare institutions provided services that in some places were far superior to those available in run-down government facilities. A turning point for some Egyptians came in October 1992, when Cairo was hit by a devastating earthquake, in which nearly six hundred people were killed, thousands were injured, and thousands more lost their homes. Within hours, the Islamists were on the streets, providing food and blankets, housing and tents, while the government of Mubarak was nowhere to be seen. Along with the collapse of every ideology embraced by Egyptian politicians and intellectuals since the turn of the century, government ineptitude, far more than terrorist guns and bombs, was fueling the Islamic flame.

Dr. Mohammed Abdel-Maksoud—the "popular" Sheikh of Shobra, as he is called—agreed to meet with me one afternoon in the law office of Montasir al-Zayyat. He said that it would be imprudent to meet at the Nasr al-Islam Mosque.

The sheikh is a tall, stooped man who walks with a limp, and his long black beard is flecked with gray. He wore a dark galabiya and a white prayer cap, and his hand often rested on a copy of the Koran, which he had carefully laid on a desk in front of him. I asked him to tell me a little about himself and what he believed.

He said that he was forty-five years old and had a master of science degree from Cairo University and a Ph.D. in agriculture from al-Azhar. "I was active in student politics," he said. "And I have been arrested a number of times. I haven't seen one truly fair election in this country—ever."

The sheikh went on to say that he had been a great admirer of Nasser, which did not come as a complete surprise, since a fairly significant number of former Nasserites and socialists, as well as former Marxists, are part of the Islamist movement now. The late Richard P. Mitchell, a professor at the University of Michigan, whose breakthrough book *The Society of the Muslim Brothers* was first published in 1969, had frequently posed the question: Cannot Islamist activism translate into Egyptian nationalism? Over the years, the question has been answered in the affirmative. For the bonding of Egypt's Islamist right and its Marxist left was not as odd a coupling as it might appear. The two had first come together during my student days in their shared opposition to Sadat's authoritarian rule and, more particularly, in their shared antipathy toward the Egyptian-Israeli peace accord. Over the years, the Islamists, who have always espoused an ambitious program of social reform, found that their ideas were not as alien to the Marxists as they initially thought. For their part, the Marxists—largely academics and professionals who had once embraced the Pan-Arabism and socialism of Nasser's days—scrambled aboard the Islamic bandwagon in the cause of revolution in Egypt. Their own atheism became almost an afterthought.

"After Nasser died," Sheikh Abdel-Maksoud continued, "I met some Islamists: I became closer to religion—began praying regularly and let my beard grow. There was such turmoil in this country then, and it was during that time that I began to realize that we had only to apply the Koran. All the answers are there. So in 1977 I became a sheikh."

After a moment, he said, "Islam is the religion of bad times, and these, too, are decidedly very bad times. Sadat told us that 1981 would be a year of luxury. He would appear on television in the midst of fields with green peppers as large as cauliflowers, and chickens that would lay a million eggs. When he was assassinated that year we learned that our debts had gone up eleven times in the eleven years that he had been in power. Quite bluntly, he had lied. Then Mubarak came along and said, 'These are difficult years, but the coming years will be better.' " The Sheikh of Shobra obviously didn't agree. Now he began to shout: "Look at the figures! In your [1992] election campaign, Clinton kept asking, 'Are things better now than they were ten years ago?' Well, that also applies here, and things are far, far worse. And for those of us in the Islamic movement, even if the government gives us a lamb or a sheep to eat for every meal, we will never accept Mubarak until he gives us the Koran—and until he gives us power. Is it not honest, and courageous, to have a referendum on applying Shariah law? This regime would never dare to do it; they're terrified."

He threw up his arms in a sign of victory, and a group of his followers who had accompanied him beamed.

"We know that the West—especially the United States—is concentrating on hitting the Islamist movement in Egypt," he went on. "We're the most important country in the Middle East, and there's a domino effect. If Egypt goes Islamic, this will have a far more profound effect on the region than Khomeini's revolution in Iran."

The sheikh excused himself briefly; it was Ramadan, and he went into another office to say midday prayers.

When he returned, I asked him whether he felt threatened, in view of the fact that the government had recently issued a decree that all mosques would come under state control. Was it possible that the government would take over Nasr al-Islam?

"Yes, theoretically Nasr al-Islam could be nationalized," he replied. "But the government is very hesitant to take this step, because it could prove to be quite dangerous. Closing the 'popular' mosques will drive *us* to take a new step. We will go to the people and bring them into the streets. We will go to the syndicates, the markets, the unions. We will paralyze the country, just as *they* did in Iran. The result could be bloodshed, but we know we are justified from the words in the Koran."

Eventually, the conversation shifted—as many conversations in Egypt do—to Sheikh Omar and the Gama'a. I asked Sheikh Abdel-Maksoud what, in his view, formed the basis of Sheikh Omar's popular appeal.

"There is a saying of the Prophet that you can change things with your hands, your tongue, or your heart, and there are several people who are trying to change things now, in different ways," he replied. "Sheikh Omar is able to combine two things: He's an al-Azhari, which means that he has knowledge—and, as opposed to the rotten eggs now sitting at al-Azhar, he is able to articulate that knowledge. And he speaks out. He tells the truth; he doesn't dissemble. He has gone through a lot, despite his well-known handicaps."

"Is he really the most powerful and most popular sheikh among the people here?"

"He's the first among equals. It is a large blessing of God that everything is not concentrated in one person, because if that were the case, and that person were struck down, the movement would collapse."

Ambassador Hussein Amin, a career diplomat and prominent intellectual who has taken a publicly critical view of the militants, believes that an Egyptian Islamic state is inevitable. When I visited him one morning at his bungalow in the exclusive Heliopolis neighborhood, I asked him to explain that belief.

"Unfortunately, economic and social reforms can never catch up with the rising Islamic tide," he said.

"Every day there are thousands of new recruits who join the movement—young people who cannot find jobs, who cannot marry, who cannot find apartments. In time, they will effect a coup. How? There are three possible scenarios. The former Minister of the Interior Zaki Badr has said that if Mubarak dies or is assassinated today, an army officer will take over, and not the speaker of the house. Yet no army officer enjoys sufficient popularity to guarantee him popular support unless—and this is the key—he tells the people that he intends to apply Shariah law. That is one scenario that seems to me quite probable.

"Another scenario is a violent takeover. The present economic and social situation is so bad that a spark could ignite massive conflict. The 1986 riots"—when Central Security Forces recruits, demanding better pay, took to the streets and presented Mubarak with the greatest challenge of his presidency—"could well happen again, starting with a minor incident, and the Army could be forced to intervene. And such an incident could well happen. People have had it up to here." He held a finger beneath his chin. "Prices are rising, inflation is up, housing conditions are deplorable. Actually, everything is falling apart. For the majority of the people, the last one hundred years has been little but a continuous experiment. We have tried everything from liberalism to fascism to capitalism to the open-door economic policies of Sadat. Nothing worked. So, many are now asking: What do we have left to try, except an Islamic solution? The only thing that we have never tried before is God-made laws instead of man-made laws."

A number of Amin's friends and fellow intellectuals supported this view, so I asked the ambassador what he thought.

"There is an inherent fallacy in this argument," he replied. "We never *had* a real democracy here, or a real liberalism, as a matter of fact. The socialism of Nasser made grievous mistakes. And Sadat's open-door economic policy [the *infitah*] merely allowed the rich to get richer. It was all very dubious. And the majority belief that an Islamic economy would save us is simply false —there is no such thing. It will be downright capitalism under an Islamic regime."

"Then, finally," the ambassador said, leaning back in his chair, "there's the scenario of the Muslim Brotherhood coming to power through the slow, steady route of politics as usual. They're now in the mainstream of political life, but don't make the mistake of assuming that the Brotherhood has totally renounced violence. When they think they're ready to assume power, then you'll see a liaison, if only a temporary one, between the Brothers and the militants. Meanwhile, each profits from the other's acts: each violent act of Gama'a makes the Brothers look like an agreeable alternative. And Gama'a benefits from the Brotherhood's lobbying and its tolerated, if not altogether legal, presence in politics."

Amin paused and called for coffee. He is a large man, with a pleasant face, who had served most recently as ambassador to Algeria, and was there in 1992 when Algeria's army took control and canceled elections to prevent an Islamist victory at the polls. Amin went on to say that Islamism was gaining ground even among his colleagues. "You know, it's really quite serious. The Egyptian diplomatic service is supposed to be the cream of society—we speak several languages, we've been exposed to foreign travel and the outside world. But you cannot imagine how this trend is rising within the Ministry of Foreign Affairs. I attended a dinner at the Diplomatic Club a few nights ago, and during the evening call to prayers three-quarters of those around the table left the room."

He said that Islamism was rising in the Army as well, even among the higher ranks, and he laid the blame for this on Mubarak's government, which, in its effort to co-opt political Islam, had saturated the country with religion: in the print media, on the radio, and on TV. It was, in effect, a new form of "official Islam." "It was Mubarak who spurred these movements on." Amin shook his head. "He made concessions—he set up a committee to study the imposition of Shariah law, though I'm quite certain he has no intention of ever imposing it. It was only when the militants stepped up their attacks on the Copts, burned churches and Christian shops, killed Christians in Upper Egypt, and then started attacking tourists and intellectuals that Mubarak came to believe in the inevitability of a downright confrontation with the Islamists, and that is what we are witnessing now."

I asked the ambassador if, in his view, Egypt could become another Lebanon.

"In the sense of intercommunal warfare between the Copts and the Muslims, no. Lebanon is divided equally between Christians and Muslims. The Copts here are a minority, which cannot cope with the Muslims in an intercommunal fight. They would be swept away in hours if they attempted to resist a takeover by the Islamists. But if it's a question of a war between the *government* and the Islamists—absolutely, yes. It's taking place already, and the government admits that it's finding it difficult to cope. The police force is not that efficient, and there are many soldiers and members of the services who are very reluctant to use force against those who carry the Koran. There are others who believe that the Islamists will come to power anyway, so it's better not to alienate them and get on their lists. And there are still others who believe it is not a worthy cause to defend a corrupt regime."

One government official had told me earlier that the Islamist groups had received millions of dollars from the Islamic government in Iran and that some twenty-five hundred activists had received training in a string of camps just across the border in the Sudan.

Amin disputed that view. "The support they get from these countries is minimal," he said. "Yes, there is some training in Sudan, and they get some Iranian arms. But this is an indigenous movement. All government claims to the contrary are merely attempts to conceal the real problem. But, that being said, there is some coordination internationally, and if you want to find the key, look to the Sudan and Hassan al-Turabi."

The banned but still tolerated Muslim Brotherhood, or al-Ikhwan al-Muslimun, had its headquarters, until recently, in an unobtrusive building in downtown Cairo, set in the midst of a bustling food-and-vegetable market on a dirt road. Its emblem and sign—two white crossed swords and a red Koran set in the middle of a vibrant green flag—was prominent on the door.

The Brotherhood remained the Islamist movement's strongest voice, and many Egyptians told me that during the previous year it had made further significant progress toward its aim—in a nation whose population was nearly 90 percent Muslim—of usurping power by stealth. It had not only set up an impressive social structure, but also controlled some of the country's most important unions, student organizations, and syndicates. The key question about the Brotherhood—one that has proved vexing to Egypt's nervous bourgeoisie and to many of its Western friends—is whether it has really renounced violence. It maintains that it has no direct control over groups like Gama'a, but some Egyptians and Westerners aren't convinced.

The Brotherhood's deputy leader, Mustafa Mashour (who became its leader in 1996), greeted me warmly when I met him. He is a small man in his seventies with a white beard. A meteorologist by profession, he was dressed in a suit and tie. He is also a politician of long standing, and had spent more than twenty years in jail. Even before I could pose a question, he said, "You are now seeing a struggle between the Islamist movement and other political trends, but I can assure you that the Islamists will win, because we're an Islamic people." He spoke calmly but deliberately.

"Does the Brotherhood believe in revolution?" I asked.

"No. And we don't agree with these young people who are using force and calling for jihad. Their use of violence could jeopardize this movement and set us back by years. We've already suffered seventy years of often crippling blows. We now have a stake in the future of this country, and we're not about to give it up. Our approach—evolution, so to speak—could take longer, but we can be sure of the final result. We could assume power, through a coup d'état, but if the majority of the people are not yet ready for us, what could we gain? We would simply be overthrown by a countercoup."

I was taken aback by the mention of a coup. I asked what the Brotherhood's strength in the Army was.

He hesitated, and didn't reply directly. Instead, choosing his words carefully, he said, "I don't mean a coup unless the majority of the people support us and we are prevented from assuming power, as happened in Algeria. We have no active cadres within the Army, but we know the general mood. The Army is religious, it's part of the people, and it's as close to Islam as we are."

I asked Mashour what the effect on the Brotherhood was of still being banned.

"Well, quite frankly, it's awful," he said. "We operate as much as we can aboveground—through the students, the syndicates, and the mosques. These are the methods which are apparent and obvious." I waited for him to continue, but he said nothing more.

Did the ban, which forced the Brotherhood to operate, at least partially, underground, play into the hands of the Islamist militants? I asked.

"Of course it does," he replied. "And more extreme groups are popping up every day. *They* need no government clearance to operate. And there's no doubt that people are turning increasingly to the violent groups because they feel the Ikhwan has been ineffective precisely because we can't even get the banning order reversed." He paused for a moment, and then he said that a dialogue between the government and Ikhwan on having the ban lifted was still going on "in fits and starts" but Mubarak simply refused to sanction a political party based on Islam, fearing that it would cause strife between Muslims and Christian Copts.

I had been told by a Western diplomat that Mashour, who was already regarded as the effective head of the Brotherhood, was believed to be the link between the Brotherhood and the more radical groups. I asked him if that was true.

"At the moment, there's no link," he replied. "In the past, we tried to convince some of these activists that their tactics were wrong, their methods were wrong, and their violence was wrong. But, unhappily, they were not convinced. We are still trying. A dialogue is now under way in prison between us and them."

People came and went from his office as we talked, including Dr. Isam al-Ariyan, a prominent pathologist who had been an important voice in the Egyptian parliament when the Brotherhood led the opposition from 1987 to 1990, prior to its boycott of the elections that year. Before joining Ikhwan, Ariyan had been a "prince" in Gama'a, so I asked him if he could arrange for me to meet one of their fighters who had recently returned from Afghanistan. He seemed somewhat startled by the question, and then replied, "It's impossible. These young men are being hounded—they're either in jail or underground. It's a reverse Vietnam syndrome, in a sense. They went off to fight in a popular war. But they are being rounded up, tried, and executed on their return."

Earlier, a political scientist who had studied the Brotherhood for a number of years told me he did not believe that violence was any longer part of its policy. Nevertheless, he said that he could not find a single case where the Brotherhood had condemned Gama'a. It had condemned acts of violence by the state—but not by Gama'a.

The previous evening—within forty-five minutes of the bombing of the World Trade Center in New York—a bomb had exploded in a café in Tahrir Square, killing four people, two of them tourists, and injuring eighteen. I asked Mashour why the Brotherhood, if it was opposed to violence, had not renounced the violent acts of groups like Gama'a. (A spokesman for the organization in Upper Egypt had claimed responsibility for the Tahrir bomb.)

"We have deplored these acts, and said they're not acceptable," he replied.

"When?"

"We do it all the time."

"Now, for the record, will you denounce last night's bombing?"

He hesitated, and then said, "Well, we can't denounce every specific incident, since we've said it all before."

As he walked with me to the door, I said I wondered if there was not a danger that Egypt's old-guard Islamic movement would be hijacked, as the Bani-Sadr people in Iran were, by their more extreme revolutionary counterparts.

For a moment, I thought I detected sadness on his face. Then he shrugged. "There's always a potential danger, but I don't think it will occur. Because when we come to power we will be led by a non-theologian—not by a sheikh."

The mud lanes of Bulaq, the fetid slum just across the Nile from Cairo University, are little more than dark, rutted tracks that cut between mud-brick hovels and cramped, dark shops. To enter them is to enter a rarely visited, unknown world of sorts. It is easy to understand how Anwar Sadat's assassins met undetected here. For there was no government presence: no services, no schools, no mail delivery, no fire station, and, for all intents and purposes, no police. The security officials withdrew from Bulaq after dark.

I had come here with a woman whom I will call Nadia in order to meet her brother, a Gama'a "Afghani," as those who fought in Afghanistan are called. He had recently returned to Egypt and was on the run; through a series of endless negotiations with interme-diaries, he had agreed to see me at a neighborhood mosque.

When we arrived, I happened to notice a face in the crowd—a small, anemic-looking man, probably in his twenties, with a thin wisp of beard and dressed in a white robe. He was having *iftar*, the evening meal during Ramadan. After the meal, Nadia took me to the courtyard of the mosque and introduced me to her brother. I will call him Gamal.

He told me that there were still about a thousand Egyptians fighting in the civil war in Afghanistan, including Mohammed al-Islambouli, the brother of Sadat's assassin, and the two eldest sons of Sheikh Omar Abdel-Rahman. They were based primarily in two training camps of the Hisb-i-Islami—the guerrilla organization of Gulbadin Hekmatyar—on the outskirts of Kabul, but they moved with ease across the border into Pakistan, he said. Their organiza-tional base was in Peshawar, and from there they traveled to Egypt via the Sudan and crossed the porous border, which he called a *cordon sanitaire.*

After thirty minutes or so, Gamal excused himself and left the mosque with some of his friends—including the young man I had noticed earlier—leaving me with no phone number and only a nom de guerre.

Several evenings later, I accompanied a friend from an international human rights organization to a fashionable private club, where she was going to take testimony from a man who had been badly tortured. He turned out to be the anemic-looking man at the mosque. He asked me to identify him by a pseudonym, Abou Juhaiman.

"It happened at the headquarters of the SSI—the State Security Investigation," he said. "I was stripped naked and blindfolded. Then they took me to what they call the ward, and electricity was applied to my lips, my genitals, and my fingertips. I think there was a doctor present, because, as far as I can recall, at certain intervals someone told them to stop. Then I was suspended—my wrists were tied to the bars of a high window, and my feet were off the ground. For about three hours, with intermittent questioning, they beat me with metal bars. It lasted for thirteen days. When I was released, I went underground." That was in 1988. Today, Abou Juhaiman is a spokesman for al-Jihad.

I asked him if we could meet again, and he agreed. "Here at the club?" he asked. I was somewhat startled, and he explained that his father was a member of Mubarak's establishment.

Over the following days, we met twice, on the club veranda. He looked very different from the man I had first seen at the Bulaq mosque. He was dressed in a suit and tie, and nodded to club members as they passed. One evening, a member of Mubarak's cabinet happened to be sitting at the next table. Overhead we heard rotors beating the air, and a helicopter came into view. "It's security for the minister," Abou Juhaiman told me with a smile.

He was an economics graduate of Cairo University, and was twenty-six, he said, and, like so many others whose stories I had heard, he had been radicalized in prison. He was embittered and hard.

"Does your father know?" I asked him.

"Yes," he replied. Then he quickly steered the conversation away from his family.

He told me that al-Jihad and Gama'a were still two separate groups, but that they now had three joint committees: for operations, for propaganda, and for finance. He served on the second, and described himself as "under the general command of Colonel Abbud al-Zumur," the former military intelligence officer who was now serving his twelfth year in prison for the assassination of Sadat. "That's why I chose al-Jihad," he said. "I would much rather be under the command of a military officer who fought in the 1967 and 1973 wars. He *knows* how to change the political regime by force. We only hit targets at the top, like ministers, the speaker of parliament, and Sadat." He was describing men who moved in the same circles as his father did. "We're not interested in minor acts of terrorism, like Gama'a—the attacks on tourists and low-ranking police. And this is a major strategic difference: Gama'a attacks from below, Jihad from the top."

I asked him how the groups were organized.

"Like a bunch of grapes," he said, and he went on to explain that the movement consisted essentially of clusters of independent cells, with no connection between the cells but with a strong, charismatic leader at the top. No one person had a clear view of the entire network, he said, and it was really not necessary to attempt to count the groups, because their ideology was essentially the same: the proliferation of cells was based largely on personality differences and on the need for security. The only leaders who were universally known were Colonel Zumur and Sheikh Omar.

I asked Abou Juhaiman about the sheikh and what his significance to the movement was.

"Many of the Gama'a cadres have no religious background or training," he replied. "That's unlike al-Jihad, where our recruitment practices are far more precise—anyone who joins us has to know the Koran and the entire Islamic legal system as a prerequisite. But the others need religious counsel and guidance for their acts, so they look to people like Sheikh Omar for fatwas to sanction those acts."

He offered an example. "Some years ago, we were short of funds, and someone suggested that we kill gold merchants and seize their property. But there was a dispute over whether this was justified, so we asked Sheikh Omar for his opinion, and he issued a fatwa. But there was a condition attached: only a merchant who was acting against Islam could be hit."

"Christian Copts?"

"Precisely," Abou Juhaiman replied.

As we continued talking, he fingered a copy of the Koran. I lit a cigarette and looked out across the Nile, which was ablaze with lights as small boats skirted by.

"I don't approve of smoking," Abou Juhaiman said. He said it the way he said everything: in short sentences, didactic and direct.

I asked him if he had ever been to Afghanistan. He replied that he had not but that he knew the Afghans well. "They're extremely skilled in combat, and they know how to plant car bombs." He began giggling. At times, he seemed exceedingly high-strung.

"Do you by any chance know Abdel-Nebi Khalifa?" I asked.

"Yes," he replied. "We worked together for a while. He was in the propaganda unit and printed anti-government tracts, primarily in Peshawar. That's all he did. But in the eyes of this regime, once you've been to Afghanistan you're a lifelong enemy of the state."*

A Western diplomat had told me that the Islamist movement's primary sources of funds were still Saudi Arabia and the Gulf states—only Kuwait had suspended funding after the Gulf War—and the Muslim Brotherhood's own financial base, which included a vast network of Islamic investment firms abroad, with holdings currently estimated at some $8 billion. Additional revenue poured in from Brothers working in the oil-rich Gulf, particularly in Saudi Arabia. When I asked Abou Juhaiman if that was true, he said, "That's not my department." But he was able to confirm a suspicion

---

*Although I made repeated requests for an interview with the Minister of the Interior, or someone from his staff, to answer such allegations, I was consistently turned down.

held by many Western diplomats that Peshawar was emerging as a key organizational base for Egypt's militant Islamic groups and that there were direct links among it, the military training camps in northern Sudan, and those outside Kabul. I remembered something that Ambassador Amin had said about the leader of Sudan's National Islamic Front: "Hassan al-Turabi is the most influential leader in the Sunni world today. He is the coordinator, and he is doing a very efficient job indeed."

As much as anyone else, Hassan al-Turabi had inherited the spoils of the U.S.-sponsored Afghanistan jihad.

There was no Politburo or Cominform of the Islamic world; its closest equivalent had been the Caliphate, which was abolished in 1924 by the Turkish leader Kemal Atatürk. But a strategic alliance grouping the Sudan, Pakistan, and Afghanistan (and underwritten by Saudi Arabia) had by now emerged as a crucial axis for the forces of militant Islam. Paradoxically, it may never have come into being had there not been a decade-long jihad in Afghanistan. Washington and Saudi Arabia (and the generals of Pakistan and, to a lesser extent, the generals of the Sudan) had been obsessed with driving out the Soviets. As a result, thousands of Islamic militants from around the world had streamed into Afghanistan to fight in the CIA's jihad. One of the most startling ironies of today's militant Islamist movement is that the vast majority of its leaders were funded, armed, and trained on the battlefields of Afghanistan—by the United States.

The erudite Turabi, one of militant Islam's most prominent ideologues, provided additional training camps, safe houses, and logistical support. The Sudan over which he presided was the world's only Sunni Islamic state in which a rigid, theocratic regime had taken root—except for the feudal dynasty of Saudi Arabia. I always found the Saudi presence in the world of militant Islam to be a curious one. Its lavish and often indiscriminate funding of many of the Islamist groups was partly motivated by its geopolitical concerns and its proxy war for supremacy in the Persian Gulf with Shi'ite Iran; it was also partly an attempt, rather shortsighted I thought, to buy protection for its beleaguered regime and to placate its own expanding fundamentalist constituency. By the late 1990s, Saudi Arabia's princes and the Saudi throne itself would be shaken out of their placidity.

I asked Abou Juhaiman what he thought of the Saudi rulers. "Corrupt," he replied. "But that doesn't mean that we'll refuse to take their money." He glanced around the well-appointed veranda, and then he smiled.

The last evening that Abou Juhaiman and I met at the club, he asked if I could help him get a visa for the United States. He had already applied and been rejected twice, on two different passports, he said. I told him I didn't think it was possible, and we said our goodbyes. I watched him as he walked away down the empty street—a slight, innocuous-looking man who became smaller and smaller as he was engulfed by the mist coming off the Nile.

The crackdown of Mubarak's security forces in March 1993 was on a scale not seen since the assassination of Sadat. Homes, mosques, and entire villages were raided, and there was a massive wave of arrests; at least forty-five people died during the raids. It was almost as if anyone who had a beard and lived in the alleys of the "popular" neighborhoods was being rounded up. Even the Muslim Brotherhood came under attack and was being forced to relinquish its control of the professional syndicates. For their part, the militants stepped up their attacks on the security forces and foreign tourists—there were even incidents in which foreign women had acid splashed on their bare legs.

Meanwhile, Sheikh Omar Abdel-Rahman was denied political asylum in the United States, and received a deportation order from the INS; at nearly the same time, he was ordered retried, along with forty-six of his followers, before an emergency high-state-security court in Faiyum, on charges arising from an anti-government demonstration in April 1989. In 1990 the men had been acquitted of all charges in the case because of discrepancies in witnesses' statements and lack of evidence. At the retrial, however, the blind cleric was sentenced to seven years of hard labor for throwing rocks at security men.

After my return from Cairo, in the last days of March, Sheikh Omar agreed to give me my first interview.

We met at his apartment in Jersey City, on the fourth floor of a nondescript brick building. Before we entered the living room, one of his aides, Ahmad Sattar—who was acting as interpreter—and I removed our shoes. No sooner had we sat down on two overstuffed beige sofas than Sheikh Omar came in. He wore a gray robe of homespun cloth over a white galabiya, the crimson turban of al-Azhar, and a pair of woolly white socks. His eyes were covered by heavy black glasses, and he walked, unassisted, to one of the sofas. On a table beside it was a copy of the Koran.

He greeted me cordially, and after we had both tested our tape recorders (I had a tiny Sony, he had an immense boom box), I asked him if he had played any role in the World Trade Center bombing.

"None, none whatsoever," he said. "I had no connection at all, and the bombing of the Trade Center was absolutely contrary to Islam. Yet every time I pick up the newspapers or turn on the TV, there I am—there is the al-Salam Mosque, which is described as a headquarters of terrorists! This is pure hypocrisy on the part of the press. Look at this man in Texas—the one who claims to be Jesus Christ. [He was referring to David Koresh.] Have Christian churches been blamed for what he's done? And when Jonathan Pollard was convicted of spying for Israel, did anybody accuse Jewish rabbis or Jewish temples of being traitors to the United States?"

He threw up his arms. Then he settled himself more comfortably on the sofa.

I asked the sheikh what, in his view, was the single most important cause of the rise in Egypt of political Islam.

"There are many factors involved—political, economic, social, and religious," he replied. "People are suffering. They live below the poverty level, while Hosni Mubarak and his gang deposit billions of dollars in American and Swiss banks. The jails are full of Islamist prisoners, who are tortured in the most heinous ways. And now even detention is not enough. Now he's begun killing people inside mosques. It happened most recently in Asyut and Aswan earlier this month, but it's happening all over Egypt. It's systematic now. Mubarak rules Egypt with an iron fist, under emergency law. People live in a police state, and I challenge Mubarak now—through your pen—to rule Egypt for one hour without emergency law. He would be unable to do it for one minute."

After a brief pause, he went on. "Then there's the positive side of the Islamic wave—what Gama'a and the other groups are doing to set up an infrastructure of hospitals, clinics, and schools. And they are preaching to show the true meaning of Islam. This movement isn't unique to Egypt; it's happening all over the Islamic world—in Tunisia, Algeria, the Gulf countries, and Saudi Arabia. People are thirsty for Islam, and there is no power on earth that can stop this movement. None."

"Are Gama'a and al-Jihad religious movements or political movements?"

"In Christianity, you have a separation of church and state," Sheikh Omar replied. "Because the church resisted the modernization of Europe, it was pushed aside. But Islam is very different: it covers every aspect of life—politics and economics, religion and social issues, science and knowledge. Therefore, it is not possible to differentiate between religion and politics. In Islam, you cannot be a Muslim unless you know politics. We do not follow your axiom 'Leave what is for Caesar for Caesar and what is for God for God.' "

He called for tea and coffee, and I glanced around his spartan living room, which had a transient air. Boxes and cartons were piled up in the corners, and only a calendar and a Koranic inscription hung on the walls. "At your trial in the Sadat assassination case," I said, "you told the judge that it was lawful to shed the blood of a ruler who does not rule according to God's ordinances—"

"Yes," he interrupted. "I told the judge that whoever does not rule as God orders is an infidel. And if you apply that rule to Nasser, Sadat, and Mubarak, they are all infidels."

"Then you did issue a fatwa against Sadat by declaring him an infidel?"

"I am not here to deny it, or say yes or no; the Egyptian justice system said that I was innocent and that I didn't issue such a fatwa."

There was a momentary silence. Then Sheikh Omar said, his voice rising, "It was Sadat himself who issued the fatwa to be killed, by moving away from his religion and imprisoning his people. And it was *his own people* who killed him, and this will be Mubarak's fate as well."

Calming down, he adjusted his turban. Then he asked me, "Do you consider what I've just said to be a fatwa?" Before I could reply, he went on: "It's only my opinion." And then he smiled.

"Were the attacks against tourists in Egypt justified?" I asked.

"Tourists are not being attacked; tourism is," he replied. "Although I must add that tourists should respect our religion and culture—tourism is not alcohol, gambling, and nightclubs. But to prove my original point that it's the industry that's under attack, four tour buses were blown up recently outside the museum in Cairo, but only after the tourists had left them and gone inside. The goal of these attacks is to put pressure on the Egyptian regime to release the thousands of Muslims now being detained. Did you know that many of those staging the attacks are the fathers and uncles and brothers of those who are now in jail? So killing the tourists is not our goal."

He asked an aide to bring him a glass of water—something he did frequently during the interview. Then he tucked his right leg into a half-lotus position. He appeared relaxed and at ease.

I said that some Egyptians were predicting that within one or two years Egypt would be an Islamic state.

"When is not important. We cannot predict a time frame, but I agree that the Mubarak regime will fall. He has reached a point that no dictator has ever reached in Egypt before. Ah, King Hosni!" The sheikh threw up his arms, his sarcasm unconcealed. "King Hosni ruling us for eleven years. And now they're asking him to run for another six-year term, and then they'll make him President for life. So you see"—he turned his face toward me—"there's really no difference between King Hosni and King Hussein and Morocco's King Hassan."

When the laughter of the sheikh and his aides subsided, I asked what kind of Islamic state he wanted in Egypt. What was the role model? Iran? Saudi Arabia? Sudan?

"It will be closer to the example of Sudan," he replied. "Saudi Arabia does not apply Islamic rules. The princes spend billions of dollars at casinos, nightclubs, and bars. The King and his family have billions, billions of dollars, so why should there be poverty in Saudi Arabia? They give their people absolutely no freedoms. Their jails are full—full of innocent people. This is not Islam. Their Islam is cosmetic, with only one purpose in mind: to keep the ruling family on the throne. What we want is a true Islamic state. We want a state where there will be no poverty, where freedom is guaranteed. We will rule through a *shura*, or consultative council, which in the West you call democracy."

"What would the imposition of Shariah law mean for Egypt's non-Muslims—the Christian Copts?" I asked.

"Islam guarantees the rights of Jews and Christians under Islamic law: let them practice their religion and protect their houses of worship. There will be no pressure to convert. But in the meantime it is very well known that no minority in any country has its own laws. Do American Black Muslims have their own laws? In Islam, we're permitted to take more than one wife—we can be polygamous. But American law prohibits this, and therefore we're punished and prevented from practicing our own laws here."

"How many wives do you have—two or three?" I asked.

"I have only one, but I would like to have three more."

"But I met one in Egypt, and spoke to another on the phone," I replied. "Have you recently divorced?"

"Your meeting two means nothing," he said. "Even if I divorce a wife, I still have an obligation to support her and my children. They are my children, after all."

He then turned to our interpreter and said *"Bass"*—"Enough."

"Under what circumstances is jihad justified in Islam?" I asked. "And was Afghanistan one such circumstance?"

"In Afghanistan, yes, it was justified, and it was one of the best jihads we've had in modern times. The Soviet Union attacked a Muslim country, so it was absolutely imperative for the Muslims to defend it. If they hadn't, there would still be a Communist regime in Afghanistan right now."

I asked Sheikh Omar how he explained the fact that Egyptians who had been recruited by their own government and by Saudi Arabia and the United States to go to Afghanistan to fight were now being treated as terrorists on their return.

"An unjust ruler is always frightened if his people are trained as fighters and soldiers, and these young men are very highly trained. He is frightened that they might overthrow him one day, so his natural instinct is to put them in jail or get rid of them. It's happening not just in Egypt but in Saudi Arabia and Libya as well."

"How many times have you been to Afghanistan?" I asked.

"I can't remember how many times. I've been there a few times." His voice turned melancholy. "We would go from Pakistan to the forward positions inside Afghanistan."

"With Gulbadin Hekmatyar?"

He avoided a direct answer. "I went in with all of the mujahideen leaders," he eventually replied.

"What do you think of Hekmatyar?" I asked.

"How many other leaders are you going to ask me about?" he said.

"Only two," I replied. "Ayatollah Khomeini and Hassan al-Turabi."

"They are all great men who tried to help their religion and serve their countries," he said. "I admire them all enormously."

I asked him if he felt that the news media's tendency to compare him with Iran's Ayatollah Khomeini was justified.

"I serve my religion and I call for the establishment of an Islamic state. That's all I'm asking for. And when this state is established in Egypt I will be a servant to this state. I am not looking for leadership."

"But if you were offered the position of Grand Sheikh of al-Azhar"—the most prominent religious office in the country—"I presume that you wouldn't turn it down?"

"If I wanted to be the Grand Sheikh of al-Azhar, I would be that right now."

I asked Sheikh Omar how a poor, blind, diabetic child could rise from the slums to become a leader of Egypt's largest militant Islamic group.

"With the help of Allah. There was no one turning point for me. But Allah helps whomever he wants. How could the Afghan people have expelled a superpower? It was only with Allah's help."

"What about the three billion dollars supplied by the CIA?" I asked.

The sheikh roared with laughter. Then he said, "Without Allah, it would not have been possible with three *hundred* billion dollars. Allah is the stronger partner of the two. The U.S. government had been trying to destroy the Soviet Union since 1945. It could never have done it alone."

Many people in Cairo, both Egyptians and foreign diplomats, were highly skeptical of the report that Sheikh Omar's United States visa was granted in error, and I had been reliably told that Hassan al-Turabi had intervened on the sheikh's behalf, assisted by U.S. intelligence officials who had known Sheikh Omar during the days of the war in Afghanistan. So I now asked him to tell me exactly how he had got his visa in Khartoum.

"In a very natural way, like anyone else," he replied. "Through the proper channels. And I am going to give you no more details."

"But how could so many U.S. government departments have made so many mistakes and at so many different times? There is wide speculation that the U.S. government sponsored your admission here."

"I suggest that you pose those questions to your own government," he said.

Sheikh Omar had been animated during our two-hour interview, but now he seemed tired, his chin resting on his chest. He suffered from both diabetes and a heart condition, and many of his supporters had become increasingly concerned about his failing health. Only the week before, on the final day of Ramadan, he had sent a taped message to his followers around the world, which was played in all of Egypt's "popular" mosques. In the message, which he called "A Will to the People of Egypt," he had said, "The end of my life and the time to meet Allah are near." So I asked Sheikh Omar if he was dying and what the message meant.

He rested his head on the back of the sofa and didn't reply

immediately. After a few seconds, he turned toward me and said, "When the FBI is asked why they are following me, they say it's because I have many enemies"—including militant Jewish groups and the Egyptian government—"and they are protecting me from them. So it's possible that something could happen—quite possible."

I asked Sheikh Omar about his connection with Gama'a and al-Jihad.

"I am merely a Muslim scholar who speaks the truth," he replied.

I persisted, and he laughed and said, "Enough, enough! Describe me as the spiritual mentor of Gama'a."

LIFE IN THE ALLEYS

NAGUIB MAHFOUZ, THE ARAB WORLD'S ONLY NOBEL LAU-
reate in literature, leaves nothing to chance. There is a precision and an economy about him, and he measures his
daily life down to the minute. Thus, on the afternoon of
October 14, 1994—as he had done every Friday afternoon
for seven years—the eighty-two-year-old writer left his
apartment building in the Agouza section of Cairo at exactly ten minutes before five, and walked outside. It seemed
to him unusually quiet that afternoon as he glanced around
the street—a rather ordinary, rather characterless block,
where old houses of ocher and beige are interspersed with
taller concrete buildings from the 1950s and where there
are shops of all kinds, offices and apartment buildings, and,
usually, traffic jams and noise.

A small, frail figure, he walked slightly stooped, assisted
by a cane; his face was half obscured by heavy dark glasses.
(His eyes were failing and sensitive.) He was somewhat irritated, he later recalled, because he did not immediately
spot Dr. Fathi Hashem's waiting car. Fathi, a forty-eight-
year-old veterinarian, had been picking him up every Friday
afternoon for seven years to drive him the ten minutes or
so to the Kasr al-Nil, a fashionable café overlooking the
Nile, where every Friday evening for thirty years Mahfouz
had met with like-minded writers, intellectuals, and disciples. The "Friday sitting" had become a ritual for him.

"The moment I saw him, I jumped out of the car,
walked the few feet to where he stood, and gave him my

arm," Fathi told me as we sat, with a group of friends, at the Mahfouz table at the Kasr al-Nil a few weeks afterward. "I opened the right front door of my car for him, he sat down, and I closed the door. Everything seemed normal—except for the lack of people. At least, at first."

Fathi went on: "It was only as I circled the car that I saw the young man approach. He went directly to Mr. Mahfouz's side of the car; I assumed that he wanted to shake his hand, as many people do. The right front window was open, and Mr. Mahfouz extended his hand. It was only when I got into the driver's seat that I noticed that Mr. Mahfouz's body was shaking. I thought the young man was shaking him, and I screamed, 'What are you doing? Are you mad?' It was the only eye contact I had with the man. When I shouted, he hesitated, and for a few seconds his eyes locked with mine. I couldn't see his face, only his forehead and his eyes—they were aggressive and afraid at the same time. He had very dark skin, not like us." Fathi encompassed the table with a sweep of his hand. "Then, in an instant, the young man turned and ran. It was only then that I saw something brown lying on Mr. Mahfouz's shoulder. It was the handle of a knife." He paused for a moment, then added, "The blade was still in his neck, on the right side."

Mahfouz was conscious, but he said nothing as Fathi leaned over and carefully removed the knife. He threw it out of the car, onto the street, and then placed his hand directly over the wound, which was dangerously close to the central carotid artery.

Realizing what had happened, Fathi began shouting for help. People began to appear: *bawabs*, or doormen of sorts, from the apartment buildings, who were dressed mostly in turbans and long, flowing galabiyas; customers from a corner sandwich shop; guards from the Police Hospital, across the street; and a few young men dressed in Western shirts and trousers. Fathi remembers that none of them had a beard.

Keeping his right hand on the right side of Naguib Mahfouz's neck, Fathi backed his car out of its parking place, and sped, in reverse, to the main gate of the Police Hospital, some fifty yards away. "It was five minutes total," Fathi told me. "For everything."

When they reached the hospital, Mahfouz insisted, quite emphatically, that he wanted to leave the car unassisted, and Fathi complied. The moment he removed his hand from the author's neck, however, Mahfouz began bleeding copiously. The doctor who admitted him later recalled a small, frail man, a diabetic with a heart condition, nearly blind and nearly deaf, holding his hand to the right side of his neck. "He said, 'There's a bit of blood here. You might want to look at it. I also have some coldness in my arm.' The moment he removed his hand, blood spurted all over, yet he remained calm. He sat in a chair and waited. In ten minutes, we took him into surgery, for a five-hour operation."

Mahfouz had left behind him, outside the hospital's towering concrete walls, in the streets and alleyways, an increasingly cacophonous crowd of *bawabs* and neighbors, street vendors and hawkers, café patrons, and merely curious passersby, who now mingled with hundreds of uniformed police. Their voices rose and fell, and they flailed their arms, sometimes so violently that turbans came unwound. Mahfouz had spent an entire lifetime documenting just such scenes—of chaos and confusion, of contradiction spliced with chicanery, of situations in which nothing is what it appears to be—as he perfected the novel form in Arabic literature. He had presented in close, rich detail the intricacies of life in the margins and in the alleyways; his often idiosyncratic characters, from the lower and middle classes, argue over matters of justice and injustice, expectation and disillusionment, and belief in God. His portraits of the city, though they are often compared to Dickens's portraits of London or Zola's of Paris, are preeminently Cairene, as his characters struggle, caught between an uncertain future and the weight of the past.

When Mahfouz's friends heard of the stabbing, they rushed to the Police Hospital, and so did his two daughters and his wife. Like most Cairenes, they were all stunned by the news. It was the most controversial act of violence in Egypt in years.

There are many versions of what happened, some of them absurd. But the key questions remain: If it was in fact an assassination attempt, why Naguib Mahfouz? Who was responsible? And, perhaps as important, why did it happen just then?

The government was quick to blame the Gama'a al-Islamiya, which had emerged as the largest and the strongest of the underground Islamic groups.

By the time Naguib Mahfouz was attacked, the battle between the Islamists and the regime had entered its third year, and both sides, in an altogether too familiar pattern now, had raised the stakes in their increasingly vengeful warfare to a new height. The militants had accelerated attacks on foreign tourists, Coptic Christians, security forces, cabinet ministers, and the police. The government had responded ever more brutally.

Within an hour of the attack on Mahfouz, the hard-line Minister of the Interior, General Hassan al-Alfi, arrived at the Police Hospital, surrounded by ten or fifteen ranking aides. In quick succession, he was followed by the Ministers of Information, of Culture, and of Health, three camera crews, and an assortment of reporters from government-controlled television and radio. No sooner had they arrived than the government announced—to everyone's astonishment—that an arrest would be made that night; the following morning, seven young men were arrested, and an eighth was killed by police gunfire. One skeptical Cairene told me that the police action reminded him of Claude Rains when he said, "Round up the usual suspects." Ultimately, sixteen alleged Islamic militants were tried by a special, in-camera military court. (A number of these courts, against which there is no appeal, had been set up by Mubarak, and Amnesty International had described them as consistently conducting "grossly unfair trials." By the end of 1997, they had sentenced nearly a hundred militants to death—the largest number of executions for political crimes in this century.) Some of the defendants in the Mahfouz trial were charged with attempted murder, others with the illegal possession of explosives and arms—and all of them with membership in Gama'a. Every defendant denied the charges. In January 1995, the court sentenced two of the defendants to death, and two others to life imprisonment.

Mahfouz had openly criticized the violent tactics of the underground Islamic groups, as he had openly criticized the tactics and, in many cases, the policies of the Mubarak government. He first came to the Islamists' attention more than thirty years ago, when the powerful religious institution of al-Azhar had judged one of his books, *Children of Gebelaawi,* to be heretical. The novel is filled with allegorical characters who resemble figures from the Bible and the Koran, and describes the complex relationship of a group of Cairo slum dwellers with their various prophets and with God. After being serialized in the prestigious daily newspaper *al-Ahram,* the novel was banned, and no publication of it—indeed, no mention of it—was officially permitted in Egypt for thirty-five years. Then, in 1988, Mahfouz won the Nobel Prize. It was something that completely disordered his exceedingly orderly and exceedingly private life.

The following year, when the furor over Salman Rushdie's *The Satanic Verses* was sweeping the Islamic world and Iran's Ayatollah Khomeini issued a warrant for Rushdie's death, Sheikh Omar Abdel-Rahman—who was arrested in the summer of 1993, and was then awaiting trial in New York on charges of seditious conspiracy to wage a "war of urban terrorism against the United States," to assassinate Mubarak during a visit to New York, and to bomb various New York landmarks—reportedly told a journalist that Rushdie was not unlike Mahfouz: in the sheikh's opinion, both were heretics. "Islamic law calls on these people to repent, and if they do not, they will be killed," Sheikh Omar was quoted as saying at the time. "If this sentence had been passed on Naguib Mahfouz when he wrote *Children of Gebelaawi,* Salman Rushdie would have realized that he had to stay within certain bounds."

When I asked a senior Egyptian security official if in his view this amounted to a fatwa, justifying Mahfouz's death, he said that he wasn't sure but that that was the way it had been interpreted, and Egyptian militants had threatened to assassinate the author on the October anniversary of his receiving the Nobel Prize. What was even more important, the official said, was that Sheikh Omar was the spiritual mentor of Gama'a.

"I haven't believed the government's version from the very start; I think they have the wrong man," Tawfik Salah, a prize-winning film director and one of Mahfouz's closest friends, told me one afternoon a week or so after a mysterious and disheveled young man—with fair skin and an Islamic beard—had "confessed" on nationwide television to stabbing Mahfouz in what he claimed was a "kidnapping" attempt gone awry. He later retracted the statement, and most Cairo intellectuals I spoke with found the "confession" more amusing than edifying.

Tawfik went on to say: "The night before Naguib was stabbed, I picked him up for another sitting at another café. Ten minutes or so after we left his home, two dark-skinned strangers appeared. One wore a galabiya and a kaffiyeh; the other was in Western dress. They carried a bouquet of flowers and a box of chocolates and said they had come to see Naguib. His wife was slightly irritated, and told them that Naguib didn't receive people at home, but the following evening they could meet him at the Kasr al-Nil café. She took the flowers and the chocolates, and she closed the door. She told me later that neither of the young men appeared to be educated, and that they spoke Arabic with the accent of someone from the Gulf states." (According to another witness, the two men then got into a Mercedes and drove away.)

"While we were waiting at the hospital for Naguib to come out of surgery," Tawfik continued, "Fathi told us that the dark-skinned young man who had stabbed Naguib ran to a yellow Mercedes that was parked just down the road with three or four others inside, and that the car sped off toward the Gala'a Bridge. The Interior Ministry gloated over that revelation for two days; then all talk of the Mercedes suddenly stopped. The police claimed that Fathi had been mistaken [despite the fact that Fathi had chased the assailant toward the car] and that they were now quite certain that there *was* no car. Then, a few days later, when they put this fair-skinned young man on TV to confess, he confirmed their account: he said that he had hailed a taxi and gone to Tahrir Square, where he boarded a bus. Yet he had just said that he planned to *kidnap* Naguib! What was he going to do, kidnap him on a bus?"

As far as the mysterious Gulf Arabs were concerned, Mahfouz's wife was unable to identify them from a stock of police photographs of those under arrest—including a photograph of the fair-skinned, bearded young man. Yet when his TV confession was aired, she told friends that he was indeed the same young man who had given her a box of chocolates and a floral bouquet the night before her husband was stabbed. Mahfouz's friends puzzled over this, for as they listened to the "confession," none of them detected a Gulf accent.

Months later, the bearded, fair-skinned young man—an electrical appliance repairman named Mohammed Nagi Mustafa—was hanged. And, given the secrecy of his trial, it is unlikely that the many puzzles surrounding Mahfouz's stabbing will ever be fully solved.

"It is indeed bizarre," a Western diplomat said to me one afternoon. "It was certainly not the usual modus operandi of the Gama'a—they have never resorted to the use of primitive weapons in their attacks. Why use a kitchen knife, which requires a great deal of skill, when the chances of success are far greater if you use a gun? This was an extremely amateurish act, and Gama'a is not an unsophisticated group. So does this mean that the movement is splintering even more, and that we're now seeing the emergence of still more fanatic groups? We have got to assume, in the absence of a smoking gun, that the attacker came from the Islamic underground. But a key question is: What does it mean?"

Egyptian intellectuals worried aloud that the attack could portend yet another escalation in the Islamists' battle against secular thought and the introduction of Algerian-style tactics here. (In Algeria, a number of intellectuals have had their throats slit by the Islamists, in front of their families.) In the offices of human rights organizations, in both Cairo and New York, officials worried as well, over the alacrity of the arrests and over all of the contradictions involved. It appeared to be an intensification of the government's policy of "collective arrest," in which fifty or so people are rounded up, then frequently tortured, in order to find one. And, far from the Police Hospital, in the "popular" neighborhoods and in Mahfouz's alleyways, worry gave way to fear, and scores of men went underground if they were young or had a beard.

Naguib Mahfouz was born in a warren of ancient alleys in the heart of Islamic Cairo, behind the al-Hussein Mosque, in the neighborhood of Gamaliya, in December 1911. His father, a minor civil servant who later became a business manager for a merchant in the Khan el-Khalili Bazaar, was highly traditional, and highly distant from his youngest son; his mother was doting and became his closest friend. His childhood was often lonely but otherwise unremarkable. After attending Islamic elementary schools and a secular high school, he entered Cairo (then King Fuad I) University, and in 1934 he graduated with a degree in philosophy. He remembers that period, which coincided with the anticolonial movement against the British, as the happiest of his life—as "the golden age of patriotism . . . when the times themselves were listening to you," he wrote in his 1961 novel *The Thief and the Dogs*.

Until 1971, all his works were written late at night, for he spent his days as a government bureaucrat: as an official film censor, an adviser on the arts, and a minor functionary in various ministries, including the Ministry of Religious Affairs.

A private, timid man who married late in life, Mahfouz is a strong believer, a bit of a mystic, and a Fabian socialist of the most passionate sort. By the late 1950s, social realism had become the defining characteristic of his work. His well-ordered, punctilious daily life was the antithesis of the world he created in his books—some forty books, over forty years. The world of his characters was unsettled and difficult, informed by history and pervaded by an overwhelming sense of loss. His *Cairo Trilogy*, which was largely responsible for his receiving the Nobel Prize, is a family saga tracing three generations and spanning both world wars. In it he tackled not only religious and political themes, which are his normal forte, but prostitution, drug addiction, and the degradation of the urban poor. In 1979, when he was among the first to support the peace treaty between Egypt and Israel, the *Trilogy* and a number of his other works were banned in much of the Arab world.

As the years went by, his novels became increasingly hard-edged and stark, and the failures of contemporary Egypt were his stage. "We live in a repugnant age of slogans," one of the characters in a novella entitled *The Day the President Was Killed* laments. "And between the slogans and the truth is an abyss, into which we have all fallen and lost ourselves." Published more than a decade ago, the novella has all the elements of Mahfouz's prophetic fictional world: the decline of the Egyptian system; the emergence of an authoritarian state; a middle-class urban family torn apart by economic stagnation and uncertainty; the sexual tensions of a young couple in a society in which men and women are kept strictly apart; the rise of corruption, and of Islam, as the almost inevitable result of a system that seems to be spiraling out of control. As he follows one disillusioned young man through his day on October 6, 1981—the day that Anwar Sadat was assassinated by an army cell of al-Jihad —Mahfouz melds illusion and reality through the eyes of his protagonist, Ilwan, and flashes of memory leap about in time. Unable to marry because he cannot find a well-paying job or buy or furnish an apartment, Ilwan, who graduated with honors in philosophy, shares a cramped, dingy room with his grandfather, who lived through the Revolution of 1919, in which Egypt was meant to come of age. Now Ilwan sits in a coffeehouse, with "light streaming from its electric lamps, their wires covered with flies," and begins a monologue:

> *We are a people more acclimatized to defeat than to victory. It is just a Mafia which controls us—no more, no less. Where are the good old days? . . . My pride wounded, my heart broken, I have come to this café as a refuge from the pain of loneliness. . . . How many nations live here side by side in this one nation of ours? How many millionaires are there? Relatives and parasites? Smugglers and pimps? Shi'ites and Sunnis?—stories far better than* A Thousand and One Nights *. . . What do eggs cost today? This is my concern. Yet, at the same time, singers and belly dancers in the nightclubs on Pyramid Road are showered with gratuities and banknotes. What did the imam of the mosque say within earshot of the soldiers of the Central Security Force? There is not one public lavatory in this entire neighborhood . . . [Sadat] He's a failure—"my friend [Menachem] Begin, my friend [Henry] Kissinger," is all he can say; his uniform is Hitler's; his act, the act of*

*Charlie Chaplin. He's rented our entire country—furnished—to the United States . . .**

One evening, three and a half weeks after the attack on him, Mahfouz agreed to meet me at the Police Hospital, a large complex of glass and chrome. Security was tight when I arrived at the main gate, accompanied by one of Mahfouz's friends, a poet named Naim Sabry. Only after passing through a metal detector, presenting identity cards, and having our bags searched twice were we permitted to enter the grounds. We found Mahfouz in his room, on one of the upper floors, with his wife and daughters. A nurse sat at the entrance to the room, and outside the door three security men in plain clothes fidgeted with their Kalashnikovs.

Mahfouz greeted us with a weak wave of his hand. I was surprised at how frail he was and how small he seemed—far smaller than his five-foot-three frame. Dressed in a navy-blue robe and pajamas, he sat, slightly stooped, on a wooden chair between two single beds. He spoke in halting English and asked me to sit on the bed to his left, because he was deaf in his right ear. He had lost a great deal of blood, and had required numerous transfusions. "Concentration tires me," he said, "so don't expect much."

I began by asking Mahfouz the questions that everyone in Cairo was asking: "Why you? Why now?"

His eyes seemed to mist over, and then he said, "I simply got caught in the middle, in the battle between the system and the Islamists. 'Why now?' is not the question—perhaps circumstance or fate—yet it could have happened anytime, for I'm convinced that the battle will continue, and that both sides will take it as far as they can. Why me? Why others?" He shrugged and gave me a sad smile.

"In *The Day the President Was Killed*, Ilwan searches for order

---

*Translated from the Arabic by Tawfik Salah.

and reason and grapples with God," I said. "Yet nothing in the alleys is as it appears to be."

"Yes," he interrupted, before I could finish my thought. "It's interesting that you chose that book, and obviously what you mean to ask is: Did I somehow prophesy my own attack? Yes, perhaps I did. But then so much of what is now happening in Egypt is, in a sense, Mahfouzian."

At the street level, Egypt is a police state that is never quite in control; where expectations and accomplishments rarely, if ever, meet anymore; where rogues are celebrated for their courage and craft; and where educated, angry young men sit in coffeehouses in the alleyways or in the cafés along the Nile, idling away their days. Like Egypt itself, their achievements are far fewer than their dreams.

The country's identity has increasingly been defined by irresolution and drift. In Cairo, in particular, people seem to be living on the edge, as much of the city's infrastructure, like its ancient monuments, is being reduced to dust. Corruption flourishes, and political stagnation ossifies. The number of Cairenes continues to increase by nearly a thousand every day, in a country whose population—more than half under the age of fifteen—has, since the early 1990s, grown by more than a million every year. Yet 95 percent of that population continues to live on less than 5 percent of the land. Every year, Egypt produces more than a hundred thousand university graduates, many of whom cannot find jobs—in a country whose literacy rate has remained frozen at about 50 percent, while its per capita GNP has remained frozen at about $700 a year. The city's once astonishing diversity of cultures and social strata has seemingly been reduced to two starkly contrasting poles: crippling poverty and extraordinary wealth.

All across Cairo, it is easy to spot soaring new apartment buildings of glass and polished chrome and, immediately behind them, narrow, labyrinthine lanes where half-naked children play—as they do in *Midaq Alley*, one of Mahfouz's most popular books—with cockroaches, in mud and dust. Zaita, the cripple-maker of the same novel, could have been the beggar on the bridge that separates

Tahrir Square, the hub of downtown Cairo, and Agouza, where Mahfouz lives. I watched him as he weaved his way among the Mercedeses and Toyotas stuck in a perpetual traffic jam. One of his legs was missing, and his only foot was bare. He wore a tattered galabiya, and he thrust his upper torso into the open windows of the cars, nodding toward his breast pocket. He had no arms.

One afternoon, as I retraced my steps to Tahrir Square, everything there seemed dwarfed by a gray and bulbous twelve-story structure, Stalinesque in design: the Mugamma—the headquarters of Egypt's equally bulbous state bureaucracy, three million strong. Many Cairenes say that more souls are at rest in the Mugamma than in the City of the Dead. (According to a recent study, the average Egyptian bureaucrat works twenty-seven minutes a day.) As I stared at the building, I was struck by the fact that the Mugamma, perhaps more than anything else, has come to symbolize the system that had been created by Colonel Gamal Abdel Nasser in 1952 but was now exhausted and in steady decline.

Mubarak had been the coincidental—and the reluctant—inheritor of that system in 1981, when Anwar Sadat was gunned down. And although it was a mantle he had never sought, he had grown, over seventeen years, to embrace it, tenaciously. (He is now the longest-serving President in Egyptian history.) As the third generation of the revolution, Mubarak lacked the charisma of Nasser and the vision of Sadat, and many Cairenes say that he is a bit like a Mahfouz bureaucrat: gray, one-dimensional, almost smaller than life.

Mubarak is a difficult man to define, for he reveals little about himself and is obsessed with privacy. When asked by Egyptian television what his favorite pastime was, he replied that he had none. After nearly two decades in power, he is, in many ways, as enigmatic to Egyptians as he was on the day he was sworn in. It is actually quite hard to say who Hosni Mubarak really is.

His official government biography, which was drawn up when he was appointed Vice President, consists of six lines; his official presidential biography is less than a page, supplemented by three pages of the medals and decorations which he has received. Most people who know him describe him with stock phrases: "He's a balancer who treads warily," or "He's an implementer, not an innovator," or "He's a military man accustomed to routine, imposed by a chain of command or a bureaucracy." But they are used only after considerable thought. For Mubarak is not an easy man to talk to or to know, according to his friends. He doesn't like discussing emotions—you have to read between the lines.

He had been cautious and self-effacing throughout his military life, uncomfortable with politicians and with small talk, and had seemed an unlikely choice when Sadat appointed him Vice President in April 1975: many of Sadat's aides reacted with shock and disbelief. Yet on assuming his presidency, Mubarak moved deftly to consolidate his power; imposed emergency law; and retired potential rivals, most importantly, Field Marshal Abdel-Halim Abu Ghazala, the powerful, pro-American Minister of Defense. As an Air Force outsider, Mubarak thus managed to stay ahead of his restive army, whose leaders remain the arbiters of power in Egypt, as they have been for more than forty-five years.

Like most military men, Mubarak lives surrounded by trophies, photographs, regimental badges, and other emblems of a military career. He has never moved into one of Sadat's opulent palaces, but has remained instead in his modest villa in the exclusive Heliopolis neighborhood, only a short drive from the Cairo West Air Base, where he spent much of his adult life. One sensed that the man who would rule Egypt longer than any other leader in its modern history was far more comfortable there, amid daily reminders of a soldier's life.

When he assumed office in 1981, Mubarak spoke of limited presidential terms, of opening Egypt to democracy, of his own need for outside help and advice, and of the imperative to reform the country's stagnant economy—nearly 70 percent of which was dominated by bloated and inefficient public-sector factories and businesses, part of Nasser's Soviet-style economic legacy. But, according to his critics, he has grown increasingly out of touch in recent years, surrounding himself with sycophants and old military friends and issuing ever more authoritarian decrees, in the same manner that doomed Anwar Sadat and the Egyptian monarchy. His increasingly imperial tone has stunned many who knew him as a quiet and unpretentious general and Vice President.

"The President has fallen into a form of political narcissism," Tahseen Basheer, a highly respected former ambassador who lectures frequently on militant Islam, told me recently. "He looks around him and he sees people who support him a hundred and ten percent. He no longer acknowledges the problems in Egypt, and if he does acknowledge them, he blames them on conspiracies launched by his enemies. The objective reality that is pushing young people to rebel is simply beyond his grasp."

A Western ambassador says, "Mubarak *likes* being President. He's confident in what he's doing, and, if you look around the Middle East, you see that politics is highly personalized. The way in which the Mubaraks, the Assads (of Syria), and the Fahds (of Saudi Arabia) interact, the way they play the game in a very personal way, is like a high-powered game of poker or chess. And on that playing board, Mubarak does very well indeed. Internally, his National Democratic Party has been so successful in monopolizing the political levers of power, the patronage flow, that the secular opposition has been marginalized to the point of extinction; they play no relevant role in the political debate. This is the demon of the NDP's success: a government which functions largely as a support system for the President."

When Mubarak, in 1993, presented himself for a third, and unprecedented, six-year term—in a referendum in which voters had the choice of voting "yes" or "no," and in which no opposition candidate was permitted to stand—he had hoped to bolster his legitimacy. For a key difference between Mubarak and his predecessors is that both Nasser and Sadat, in different ways, had seized power: Nasser by deposing King Farouk, and Sadat, with the assistance of the Islamists, by his defeat of the left. Both then established their own, very distinctive governments. Nasser cemented his authority with his nationalization of the Suez Canal and his leadership of the Arab world; Sadat by his recapture of Egyptian land during the October War. Their actions gave to their regimes an unchallengeable legitimacy. But Mubarak had never seized power as his predecessors had. He had merely inherited it.

And his inability, or unwillingness, to come to grips with the monumental problems that Egypt faces has led to a widespread perception that the Arab world's largest country is badly adrift. After seventeen years in power, he sometimes still appears to be a caretaker buying time. Like the anguished government official at the beginning of Mahfouz's *Autumn Quail*, Mubarak seems to be "standing in the middle of nowhere."

The Mubarak government's reputation for rampant corruption is fueling popular discontent and is being exploited by the Islamists; it is also leading to growing consternation among Western donors and diplomats. Particularly nettlesome are the mounting accusations against the Gang of Sons, as the wheeling-and-dealing offspring of a number of key Mubarak officials are called; two of the most frequently mentioned are the sons of the President. Accusations that the Gang of Sons—and, by extension, the Mubarak government—is actively assisting neighboring Libya in circumventing United Nations sanctions have led to a number of recent rebukes from the United States. (Equally distasteful to Washington was the confirmation, in September 1997, by the CIA that Egyptian security officials, in December 1993, had abducted a prominent Libyan dissident, who was about to receive U.S. citizenship, from his Cairo hotel and had turned him over to Colonel Muammar al-Qaddafi's viscerally anti-American regime. According to the CIA, Mansour Kikhia—who, prior to his defection to the United States, was Qaddafi's ambassador to the United Nations and his Minister of Foreign Affairs—was executed, without charges or trial, outside the Libyan capital in early 1994. The revelation of Egypt's role in Kikhia's abduction and death prompted an angry phone call to Mubarak from the American Vice President.)

Nevertheless, Washington continues to have an enormous stake in the Mubarak regime, for on assuming office Mubarak had immediately reaffirmed Egypt's commitment to the peace treaty with Israel, began reestablishing the nation's place as a leader in the Arab world, and set to work behind the scenes as a mediator in the on-going quest for Middle Eastern peace. Later, he, more than anyone else, gave legitimacy to the U.S.-led coalition against Iraq's Saddam Hussein in the Gulf War. (For that endeavor, Washington wrote off nearly $7 billion of Egypt's foreign debt.)

Yet for many Egyptians—Islamists, Marxists, and secularists alike—it was precisely because of these things that they found themselves more and more estranged from their President. Washington's seemingly petulant behavior toward Saddam Hussein and its failure to push the fledgling Palestinian-Israeli peace process along are generally perceived—not only in Egypt, but across the Middle East—to be emblematic of a largely one-sided American strategy, a strategy in which Washington has shown a deplorable lack of balance in its treatment of Israel and the Arab world. At the United Nations, the United States had pushed relentlessly for ever more punitive sanctions against Iraq, yet when Israel defied UN resolutions, Washington excused it with a wink and a nod. When the hard-line Israeli government of Benjamin Netanyahu all but ruptured the Oslo peace accords by refusing to relinquish more than scattered pockets of occupied Palestinian land, it appeared that Washington assumed that its allies in the Arab world—including Mubarak—could control their populations. Events made it dramatically clear that they could not. Each false step that Washington took was pounced upon.

In retrospect, it seems to me that to understand today's events in Egypt and the Middle East, the Camp David peace treaty provides the key. In a sense, everything else sprang from it: the rise of anti-Americanism and Islamist politics; Hosni Mubarak's enveloping state of siege; the bitter sense of betrayal of the Palestinians; and Egypt's transformation into a country at war with itself. Perhaps as symbolic of this as anything else was the 1981 funeral of Anwar Sadat—to many in his own country, a traitor who had been seduced by the United States into the role of leading a moderate, pro-American Arab state. His funeral, in a sense, presented a clear profile of what his country had become: three former American presidents and the Prime Minister of Israel were invited; his people were not.

Ironically, the lavish infusion of U.S. aid (nearly $40 billion since

1979) that transformed Egypt into the hub of American policy in the Middle East—and made it, after Israel, Washington's second-largest recipient of funds and the largest U.S. overseas aid operation since Vietnam—was meant to buy political stability. I was reminded graphically one morning in late 1994 how fallacious that was.

As I strolled along the Nile, retracing one of Miss Pennypecker's favorite walks, I passed clusters of riot policemen, their faces partly hidden by visored helmets, who were standing guard outside tourist centers and half-empty hotels. Below me, accompanying a cruise ship on the Nile, a dozen or so others stood at imperfect attention in a small patrol boat, their machine guns turned toward the larger ship, which carried a group of bikini-clad, sunbathing Greek tourists, whom they were meant to protect. The campaign by Islamic militants to cripple Egypt's economy through attacks on tourism— the country's number one source of foreign exchange (followed closely by remittances from workers in the Gulf countries and American aid)—had cost the Mubarak government $1.5 billion in 1994, and had decimated the tourist industry. Combined with an admittedly timid government attempt at privatization and structural economic reform, the growing reluctance of foreign investors to consider Egypt potentially promising anymore had only served to widen the gap between the rulers and the ruled. And the social and economic alienation that was largely fueling the Islamic flame was almost certainly going to get worse. Waging war on the Islamists will not change that.

When I asked a Western ambassador what he thought, he replied, "Unlike Algeria, Egypt's Islamist groups are not regime-threatening—at least, not yet—but if the government continues to refuse to address the root causes of this revolt, and persists in treating it as merely a law-and-order problem, I'll be a little less certain about that. Mubarak has a mind-set about the Islamists, and he keeps insisting to us that they're a creation of Iran and Sudan, but he doesn't produce a shred of evidence. Yes, some Iranian money is coming in, and some Egyptians are training in Sudanese camps, but it is very wrong—indeed, potentially self-defeating—to put all the weight on external help, because the great majority of weapons, money, and recruits, and the anger that fuels them, are coming from here. Despite Mubarak's pronouncements, the problem is not Iran or Sudan. It's him."

The anger of which the ambassador spoke had increased almost palpably by the end of 1994. So had the level of violence, and the intransigence on both sides. Egypt seemed to be sliding into an incipient guerrilla war in which neither the Islamists nor the security forces had defined any front lines. Thousands of political prisoners were being systematically tortured as part of official policy; hundreds had "disappeared"; hostage-taking and collective punishment were common practices; and entire neighborhoods had been cordoned off, and mosques and houses razed.

One day I visited a group of young men, mostly students, who were hidden away in a slum neighborhood in one of Mahfouz's alleyways. They hadn't attended classes in more than a month, they said. When I asked why, one replied, "Because we're bearded, and we're young. To be young and bearded in Egypt is a crime."

What Mahfouz has termed "the concealed side"—the reality that hides behind convention and form in societies where repression has become an inescapable part of everyday life—did not express itself in a highly visible presence of crack troops or of uniformed policemen on the streets, though I did notice them from time to time. It expressed itself mostly in fear in the alleys and in outrage in sophisticated Cairo salons. It also expressed itself in a growing anti-Americanism, which I had not known in Egypt before, and in an intellectual siege in which the country's writers, directors, playwrights, and poets found themselves ever more frequently caught between the Islamists, on the one hand, and the government, on the other—especially the official sheikhs of al-Azhar, whose increasingly strident pronouncements, as they attempted to guide artistic thought, were proving as outrageous as the demands of many militants.

"What is happening to our civility?" Egypt's best filmmaker, an eccentric genius named Youssef Chahine, asked me one afternoon. His most recent film, *The Emigrant*, which was hugely successful and had broken all Egyptian attendance records, had come under attack by the militants, who alleged that it was based on the biblical travels of Joseph, and thus personalized a prophet in a human way. There were bomb threats against one of the theaters where it was being shown, and an obscure Islamist lawyer, backed by al-Azhar, had demanded that the film be banned (which happened in 1995, though the banning order was later overturned by an appeals court). "You know," Chahine told me, "prior to all this, I had a film"—a docudrama depicting the alienation of Cairo's slum dwellers— "banned by the *government*." Unlike many writers and artists, Chahine had not been fatwaed by the militants, but he felt threatened nevertheless. "All of us do," he said. "Both physically and artistically. Strangling someone's work is like hitting Naguib Mahfouz in the neck."

Mahfouz had begun receiving death threats in 1988, only days after being awarded the Nobel Prize—when the controversy over the banned *Children of Gebelaawi* was revived—but he had doggedly refused to accept armed government guards. "I walk to the coffee shop, and I don't look to the left or the right," Mahfouz said in an interview at the time. "And so what if they get me? I have lived my life and done what I wanted to do."

For six years, Mahfouz could have been targeted at any time. Yet the man from the alleys of Gamaliya, who has left Egypt only twice in his life—for three-day official trips to the former Yugoslavia and to Yemen—simply did not believe that it could ever happen to him.

He had been deeply shaken in June 1992 when his friend Farag Foda, one of Egypt's best-known writers and an iconoclastic critic, not only of militant Islam but of the creeping Islamization of Egyptian life, was shot to death outside his Cairo home by two masked men from the Gama'a who riddled his body with a dozen bullets, fired at close range, after he had been accused of apostasy. It was the first assassination of an Egyptian intellectual, and for many of them it marked the beginning of the siege. Despite his acerbic writings, few Egyptians expected Farag Foda to pay with his life.

Like Foda and most other Egyptian secularists, Mahfouz—who

had frequently called on the government to enter into a dialogue with its Islamic foes—had grown concerned over the steady, consistent rise in the influence of the Islamists in the schools and universities, in the news media, in the courts, and in the arts, and over what he considered an acquiescent government response. (Clearly baffled by the movement, the government continued to veer between suppression and a highly orchestrated campaign to make itself appear more Islamic than the Islamic activists.) In January 1994, Mahfouz's concern gave way to alarm. In what, by all accounts, was an extraordinary session of parliament, a flamboyant independent-Islamist deputy, Galal Gharib—after requesting all women to leave the hall—accused the Minister of Culture, Farouq Hosni, of publishing "nude, pornographic" pictures in a government-sponsored monthly magazine; one of the pictures in question was Gustav Klimt's painting of Adam and Eve. Then, accompanied by a thunderous chorus of cheers from his supporters in the hall, Gharib attacked ballet schools in Egypt, Arabic translations of foreign literature, and the Egyptian adaptation of a play by Bertolt Brecht. Much to the sheer astonishment of secularists in the hall, Hosni agreed that any books scheduled for publication by his ministry would be sent to al-Azhar for review. Never before in the history of modern Egypt had any government agreed to such a demand. Mahfouz issued a furious statement, signed by scores of artists and writers, in which he described the assault on the arts as "intellectual terrorism," and he later told friends, "The censor in Egypt is no longer just the state. It's the gun of the fundamentalists."

The University of al-Azhar is the oldest university in the world, and attracts thousands of students each year from every part of the Muslim world. Its campus, which has become increasingly sprawling and rich—and increasingly militant—is dominated by a stunning tenth-century mosque and by five towering minarets, from which muezzins, five times a day, call the faithful to prayer. It has long been a prime recruiting ground for the Muslim Brotherhood, and its graduates have, in turn, reexported the Brotherhood's brand of militant Islam throughout the Muslim world. What is far more worrying to the Egyptian government, however, is the Brotherhood's recent success, thanks largely to funding from Saudi Arabia, in recruiting prominent sheikhs from within al-Azhar itself.

Western diplomats were thus not surprised when the seventy-seven-year-old Grand Sheikh of al-Azhar, Gad al-Haq Ali Gad al-Haq, who had been appointed by Mubarak, issued a scathing fatwa against holding a United Nations conference on population in Cairo in the fall of 1994, or when he granted the title of *shahid*, or martyr—the highest accolade that an Islamist can receive—to a young member of Gama'a who had joined forces with the Palestinian militant group Hamas in a shooting spree in Jerusalem that left sixteen wounded or dead. Both pronouncements caught the Egyptian government unawares and led to Mubarak's acute embarrassment.

The diplomats and Egypt's increasingly beleaguered secularists were nevertheless stunned when one of the world's leading moderate Islamic scholars, Sheikh Mohammed al-Ghazali, of al-Azhar, testifying for the defense at the trial of those accused of assassinating Farag Foda, effectively endorsed the extrajudicial killing of apostates or of anyone who opposed the implementation of Shariah law. For the secularists, Sheikh al-Ghazali had come to represent a dangerous convergence between Egypt's radical and moderate Islamist political trends. In their view, as the government has accommodated al-Azhar, and thus emboldened it, al-Azhar has begun adopting political ideas from the militants.

"Suddenly, we realized that within al-Azhar there are many sheikhs who aid and abet the violence, who give it credence," Tahseen Basheer, the retired Egyptian ambassador, told me over tea. "Al-Azhar has always been a center. Sheikh Yassin [the leader of Hamas] studied there; so did Hassan al-Turabi and Sheikh Omar Abdel-Rahman. And today we see the sheikhs of al-Azhar issuing fatwas as extreme as those of Gama'a, and they are doing it with the active encouragement of the Muslim Brotherhood."

The key question about the Brotherhood continued to be whether it had really renounced violence, as it claimed to have done. It continued to maintain that it had no direct control over groups like the Gama'a, but some Egyptians and Westerners remained unconvinced.

"How overt the coordination is between the groups is secondary," one Western diplomat told me when I called on him. "What matters is that all these groups have a relationship that works; their goals are the same. They could be rivals, they could be in competition, or somewhere in between. That doesn't matter. What does is that they have an effective distribution of labor, and that the glue that holds it all together is the money from Saudi Arabia and the Gulf, whether it comes from individuals or from their governments."

Imbaba, hidden away in the alleys—far from my understanding or view, when I first glimpsed it from my terrace during my student days—is only a bridge away from the affluent island of Zamalek, but it is one of Cairo's most dismal and squalid slums, holding some 800,000 people, or perhaps more.

In it, stark, sometimes tottering houses, built of stucco or brick or of corrugated iron and mud, line a labyrinth of open sewers and unpaved alleyways. The alleys are so narrow that they are little more than dark, hidden passageways. Some of them are less than six feet wide, and an attempt to navigate them by car meant lurching, no faster than a person could walk, through gullies and ravines, then negotiating one's way around chicken coops, uncollected garbage, and open cesspools. Laundry hung from rooftops and from window frames on both sides of the car, and when there was a breeze the laundry met in the middle of the alley, creating billowing barricades.

From the moment you arrive in Imbaba, the problems facing Egypt overwhelm you: the growing polarization of politics; a population that has increased by 50 percent during the Mubarak years; an economy lacking an industrial base, in which at least 15 percent of the country's eighteen million workers are unemployed and another 35 to 50 percent are underemployed. Twenty-three percent of Egypt's people live in absolute poverty.

As I glanced across the Nile, the high-rise skyline of Zamalek, punctuated by tree-lined avenues, gardens, and parks, and of the other Egypt continued to define itself.

I had come here with a graduate student—whom I will call Ahmed, since at the moment he was living underground—and we decided that it was far more practical to walk.

Walking through the alleys is, in a sense, to explore a walled, hidden city of sorts. There is almost no government presence here: few services; no sanitation; only sputtering electricity; few hospitals or schools. We had left the government behind us at the last paved road.

We had also left sunshine behind as the alleys gave way to a maze of ever-smaller muddy lanes where shabby apartment buildings with peeling façades loomed on both sides of us, blocking out the sky.

We finally reached our destination, the al-Iman Billah Mosque. One of some seventy thousand unofficial, or "popular," mosques— whose numbers had more than doubled since my student days—it was little more than a room on the ground floor of a dun-colored apartment building in Imbaba's Munira Gharbiya neighborhood. Militant Islamic slogans were defiantly scrawled across its walls, above latticed windows and brown-painted doors, which were sealed with immense padlocks. The government, in its move to crush the Islamic groups, had closed all of Munira's "popular" mosques —there were ten—and imprisoned their sheikhs. The sheikh of al-Iman Billah was a medical doctor who, without charges or trial, had been in the "punishment wards" of various Cairo prisons for more than four years. Sheikhs from the neighborhood's other "popular" mosques—including professors, lawyers, and a former Marxist economist—had been in prison just as long. But the "popular" mosques, nearly a thousand of which had been shut down nationwide, were, in a sense, like the Islamic militants themselves: quiescent in one province or in one neighborhood after a government crackdown, they would spring up in another.

Leaving the al-Iman Billah, we moved next door, to a coffeehouse, and sat at one of a number of small wicker tables spilling out into the alleyway, where, as Mahfouz once put it, "the houses bunched together untidily on both sides of the road like a row of soldiers standing at ease." On this particular day, four disagreeable-

looking plainclothes security men sat at the table next to us, fingering worry beads. As we sipped tiny cups of thick coffee, we watched
the life of the alleys pass by: a young girl on a donkey, who was
dressed in a black galabiya and wearing the traditional head scarf,
or *hijab*; birds in wicker cages, in a cart pulled by a mule; a herd of
goats waiting to be slaughtered outside a butcher shop, where car-
casses of meat hung from spikes and blew in the breeze. A group of
dark-eyed, dark-skinned men in galabiyas, with prayer caps or
floppy turbans on their heads, walked by silently in single file, as if
performing a secret military drill. The security men stared at them,
and they stared back. The dark-skinned men were mostly from the
countryside of Upper Egypt, Ahmed said, where the battle between
the Islamists and the regime was most intense. Many Cairenes worried that the chaos it had spawned was driving Upper Egypt dangerously close to civil war.

A buxom woman who had tattoos on her fingers and her nose,
and whose head was covered by a scarf, joined us; Ahmed introduced her to me as Gamila, the neighborhood prostitute. She told
me that she gave 20 percent of her earnings to a "popular" mosque.
As we continued chatting, a large, lumbering man came and sat
down; then a little girl, who told me that she had to walk two miles
each day to attend school. An alley dweller is not just a person but
part of a social network, a professor of sociology had told me earlier. And now, as I watched the life on the street, it seemed to me
that, as in so many of Mahfouz's works, two seemingly contradictory worlds coexisted in the alleys side by side: a world of extreme
Islamic activism and a world of extreme vice.

And those who lived here, tucked away from public view,
were—like the alleys—Mahfouzian. They included civil servants
and bureaucrats, the educated unemployed, laborers and shopkeepers, pensioners and petty thieves, drummers and belly dancers, drug
dealers and prostitutes. In the alleys, they had once found solace in
their anonymity, but as they measured their lives against their hopes,
they came up short, so it is hardly surprising that the alleys of Imbaba had become a stronghold of the militant Islamic groups.

They were all represented here—the Brotherhood, Gama'a, and

al-Jihad—and, in storefront groceries as well as in the "popular" mosques, it was easy to find cassettes of sermons by Sheikh Omar Abdel-Rahman. After Ahmed and I left the coffeehouse, walking deeper into the ever-smaller alleyways, they became increasingly defined by Egypt's two great themes: the faithful and the poor.

The sounds, from amplified systems or from radios, were those of the Koran. Men bowed in prayer in narrow spaces among dusty potted palms. I saw on nearly every crumbling wall we passed, and flying from balconies above, the green-and-white flags and signs of the Muslim Brotherhood. "Islam is the solution" they announced.

The Islamists, led by the Brotherhood, had built their own social and welfare system here, rivaling that of the state. Gama'a-controlled "popular" mosques had set up discount health clinics and schools, day-care centers, and furniture factories to employ the unemployed, and they provided meat, at wholesale prices, to the poor. Despite an aggressive $10 million social program launched by the government at the end of 1994, the Islamists' institutions remained generally far more efficient and far superior to run-down government facilities. Along with the collapse of every secular ideology embraced by Egyptian politicians and intellectuals during this century, it was government repression and ineptitude, far more than militants' guns and bombs, that were fueling the Islamic flame.

In Imbaba, by mid-1992, the Gama'a al-Islamiya had, in essence, created a state within a state. Dissent was rarely tolerated in the alleys under its control. Girls and women were harassed if they ventured outside without covering their heads, and I noticed that even girls as young as six—as opposed to the usual age of twelve or thirteen—had "taken the veil," and were wearing *hijabs*. Christian shopkeepers were made to pay "taxes"—forcibly, I was told—for their protection, and many had removed icons of the Virgin Mary from their walls. Groups of militants, armed with knives and guns, went around burning video shops, and there were many neighborhoods that policemen feared to enter after dark. Local emirs, or princes, were appointed—most often bearded young men wearing long white robes and crocheted prayer caps. Throughout their areas of control, they imposed Islamic law by fiat. Then, in December, the government had moved in, in an abortive attempt to crush the Islamic groups. It was a virtual invasion of some fifteen thousand troops. Raids have occurred intermittently ever since.

I found evidence of the violence everywhere I went: metal sheeting pockmarked with bullet holes; "popular" mosques whose doors had been cemented closed; the faces of mothers whose sons had disappeared; and a young boy, barely a teenager, who had been arrested and buried up to his neck for days at a time, in highly saline soil in a state security camp. His skin, discolored and disfigured, resembled that of a leper, and it was impossible to guess his age.

Ali Ismail is a lawyer who defends members of the Islamic groups, and I first met him one evening in November 1994 at his office in a flooded, unlighted Imbaba alleyway. A stocky man in his mid-thirties whose most distinguishing characteristics are deep, dark eyes and a neatly trimmed black beard, he greeted me and my interpreter warmly and offered us Pepsi when we arrived. Then he guided us from an outer office into his own, a small, bare white-washed room lit by a single electric bulb that dangled from the ceiling. The shutters on the only window were securely closed.

During the security operation in December 1992, Imbaba had been effectively sealed off from the world, so I asked Ismail to tell me what had happened then. "They cordoned off the entire area at four or five strategic points," he said. "People woke up in the morning to find themselves under siege. There had been so many police operations here before that people got used to it. But there had never been anything like this. It was unprecedented in its intensity, in its viciousness, in its length of time, and in the number of arrests. Not even in the worst of times—when Sadat was assassinated, for example—had there been anything like this. It went on night and day, for five weeks. By the first evening, the idea of collective punishment was the defining line: they would arrest all those who were bearded and young, their mothers and fathers, their children and wives. *Babies* were even taken in. And children less than ten years old were herded into police stations and tortured, to pressure their fathers to turn themselves in.

"Women were tortured with electroshocks and beaten in the streets—dragged by their hair, after their *hijabs* were savagely torn off their heads. Altogether, there were no fewer than five thousand long-term arrests. Over the next year, some forty-five hundred people were released; they were never charged or tried. Many of them have no idea why they were arrested—except that they lived in Imbaba's alleyways."

"What about the five hundred others?" I asked.

"They're all still in prison," he said. "Some of them were charged and tried, and most were acquitted and ordered released by the courts. Others—the great majority, four hundred or so—were never brought to trial, because the courts ordered their release for lack of evidence." He paused for a moment, and then he continued: "But under our emergency law"—which in 1997 was again extended for an additional three years, meaning that it will have been in effect for an unprecedented twenty years—"when you go to prison in Egypt there's no hope of getting out."

According to Human Rights Watch, the number of Islamists in Egyptian jails in 1994 was over twenty thousand—as opposed to some six thousand the previous year. When I called on General Hassan al-Alfi, the hard-line Minister of the Interior, he became increasingly agitated, and said that these figures were totally wrong. He refused to provide an alternative number, however, and would only say that some four thousand Islamists had been arrested in 1994. Ismail told me that a total of nearly thirty-eight thousand were being held. It was the largest number of political prisoners in Egypt's modern history, and the vast majority of those prisoners had been ordered released by civilian courts.

Ismail explained the way the Orwellian system worked. When Islamists are acquitted by the courts, most of them are transferred almost immediately to the headquarters of the dreaded State Security Investigation, or SSI, an arm of the Interior Ministry, and they are kept there for anything from a week to a month. Then a new order is issued for their arrest, signed by the Minister of the Interior himself. During the period between a person's acquittal and his rearrest, an SSI official draws up documents claiming that he has been released. "And who would know?" Ismail said. "They've been in SSI headquarters all along. This has happened in Egypt before. But what is noteworthy, and alarming, is that it's the usual procedure now."

I asked him to give me an example, and he spoke of Hassan al-Garabawi, a lawyer from the Cairo slum area of Ayn Shams. He had been arrested in January 1989 and acquitted in May of the following year. Since that time, thirty court orders had been issued for his release and thirty new detention orders filed. Hassan al-Garabawi had been in prison for six years. He had never left jail, even though he had been ordered released by five different judges five times a year.

"I have fifty cases of such severity," Ismail said. "They are doctors, lawyers, architects who are being held incommunicado in what is called 'the highly guarded prison'—the Scorpion." (The Scorpion, a new prison within the high-security section of Cairo's Tora Prison complex, is one of Egypt's most dreaded detention sites. A number of lawyers and judges told me that it had been built at least partly with aid from the United States.) "And this is *illegal*," Ismail went on. "Here are the court rulings." He waved a sheaf of papers in the air. "Abdel-Harith Madani was one of the attorneys who challenged this. He was not the most prominent or the most forceful, but he could have paid the price with his life."

I had met Abdel-Harith Madani—a handsome young man of thirty, with intense dark eyes, a square black beard, and short black hair—in the office of another Islamist lawyer in Cairo in 1993. Soft-spoken, almost shy, Abdel-Harith had defended many Islamic militants, including some (there had been fifty-six by then) who had been sentenced to death. In April 1994, he was arrested by the SSI. "I know the case dot for dot," Ismail said. "He was my friend." The account he gave me was later confirmed by Human Rights Watch and Amnesty International.*

Human Rights Watch World Report, 1995 (New York: Human Rights Watch, 1994). *Amnesty International Report* (London: Amnesty International, 1995).

April 26 was a beautiful early-summer day, and Abdel-Harith, after spending the day in court, returned home for an early dinner with his twenty-one-year-old wife and their two infant daughters. Then, as was his custom, he jogged along the Nile; jogging and soccer were passions of his. He was particularly pleased with himself that evening, for only a few days earlier he had won an important case: a court had ruled that the incommunicado detention of prisoners in the Scorpion was contrary to the Egyptian Constitution and the penal code. Just the previous morning, he had had the documents hand-carried to the director of the Scorpion.

Abdel-Harith had often told friends that the spiraling violence in his country appalled him, and now he was attempting to broker a cease-fire between the two sides, through a respected opposition member of parliament, Kamal Khalid. He hoped to have word from Khalid later that evening on the government's response.

He arrived at his law office, in the fashionable area of Giza, at around eight o'clock that evening, and he apparently didn't notice that unmarked SSI cars were parked just down the block. Three lawyers with whom he shared the office were already there. Like Abdel-Harith, they were members of the Egyptian Organization for Human Rights, and, like him, they headed a legal-aid fund—reliably said to be underwritten by Saudi Arabia—for Islamist detainees. Khalid had called him, one of the other lawyers said, but Abdel-Harith was never able to return the call. Nine SSI officers stormed the office, breaking down the door. Several others cordoned off the building. The four young lawyers were told to stand up and face the wall, with their arms raised above their heads. They remained there for three hours, as the SSI officers tore the office apart.

Abdel-Harith was then driven blindfolded to his home by the SSI. (The three other lawyers were released.) The officers ransacked his apartment, terrifying his wife and his daughters. Then they drove him to the SSI headquarters in Giza. It was just past midnight.

Across Giza, in the small rooftop extension on the eighth floor of the Kasr al-Ayni Hospital, which had been transformed into a secret prison ward, doctors remember that Abdel-Harith was carried in just before dawn. He was bleeding profusely and was in a severe state of shock. Within an hour, he was dead. According to a still unreleased autopsy report, he had been beaten to death. Seventeen wounds were found on his body, including punctures with a sharp instrument. The fatal blow had been delivered by a club, to the back of his neck.

Yet no one told his family or his friends for eleven days. It was only on May 7, at dawn, that his wife was told to come and pick up her husband's body at the central morgue. (The Ministry of the Interior later announced that Abdel-Harith had died of lung failure caused by an asthma attack, and a spokesman told the press, "What do you expect the government to say? We never violate human rights. He died God's death.")

At the same time that Abdel-Harith's wife received the telephone call, the SSI arrested his mother-in-law, one of his cousins, and a cousin of his wife's, and they were held, virtually as hostages, until the family would agree to pick up the body and bury it immediately. But the family refused, demanding that the autopsy report be released, and that a second, independent autopsy be performed. They were backed by the powerful syndicates of lawyers and doctors— both of which the Islamists controlled—and later by the American State Department, Amnesty International, and Human Rights Watch.

Nevertheless, the family's protest did not last long. The next evening, Abdel-Harith's cousin Amir, who had spent two days at the SSI, returned home. He had been tortured. The following morning at dawn, the family went to the Zeinhum Morgue and retrieved the corpse.

The SSI had arranged for a plane to fly Amir and the coffin containing Abdel-Harith to the tiny village of Qimaan al-Mataana, in Upper Egypt, where Abdel-Harith's parents live. But neither of his parents was permitted to attend the burial; nor, for that matter, was anyone else. And the family and the villagers were warned that if they complained, Abdel-Harith's younger brother, Salah, who was in prison after being accused of killing an undercover SSI officer in 1992, could meet the same fate that Abdel-Harith had met.

The SSI buried Abdel-Harith in an unmarked grave in al-Mataana's cemetery, near the banks of the Nile, and for the forty days of official mourning SSI officers stood guard by it. Nobody was permitted to come to pray, or to pay final respects. And every morning during the forty days, the women of al-Mataana, dressed in black shawls, passing by the cemetery on their way to the village well, craned their necks forward and tried to find the grave. It was identifiable only by the presence of the security men. Otherwise, it was just a pile of stones covered with dust and sand.

Since the days when the schoolteacher Hassan al-Banna founded the Muslim Brotherhood seventy years ago, Egypt's twenty-five thousand schools—which have 850,000 poorly paid teachers—have proved fertile ground for the spread of political Islam. And, by late 1994, it was in the schools that one of the fiercest battles between the Islamists and the government was being played out. In classrooms around the country, especially in Upper Egypt, the Islamists had basically seized control of the educational system, assaulting secular thought, altering school texts, and playing cassettes of radical sermons by "popular" sheikhs in class. And as the battle lines became increasingly drawn, they had most symbolically been expressed in a growing tussle over whether female students and teachers could attend classes veiled.

So one evening in November I called on Dr. Hussein Kamel Baha al-Din, who has what is probably Egypt's most difficult job. As Minister of Education, he is charged with combating Islamic activism in the schools. In 1993, he had banned the *niqab*—a shawl-like garment that covers the face, hair, and neck—from the classrooms, but when he banned the less extreme *hijab* the following year, he was, much to his astonishment, overruled by the courts. Emboldened, the Islamists had now forcefully challenged him on the *niqab*. Like so much else that is happening in Egypt, the government's campaign against the head scarves has only served to harden the Islamists' resolve.

There were demonstrations nearly every other day and, often, violent clashes, as bands of young girls dressed in *niqabs* stormed government schools. One afternoon in Imbaba, I watched a number of girls being rounded up—some as young as ten. They refused to enter a police van, because, they said, it was a symbol of the regime, but they were picked up and carried into it anyway, flailing their arms and singing verses from the Koran.

Baha al-Din—a medical doctor and former professor, who is one of only a handful of intellectuals in Mubarak's cabinet—had stunned Cairenes in an interview earlier that year by saying that the Islamists had successfully infiltrated primary, preparatory, and secondary schools all over Egypt. When I visited him, I asked him to explain.

"I couldn't believe how many fundamentalist teachers we had in the schools," he said. "I've transferred more than a thousand teachers out of their jobs and put them into administrative posts; then I went through the libraries, which were full of fundamentalist tracts, and had them all removed. And then, of course, there's the matter of the *niqab* and the *hijab*. And this matter is a matter of actual war. When I tried to ban them, there was an immense uproar. Everyone fought me ferociously—the media, the teachers, al-Azhar. The fundamentalists have forced entire schools to wear the *hijab*. I found schools in which little girls as young as six, seven, eight were being forced to wear it; schools where teachers were preventing students from singing the national anthem or saluting the flag. In other words, there was to be no national identity—only an Islamic one. Music, theater, anything relating to the arts was being proscribed. The fundamentalists disapprove of drama clubs, so on the night of a performance they would surround a theater, kneeling in prayer and blocking all the entrances so that no one could get in. One woman was forced to divorce her husband because he had sent their children to a particular school. They told her that her husband was heretical.

"It's an *immense* problem," Baha al-Din went on. "The leaders of this movement are *very* well educated, and they know exactly what they want. They want to seize power, and our educational system offers them a very convenient route. In order to change this, we have got to change the *entire* system of rote learning. I've begun to do this at the primary level, but it's going to take time."

Since the Islamist tide not only was sweeping through the secondary schools and the universities but had also begun to express itself in publishing and the arts, I asked Baha al-Din how al-Azhar was affecting education and intellectual thought.

"I went to al-Azhar and met with fifteen hundred of them to defend my views on the *hijab*," he replied, "and they fought me every step of the way. They issued a verdict"—not a fatwa— "against me, and they are still trying to force me to change."

Baha al-Din refused to comment on the rise of Saudi Arabian influence in evidence at al-Azhar—and in the Egyptian Islamist movement at large—but one of his key advisers had told me earlier that considerable amounts of Saudi money were coming in, and that they had increased substantially over the previous year.

When I asked a Western diplomat later how the funding of Egypt's Islamic underground worked, he replied, "It's mostly legitimate, but it's all managed behind the scenes: through banks, insurance companies, foundations, front organizations, and mosques." What had changed during 1993 and 1994, he said, was the increasing amount of money, in terms of percentage, that was coming from Europe and the United States.

As early as 1995, Egypt's militant Islamic groups had support offices in some thirty countries, one Western ambassador told me at the time. Generally, he said, these supporters worked under the cover of a religious front, from which they collected money, set up organizational cells, and purchased explosives and arms—not only for the Egyptian groups but also for the Palestinian organization Hamas. I learned later, from a ranking official of the Egyptian government, that its assessment was that in 1994 over $15 million had been collected in, or channeled through, the United States. According to the official, the bulk of it had gone to Hamas.

The funding would continue over the coming years, and, by mid-1998, millions more dollars would have reached Egypt, Jordan, the West Bank, and the Gaza Strip from the United States.

Sheikh Omar Abdel-Rahman had arrived in the United States, quietly and without attracting attention, in July 1990, via Saudi Arabia, Afghanistan, and the Sudan, on his much-disputed tourist visa

—the sixth visa he had been granted by the United States. What is perhaps as interesting as how he entered this country is why he decided to come. I had learned in Cairo that his primary purpose was to set up a U.S. infrastructure, a funding mechanism, and an organizational base for Egypt's militant Islamist groups—an undertaking that he had largely accomplished by the time of his arrest.

One afternoon just before Christmas in 1994, after returning from Cairo to New York, I went to the Metropolitan Correctional Center, in lower Manhattan, to meet with him, in what appeared to be a recreation room, in the prison's maximum-security ward. The sheikh had been in prison for a year and a half, and his arrest, on immigration charges in July 1993, was still largely unexplained. Only a week or so earlier, U.S. officials had abruptly informed the Egyptian government that the sheikh could leave the United States for any country that would accept him—and Afghanistan had—unless the Egyptians quickly presented an extradition request. The government of Mubarak was exceedingly reluctant to do this, since it feared a confrontation with the sheikh's followers. For Egypt, it would be far more convenient if the sheikh could be held under guard in the United States indefinitely. But after twenty-four hours of sometimes heated talks between Amr Mousa, the Egyptian Minister of Foreign Affairs, and the U.S. Ambassador, Robert H. Pelletreau, an angry Egyptian government submitted the extradition request, which led to further strains in the relationship between Egypt and the United States. Mubarak, in particular, was furious, I was told by one of his aides, that Washington had shifted the responsibility for the sheikh's prosecution to Cairo. Then, to everyone's collective—and continuing—surprise, Attorney General Janet Reno ordered the sheikh's arrest.

I was accompanied to the Metropolitan Correctional Center by Ahmad Sattar, my usual interpreter, who was now serving as a paralegal for the sheikh, whose conspiracy trial would begin in Manhattan in January 1995. No sooner had we sat down, on two straight-backed chairs, than Sheikh Omar came in. He wore a blue two-piece prison uniform, brown bedroom slippers, and a pair of woolly white socks. His eyes were not covered by the heavy black glasses that he normally wears, nor was he wearing the crimson turban of al-Azhar. Instead, he had a simple white prayer cap on his head.

He greeted me cordially and opened the conversation by telling me that his twenty-year-old son, Abdullah, had just begun his first year at the University of al-Azhar, where the sheikh himself had received his Ph.D. in Islamic jurisprudence some twenty-five years before.

I asked him how he explained the new militancy at al-Azhar.

"In my view, it isn't militancy," Sheikh Omar said. "It's just a tepid whispering that has begun. You mentioned the UN population conference, and the Grand Sheikh's opposition to it. But in the final analysis, what did he *do*? We didn't see the kind of opposition that we saw from the Pope in Rome—his opposition was very forceful. I do admire that man. He opposed this conference, and the issue of abortion, in a most positive way, and he did whatever he could to prevent this conference's taking place. Everyone in the world knew what the Catholic Church's position was, so why didn't the Grand Sheikh of al-Azhar stand up and tell the world what Muslims think? No. Al-Azhar's response to this conference was not nearly adequate enough for me."

"But," I persisted, "many Egyptians believe that the al-Azhar sheikhs sense that their interpretations of Islam are being superseded by those of more militant groups, and, as a consequence, they are increasingly adopting the ideas of these groups."

"Good," the sheikh responded, "if what you say is true." After a moment's pause, he went on: "You know, if al-Azhar had not neglected its duty, had it not become only a mouthpiece of the government, had it implemented Islamic Shariah law, you would not see any Islamic groups, like Gama'a, working as they are now. They wouldn't even *exist*, for it was only after al-Azhar forfeited its historical role that all these groups began popping up to fill the void. Every Islamic group working in Egypt now is trying to fill a vacuum created by al-Azhar."

I asked him to give me an example, and he replied, "In the area of education, for one; but, most important, in the implementation of Shariah law. I can assure you, the moment that al-Azhar begins doing what it is supposed to do, you will no longer see any of these Islamic activist groups."

As the sheikh continued talking, he appeared at ease, rocking back and forth in his chair, his long white beard resting on his chest. He apologized that he could not offer me tea or soda, explaining that he was not permitted to carry money in his prison uniform.

I asked Sheikh Omar if, in his view, the attack on Naguib Mahfouz was justified.

"I don't know the circumstances, but it all seems a bit strange," he said. "It could be just another government trick to anger the people. Naguib Mahfouz has been around for years, and if our youth wanted to attack him they would have done it long ago. The main question I have is: Why now? They've charged sixteen people. It's unbelievable! They say sixteen people were needed, just to scratch a man on his neck with a knife. Now they will court-martial them all, and within a month they'll be dead. And no one will know, not even their lawyers, what really happened to Naguib Mahfouz."

"Are you absolutely certain that this attack was not carried out by Gama'a?" I asked.

"This is what I think," he replied. "Naguib Mahfouz is not a target for the Islamists. As I said before, we know where he sits, where he walks. When the pressure on the Islamic groups was not nearly as great as it is now, when they were more or less able to freely move about, they never attacked Mahfouz. So why now? And what could they hope to accomplish by killing him anyhow?"

"It has been reported that you issued a fatwa against Mahfouz by declaring him an apostate," I said.

"No, no, no," he replied, and his voice began to rise. "This whole matter is *so* misunderstood. What I said—and this was when *The Satanic Verses* was making headlines—was that if we had punished Naguib Mahfouz for what he wrote in *Children of Gebelaawi*, then Salman Rushdie never would have dared to write that book. This was a reply to a question asked by a journalist. It was a reply, an opinion. It was *not* a fatwa."

"How should Mahfouz have been punished?" I asked.

"You've got to understand the rule of Shariah law," Sheikh Omar replied. "Al-Azhar should have brought Mahfouz before a committee, where he would have been judged. He would have had an opportunity to defend himself, and if found guilty, he would have been given an opportunity to repent. But under Islamic law, any Muslim who is found to be an apostate has no other option: he *must* repent."

"And if he doesn't?"

"Then he will be executed," Sheikh Omar said.

He stopped for a moment, and then he went on: "You personally, and others in the West, may not like this; you may find it harsh. But this is our religion; it is the rule of God."

For a few moments, neither of us said anything more.

Before I left Cairo, I had asked a foreign diplomat what he anticipated was going to happen in Egypt next, and he had replied, "Egypt is not Algeria, at least not yet. There it's a civil war; here it's guerrilla attacks. But should widespread violence and unrest break out, then the key question is: What will the Army's reaction be, for it remains Mubarak's only real constituency. I suspect he will keep the troops in the barracks for as long as he can, for there are many who doubt whether the Army will fire on civilians to support an increasingly unpopular government."

By the end of 1994, former Mubarak officials were speaking of growing ties between junior military officers and the Islamic militants. There had been at least one court-martial—and probably two—that year of junior officers charged with plotting to assassinate the President. (The officers were subsequently executed by firing squad.) It was the realization of the government's worst nightmare.

So I now asked Sheikh Omar what the Islamists' strength in the Army was.

He hesitated, and didn't reply directly. Instead, choosing his words carefully, he said, "That is a very difficult question, which no one can answer right now. And even if I knew, obviously I would not tell you—which divisions, where, and how much—and allow the Egyptian government to finish them off. What I can say is that, in addition to the courts-martial, there have been at least three trials of civilians this year in which some of the defendants were officers or cadets from the Military Academy." (According to defense lawyers, there were thirteen.)

Sheikh Omar had been animated during our interview, but now he began to fidget in his chair. In an hour or so, he told me, he was meeting with former U.S. attorney general Ramsey Clark, who was heading his defense team.

"One more question," he said.

I asked him what, in his view, was the most likely scenario for the Islamists to come to power in Egypt, if they do.

"Be specific," the sheikh said. "Give me your choices."

I did. A growing number of Egyptians and foreign diplomats had come to believe that if parliamentary elections, scheduled for November 1995, were free and fair, the Islamists, led by the Muslim Brotherhood, would probably win. I now said to the sheikh that it seemed to me that the three most logical scenarios were elections; a military coup; or mass demonstrations and chaos on the streets.

"Forget about elections," he replied. "As long as this government is in power, they will *never* be free or fair. Every election in which Mubarak has stood, he has won by ninety-nine percent. Has this ever happened to an American president?" (According to Amnesty International, the elections of 1995 were "fraudulent, undemocratic, and grossly unfair.")

"As far as a coup is concerned," the sheikh went on, "the Egyptian Army is now under unprecedented surveillance and security. Military intelligence has set up a new arm—it's called the Seventy-fifth Group—and its sole purpose is to monitor junior officers and new recruits. And that monitoring tells me that there is something to be worried about. But, nevertheless, the moment they discover anyone who prays, who reads the Koran, who observes Islamic rituals, they are weeded out; thus, through attrition, they are trying to deplete the ranks.

"So," he continued, "we've eliminated two of the three choices, and the last one is the most viable for me: for people to rise up and go to the streets. You've seen the disaffection all over Egypt—we *control* the bar association, yet when lawyers demonstrate they are beaten back with tear gas and clubs. We *control* the student unions at the universities, yet the representatives are being carted off to jail. And the students, like the lawyers, are *elected* representatives. Blue-collar workers have been striking more than ever before. Everyone, from the extreme right to the extreme left, has lost faith in this regime; on every level of society, people are in conflict with this regime."

He stood up and walked me to the door, ringing a button for a guard to see me out. He seemed confident, even puckish, and I was struck by the realization that, for over a year, Sheikh Omar had been in jail. Yet even from a prison in the United States he was better informed on what was happening in Egypt than many Egyptians were.

Before I left Cairo, in November 1994, I had called on President Hosni Mubarak in the presidential palace in Heliopolis, some ten miles from the center of town, where he had set up his primary office. To walk through the palace's high-ceilinged halls, resplendent in marble, alabaster, and gold, is to enter a vanished world of monarchs and colonial powers, seemingly cut off from the rest of Egypt behind towering stucco walls.

The now seventy-year-old Mubarak is well aware of the risks involved in leaving the palace grounds. As Vice President, he had been sitting next to Sadat on the afternoon of October 6, 1981, watching the military parade, when machine-gun fire began. In forty-five seconds, Sadat was dead.

Having entered his third term, for all intents and purposes Mubarak had crowned himself President for life. He had broken the covenant with his people by steadfastly refusing to designate a successor—something that neither Sadat nor Nasser had dared to do. And he had rejected out of hand a call from a group of prominent Egyptian intellectuals and opposition leaders for a popular vote—rather than a referendum—to elect their President. He explained his reasoning to the London daily *al-Hayat*: "Money would play a big role, and someone unqualified would be elected, as has happened in Latin America."

The modest, unpretentious soldier from Kafr al-Museilha, who offers only a glimpse of himself, a fleeting sketch—projecting charm and guilelessness one moment, humility and ruthlessness the next—had dashed all hopes that he would institute real democratic reform. Many Egyptians now believe that political renewal may only come, as it has in the past, at the point of a gun.

All that I had heard about Mubarak, in the days before we met, had led me to expect a disillusioned man. He doesn't take pressure well, I was told, and tends to withdraw into himself. Only a few days earlier, he had met with President Clinton, who had stopped in Cairo en route to the signing of the peace treaty between Jordan and Israel. The meeting had not gone well, according to all accounts, and the Egyptian government had begun to sense that American foreign policy in the Middle East was no longer as inextricably tied to Cairo as it once had been.

There had also been a disaster in Upper Egypt a few days after Clinton left, in which some six hundred people died when blazing fuel from an army depot was carried by flash floods through a small town. Two years earlier, when Cairo had been hit by a devastating earthquake, the government had dithered while Islamist groups rushed in with relief. Mubarak was determined that this would not happen again. But the government stumbled, and every stumble was pounced upon.

Security at the presidential palace was unprecedented when I arrived. The outer foyer bristled with electronic equipment and metal scans. After some time I was escorted into the private office of the President. Mubarak is a thickset man of short-to-medium height with jet-black hair; there is little that is soft or tentative about him. As he greeted me and indicated that I should sit on a large gilded sofa to the left of his elegant armchair, his manner was confident, even ebullient. After an exchange of pleasantries, I asked Mubarak what concerned him most about the problems facing Egypt now.

"Our main concern is the economy," he said in English, "and we're working hard on economic reform. I suppose you're asking that question because of the [Islamic] fanatics here. They're nothing to worry about. We're used to this in Egypt; it goes up and down. And, frankly, I must tell you, this whole problem of terrorism throughout the Middle East is a by-product of our own illegal Muslim Brotherhood—whether it's al-Jihad, Hezbollah in Lebanon, or Hamas. They all sprang from underneath the umbrella of the Muslim Brotherhood."

"But the Brotherhood claims that it has now renounced violence," I said, adding that many Egyptians believed that as long as it was banned and forced to operate underground, it increasingly ran the risk of being hijacked by the more extremist groups. So I asked Mubarak if he had any plans to legalize the Muslim Brotherhood.

A hint of impatience and displeasure crossed his face. "Absolutely not! I will not *permit* another Algeria here. Oh, yes, they say they have renounced violence, but in reality they are responsible for all this violence, and the time will come when they will be uncovered." He went on to imply that a severe crackdown on the Brotherhood was imminent. (Months later, prior to the parliamentary elections of 1995, that crackdown began, and it would continue over the next three years.)

As we continued talking, Mubarak expressed both irritation and concern over what he considered to be the passive attitude of Western governments, particularly those of Britain, Germany, and the United States, in allowing Egypt's militant Islamic groups to operate freely from their soil. But he voiced his greatest concern—rage, really—over the veterans of the U.S.-sponsored Afghanistan war.

"Nearly all those who are committing these crimes, these acts of violence, were trained on the battlefield of Afghanistan," he said. "They are now reinfiltrating, all over the Middle East. They have training, money, and arms, and they're now looking for a new cause. The problem of violence in this country began when the first man returned from Afghanistan. Before that, there was a dialogue between the Gama'a al-Islamiya and the government."

When I asked him if he could give me details, he hesitated, and then said that he would prefer not to.

A number of Western diplomats had told me earlier that they

were troubled by mounting evidence not only of cooperation between Egypt's militant Islamic groups and Hamas but of recurring
reports that the Egypt-Gaza frontier had, in essence, become a *cordon sanitaire* for the smuggling of weapons and men, and the transfer of funds, in and out of Yasir Arafat's beleaguered Palestinian
Authority. I asked Mubarak—who has shown himself more inclined
toward Palestinian anxieties than Anwar Sadat had been—how concerned he was about the breakdown of law and order in the Gaza
Strip.

"I'm concerned, of course," he replied. "The last thing we want
is to have the ghost of Afghanistan haunting us again—and this time
right across our border, in the Gaza Strip. And I must be absolutely
frank: the failure of the Palestinian Governing Authority, and of
Yasir Arafat, not only will set us back by fifty years but there will
be *terrorism everywhere*! My own fear is that if there is a delay in
the peace process, if Arafat fails, all these extremists, all these terrorists trained in Afghanistan, will rush to Gaza and join Hamas. It
will be a *disaster*, and will create one hell of a problem for us."

From time to time during my interview with Mubarak, which
lasted two hours, he seemed bewildered, then annoyed, by some of
my questions—concerning, for example, the increasingly iconoclastic behavior of the Grand Sheikh of al-Azhar and the incommunicado detention of prisoners in the Scorpion—and broke into Arabic
with his Minister of Information, who was sitting next to me. I
wondered if it was possible, as I had been told by some of his aides,
that Mubarak genuinely wasn't aware of many of the things that
were happening in Egypt, though they were happening in his name.

One of his top advisers had told me earlier that, in his view, the
main irony surrounding the Middle East's militant Islamic groups
was that all of them had been spawned by the leaders of the region
themselves: Gama'a had been a creation of Egyptian intelligence to
counter the left; Hamas was a creation of Israeli intelligence to undermine the PLO; and the "Afghan Arabs," the veterans of the Afghan war, were created by the CIA and Saudi intelligence. And, as
the contacts among these various Islamic groups increased, there was
a growing resentment toward the United States; for it was Washington, in Cairo's view, that was most responsible for creating what

the adviser called a hydra-headed monster on the battlefields of Afghanistan, yet it had then refused to assist threatened Arab governments in putting the genie back into the bottle again.

So I asked Mubarak how much responsibility the government of the United States—and that of Egypt—bore for the creation of today's militant Islamic groups.

He remained quiet for a moment, and then he replied without answering, "Yes, Sadat was responsible for the formation of Gama'a. He was badly advised, and he made a big mistake. But I must tell you, even though this group calls itself Gama'a al-Islamiya, it is *not* Islamic. None of them are: they have nothing to do with Islam. They want to seize power, pure and simple, and who are they? Belly dancers and drummers from the slums. The man who tried to assassinate Naguib Mahfouz knows nothing about the Koran; he knows nothing about praying. He was simply paid to do what he did. It's all a matter of money."

"Who is paying them?" I asked.

"The financing is coming from different places," he replied. "These people have their contacts in Paris, Germany, Switzerland. They move about, from here to there. And thanks to modern technology, they make bank transfers by wire, and run the movement by conference calls and fax."

"What about the United States?" I asked.

It was clear that he was angry and bitter, even before he spoke.

"Your government is in contact with these *terrorists* from the Muslim Brotherhood," he replied. "This has all been done very secretly, without our knowledge at first. You think you can correct the mistakes that you made in Iran, where you had no contact with the Ayatollah Khomeini and *his* fanatic groups before they seized power. But I can assure you, these groups will *never* take over this country; and they will never be on good terms with the United States. These contacts will never be of any benefit to you or to any other country which supports these groups."

A year or so earlier, Mubarak had told a group of Egyptian editors that Sheikh Omar Abdel-Rahman was a paid agent of the CIA, and I now asked him if he still held that belief.

He replied that he did, and when I inquired why, he responded that he had read it in *The New York Times*. (Not surprisingly, the sheikh denied the allegation and told me that when Mubarak made the original charge, "even Warren Christopher denied that it was true.")

When Mubarak had first assumed office, he did more to bring about democracy than most Egyptians thought he would. But then, having doled out certain freedoms, he began reining them in. Now his government, according to international human rights organizations, has one of the most abusive records anywhere. So I asked the President if it wasn't a mistake to treat the Islamic movement as strictly a law-and-order problem and, in the process, come under criticism around the world.

"I do not have one political prisoner in my jails," he said. "Everyone there is a criminal who has engaged in criminal acts. Not once have I ever arrested anyone for their political beliefs. Yet the moment anyone is picked up, somebody immediately sends a fax to Amnesty International. And most of these human rights organizations abroad get their information from a so-called human rights organization here, which is controlled by members of the former" —Nasser—"regime, and is stacked with people from the Muslim Brotherhood."

He had begun shouting, and paused to take a deep breath.

I used the occasion to ask him when the autopsy report on Abdel-Harith Madani's death—which had been requested by President Clinton's aides only a few days before—would be made public.

He leaned across a table toward me, and his face hardened perceptibly.

"*Why* is there such a big fuss about Abdel-Harith Madani?" he asked, and his voice began to rise. "What about the human rights of the women and children that these people kill? *Madani was a criminal!* And those who say they're looking out for human rights are only looking out for criminals' rights. They never ask about the innocent people who have been killed in the streets. There's no balance at all! What about Naguib Mahfouz? What about his rights? What about the woman who lost all her sons—two in the wars, and one at the hands of these terrorists. *What about her?* She cannot *have* any more children. Till this day, when I see her on TV, I cannot look at her face."

The President leaned back in his chair, looking suddenly beleaguered and tired. Then he said, seemingly to no one in particular, "We are in a mess."

Naguib Mahfouz left the Police Hospital in the last days of 1994, but he never resumed his normal life moving from café to café. He now meets friends in far more controlled settings and, much to his irritation, he is surrounded by a small group of heavily armed security men. When I last saw him, in the summer of 1997, he told me that the stabbing had left his writing hand largely paralyzed. One of the Arab world's most gifted and most prolific writers can now only with difficulty sign his name.

A few weeks after the attack on Mahfouz, *Children of Gebelaawi* was serialized in the Egyptian press. It was done without his permission and, to the best of everyone's knowledge, without the permission of al-Azhar. Mahfouz was furious, and told friends that the republication of the banned novel was tantamount to "a second assassination attempt."

The controversy began when the Minister of Information—with television cameras in tow—appeared at Mahfouz's bedside and declared that the government did not support a ban on any of his works. No one was certain—including Mahfouz himself—whether the minister's statement ended the prohibition or not.

The evening that I visited Mahfouz in his hospital room, when I asked him what he thought, he merely shook his head and said, "I asked that the publication come at a later time, if the book was to be republished at all."

"Whom do you hold responsible for the attack on you?" I asked.

He answered, without hesitation, "The system, not the young man. The young man who attacked me didn't know anything about *Children of Gebelaawi*. He had never read the book."

I asked Mahfouz what troubled him most about the situation in Egypt now.

"All the young men, like the one who attacked me," he replied.

"We have alienated an entire generation—our most precious commodity, our youth."

"You've told your friends that young people today don't have the same chances that your generation did," I said.

Mahfouz smiled sadly, and nodded his head.

"Can you explain that?" I asked.

He was silent for a moment, and then he turned toward me and said, "We sat in the coffeehouses late into the night and discussed the world. We didn't have to worry about what life would bring us the following day. Our economic situation was far better, and we had more democratic rights. We could choose any political party, and we could choose our government. Some of us even had the hope to be in that government. We had the hope to rule, and to have a chance." He paused for a moment, and then he said, "But the young men of today don't have our hopes, or our opportunities. They also don't have our dreams."

الإخوان المسلمون
وأعدّوا

CHILDREN OF THE JIHAD

ONE FRIDAY EVENING, JUST AFTER SUNSET PRAYERS, SHEIKH Omar Abdel-Rahman climbed into a camouflaged truck in Peshawar, Pakistan, and set off for his first trip inside Afghanistan. It was 1985, he told me later, and he had just spent three years in Egyptian prisons, where he had been severely tortured as he awaited trial on charges of issuing the fatwa that resulted in the assassination of President Anwar Sadat, and of having conspired, along with some three hundred others, to overthrow the Egyptian government. As he settled into the back seat of the U.S.-supplied truck, the sheikh, who was then forty-seven, was helped into a flak jacket by the fundamentalist Afghan resistance leader Gulbadin Hekmatyar.

Hekmatyar was one of the most stridently anti-Western of the resistance leaders who were coordinating the U.S.-financed jihad of the 1980s against the Soviet occupation in Afghanistan; nevertheless, he was receiving roughly half the arms that the CIA was supplying to it. The sheikh had first met Hekmatyar in Saudi Arabia a number of years before, and they became fast friends. They had much in common: both were exceedingly charismatic religious populists; both had committed their lives to jihad, or struggle —or, more loosely, holy war; both were controversial, fiery orators. And although they were both given to elliptical, colorful turns of phrase, their shared message was clear: the imperative to overthrow a secular government—whether in Afghanistan or Egypt—and establish a theocratic Islamic state. For the blind Egyptian cleric and the Afghan engineer, the Soviet invasion of Afghanistan proved to be a turning point.

Outside Peshawar the mountain passes came alive with men. The mujahideen were loading their caravans with AK-47s, mortars, grenades, and mines to return to Afghanistan. Mules and ponies strained under the weight of wooden crates strapped onto their backs. There were no identifying markings on the crates, nor were there any on the contents inside, but everything was part of what would become Washington's largest covert-action program since Vietnam—equipping fighters on the last battlefield of the Cold War. The truck in which Sheikh Omar was traveling joined a convoy of six or seven others and continued toward the Khyber Pass.

The mujahideen preferred to move the arms supplied by the CIA on moonless nights, Nawab Salim, one of Hekmatyar's aides, explained later when he recounted the trip to me. Salim accompanied the sheikh and Hekmatyar into Afghanistan that night; so did Mohammed Shawky al-Islambouli, an Egyptian who was fighting in the war and who was the elder brother of Lieutenant Khaled al-Islambouli, the assassin of Anwar Sadat. Sheikh Omar said little as the convoy inched its way along the precipitous mountain road, from time to time passing desolate Afghan refugee camps where men stood or squatted around tiny wood fires and the muffled chants of a mullah could be heard from a nearby mosque. The sun was just beginning to rise when the convoy reached its destination, a battlefield headquarters in the province of Jalalabad, some fifty miles northeast of the Afghan capital, Kabul. Everything there seemed to be highly improvised, and the headquarters consisted merely of a string of battered and pockmarked buildings built into the side of a strategic hill.

For nearly two decades, Sheikh Omar had preached his message of jihad throughout the Middle East. Now he was inside Afghanistan, where a jihad was actually taking place. "My strongest emotion was pride," he told me afterward. "I felt so proud of my religion, so proud of the power that Muslims had. And I knew that Allah would aid these people and this religion, and that Islam would be victorious in the end. I had so many other feelings, which I cannot describe—I couldn't describe them then and I can't describe them now. My tongue can find no description for what was inside me then."

Guided by Islambouli and Hekmatyar, the sheikh walked to a sandbagged position on the crest of the hill. From below, in the valley, came the echo of crashing artillery shells. He stood there for perhaps five minutes. "He was weeping," Nawab Salim recalled. After a few moments Sheikh Omar turned toward Hekmatyar. "I have never asked Allah for anything," he said. "But I am under a great disadvantage now. If Allah could only give me eyes for a couple of years, or for a couple of hours, so I could fight in the jihad."

Eighteen years have passed since the CIA began providing weapons and funds—eventually totaling more than $3 billion—to a fratricidal alliance of seven Afghan resistance groups, none of whose leaders are by nature democratic, and all of whom to a greater or lesser extent are fundamentalist in religion, autocratic in politics, and venomously anti-American in both respects.

When the Soviet Union invaded Afghanistan to prop up its pro-Communist regime in the last days of December 1979, the same year that the Ayatollah Khomeini was swept into power in Iran, startled American policy makers were ill prepared for either event, and they responded in ways that would have powerful and lasting consequences. For the Reagan Administration, the jihad was a battle to "bleed the Soviets," and it was curiously popular on Capitol Hill. With bipartisan support, a zealous Congress doubled, and even tripled, the Administration's requests for assistance to Afghanistan. Tons of Soviet and Chinese weapons bought from friendly governments, including those of Egypt, China, Israel, and South Africa, were sent to the battlefield. The provision of weapons from Communist countries was meant to camouflage Washington's direct links to the war, a policy referred to—somewhat implausibly—as "plausible deniability." The American effort to punish the Soviet Union at a time when it was perceived to be overextended and potentially vulnerable was complemented by a Pan-Islamic effort to establish the "perfect Islamic state"—a return to the ideals and dreams of the

seventh-century Caliphate. The two agendas were mutually reinforcing for more than a decade.

The Islamists, the CIA, and Saudi Arabia had been obsessed with
driving out the Soviets. As a result, the CIA helped to train and fund
what eventually became an international network of highly disciplined and effective Islamic militants—and a new breed of terrorist
as well. Thus it was that when the Soviet Union left Afghanistan
and the CIA closed down its pipeline to the mujahideen, Washington
left behind tens of thousands of well-trained and well-armed Arab,
Asian, and Afghan fighters available for new jihads.

Peshawar—only thirteen miles southeast of the Khyber Pass,
with Afghanistan beyond—is a rugged, lawless sort of place, riven
by religious fervor and violence and rich in political intrigue. It has
been a battleground for imperial armies and tribal warlords for centuries. When the Soviet Union invaded Afghanistan, it was transformed into the major staging area for the jihad. It had previously
been visited only by drug dealers and spies, but during the jihad it
had swollen. Now there were gunrunners, smugglers, freedom fighters, and war victims—and drug dealers and spies.

Its densely packed mud houses, pastel villas, and streets crowded
with four-wheel-drive vehicles and donkey carts became temporary
home to thousands of "Afghan Arabs" who fought in the jihad. It
was easy to find them during the 1980s, when I covered the war, in
the posh neighborhood of University Town, or in a string of hostels
along one of the city's main thoroughfares, University Road. For
during those years, and up through 1992—three years after the Soviets had left Afghanistan and its Communist government finally
fell—some twenty-five thousand Islamists, from nearly thirty countries around the world, had streamed through Peshawar on their
way to the jihad. They came, without passports and without names,
from Egypt's Gama'a and al-Jihad; from the Palestinian organization
Hamas; from Saudi Arabia's Islamic Movement for Change; from
Algeria's Islamic Salvation Front; and from the Philippines' Moro
Liberation Front. Six years after the formal end of the jihad in February 1989, a thousand or so remained. Some were in Peshawar

itself, while others were encamped in the mountain passes of the ungovernable tribal areas on both sides of the border with Afghanistan, planning and executing what investigators now believe were terrorist acts that have reached from Pakistan to the Philippines, from Cairo to Bangkok—and, most prominently, to the streets of Riyadh, Dhahran, and New York.

When I revisited the area in the spring of 1995, American investigators who were in Pakistan attempting to garner clues to the World Trade Center bombing and to the killing of two American consulate officials in Karachi that March told me that Peshawar could now rank as one of the leading training grounds for terrorists from around the world, along with Tehran, Tripoli, and Beirut.

"They're a real disposal problem," a Western diplomat in Peshawar remarked to me at the time, as we chatted about the foreign jihadis who had stayed on after the Soviets left Afghanistan and the CIA and the Special Forces officers who had been in Peshawar overseeing the jihad closed down their training camps and their weapons pipeline and went home. "Some of those who stayed behind are absolute Islamic fanatics," the diplomat said. "Others are anti-Communist ideologues; still others came to fight because they thought it was a good thing to do or they were looking for adventure. They're basically well educated; many are university graduates, mostly from science faculties, medicine, pharmacy, and law. They're in a sense like the Abraham Lincoln Brigade that went off to fight in the Spanish Civil War. But when that war was over, those volunteers went to Paris to write."

As I wandered through Peshawar's narrow lanes, dodging huge, brightly painted trucks and eyeing, and being suspiciously eyed by, men wearing floppy turbans—many of whom carried AK-47s on their shoulders or hips—I realized that in Peshawar, more than anyplace else, you could actually see the legacy of the CIA's war: the strain on Pakistan's social and economic structure caused by the influx of millions of Afghan refugees and tens of thousands of Afghan and foreign mujahideen; a new drug-and-Kalashnikov culture, bred from the profligate leakage of arms from the CIA's pipeline; and the presence in Peshawar of the "Afghan Arabs" who had stayed behind. They were all exceedingly well trained and exceedingly well armed, and many of them were followers of Sheikh Omar.

"Even today, you can sit at the Khyber Pass and see every color, every creed, every nationality pass," a Western diplomat told me one afternoon on the veranda of his Peshawar home. "In their wildest imagination, these groups never would have met if there had been no jihad. For a Moro to get a Stinger missile! To make contacts with Islamists from North Africa! The United States created a Moscow Central in Peshawar for these groups, and the consequences for all of us are astronomical."

The diplomat went on to say that many veterans of the jihad had set up informal networks of small, loosely organized underground cells, with support centers scattered around the world: in the United States, the countries of the Persian Gulf, Germany, Switzerland, Britain, and Scandinavia—and in the Sudan, Pakistan, and Afghanistan. The days of mule trains, like the one Sheikh Omar joined en route to Afghanistan, are long gone; now E-mail and faxes drive the jihad.

The gunmen seemed so ordinary, so inconspicuous, that they would be remembered later in only the vaguest of ways: not too short but not too tall; stocky, of medium build. Their hair was dark brown, and their eyes were dark and expressionless. The maid who cleaned one of three houses they rented, in an upper-middle-class neighborhood of the Ethiopian capital, Addis Ababa, thought that they were strange. They would never permit her into the bedroom, and they never appeared to leave the house, except to go to the airport, which was nearby, or to drive up and down Bole Road, a tree-lined boulevard leading from the airport to the center of the capital. They had also removed the draperies from the windows of the house and replaced them with swaths of black cloth.

For more than a month they waited. Then, on the morning of June 26, 1995, ten of the strangers, in three rented cars led by a Toyota Land Cruiser, drove to a small side street just off Bole Road. One of the men stayed behind and, at 8:15 a.m., he scanned the airport, peering through an opening in the black cloth with a pair of high-powered binoculars affixed to a tripod. He watched the Ethiopian Prime Minister, Meles Zenawi, welcome Hosni Mubarak to Addis Ababa for a summit meeting of the Organization of African Unity. Then, as Mubarak's four-car motorcade pulled out of the airport and onto Bole Road, he flashed a radio signal to the men waiting in the Toyota. Slowly, the three cars inched their way toward the intersection, and as Mubarak's motorcade came into view, one of them careered onto the boulevard, blocking its path. In less than a minute, AK-47 machine-gun fire began. Rounds of bullets fired by three of the gunmen at close range thumped repeatedly into the President's armored limousine, one round nearly penetrating the window glass; other rounds rained down on the black Mercedes from rooftops. As Mubarak's driver spun the Mercedes around, Egyptian and Ethiopian security men opened fire, killing two of the gunmen. The others, three of whom were later killed, sped away.

Over the previous two years, at least two other plots to assassinate Mubarak had been broken up before the conspirators could act. This time he had survived—narrowly—an actual attack.

Ethiopian police would later find the Toyota and the two other cars abandoned by the would-be assassins. They contained a veritable arsenal of arms and explosives, and two rocket-propelled grenades that could have blown Mubarak's armored limousine apart. One of the great mysteries of the attack, an Ethiopian detective would later say, was "why the terrorists didn't use their grenades." Investigators could only suggest that the quick response of Mubarak's driver and his security men may have cut the attack short, and been the only thing that saved the President's life.

Anwar Sadat had died a commander celebrating his greatest military triumph, felled by the bullets of his own troops. Hosni Mubarak nearly met the same fate. His eleven assailants, and the hundred or so others who planned the operation, coordinated the transfer of weapons, and provided logistical support, had nearly all come of age on the battlefields of Afghanistan, trained and armed not only by Saudi Arabia and the United States but also, in part, by his own government and, before him, that of Anwar Sadat. They were, in every sense, Egypt's children of the jihad.

"It was a damn sophisticated operation," a Western diplomat in Cairo who was involved in the investigation remarked. "The planning itself went on for a couple of years. These guys are not a group of amateurs; they're very competent. They have vast networks, escape routes, supply routes, training camps, and an abundance of funds. It takes a huge infrastructure to keep this going; it's a real institutional service for terrorists." He paused for a moment, and then he said, "We're a long way from three years ago, when six guys from Upper Egypt would shoot at a busload of tourists, and then hide in the sugarcane fields. This is now a trade craft of professionals. When you look at the international context, the linkages, the safe houses, the safe countries, it's a very frightening thing."

The attack on Mubarak, perhaps as much as anything else, illustrates the universality of which the diplomat spoke. Mubarak's would-be assassins were all men based in Upper Egypt. Most of them came from Luxor, near the Valley of the Kings, the burial ground of the Pharaohs of the last glorious period of Egyptian history. They had been drawn much earlier into the assassination plan—one through the Muslim Brotherhood, several through mosques. They were then sent for training in Afghanistan. From there, they were based for a time in Iran, as logistics were being prepared. They then traveled, first to Yemen—where they obtained Yemeni passports—then to the Sudan, where they lived at a "safe farm" for a time, and from there they crossed the border to the staging area, the rented houses and cars, waiting for them in the Ethiopian capital of Addis Ababa.

In September 1996, three of the would-be assassins, who had been arrested in Addis Ababa, were tried there and sentenced to death. The others went underground and disappeared, first into the Sudan, and then into Afghanistan.

The attempt on Mubarak's life is said to have been masterminded by Mustafa Hamza, a soft-spoken, bespectacled Egyptian agricultural engineer who travels on a Sudanese diplomatic passport and resembles a prosperous businessman. He is also the military leader of Gama'a, a member of its exiled leadership council, and a veteran of the jihad. Like many Egyptians—two thousand or so in all—who fought in Afghanistan, Hamza had been one of the lesser defendants in the Sadat assassination trials. When those trials ended, in 1984, hundreds of the defendants left Egypt for the jihad. And like many of the others—including Sheikh Omar's two eldest sons —Hamza now moves back and forth between Europe, the Sudan, Peshawar, and his base in the mountains of Afghanistan.

After the attack, Mubarak was rushed back to Cairo full of rage against the Sudanese, whom he accused publicly, and frequently, of being responsible for the attempt on his life. Lashing out at that country's leadership, Mubarak's legendary—though normally well-controlled—temper was revealed; Hassan al-Turabi, the Sudan's Islamist leader, and its President, he charged, were "thugs, criminals, and crackpots." According to Secretary of State Madeleine Albright, who was then the U.S. representative to the United Nations, weapons for the operation had been shipped from the Sudanese capital, Khartoum, on Sudan Airways—an allegation that Mubarak's government has never confirmed.

For over a week, Egyptian and Sudanese forces clashed at the disputed Red Sea border area of Halaib, and many Egyptians worried aloud that their country might once again go to war.

As his forces exchanged artillery fire, Mubarak embarked on a highly scripted whirlwind public tour. He opened the gardens of his presidential palace and received thousands of well-wishers each day. His army repledged its loyalty to him, and his religious establishment hailed him as a just ruler who kept the faith.

And far from the presidential palace, in the ungovernable tribal areas on the Pakistan-Afghan frontier and in the training camps outside Peshawar and in Afghanistan, the armies of Sheikh Omar, Mustafa Hamza, and the Gama'a—and their religious establishment—reaffirmed their allegiance to them.

Five months later, on November 19, there was no warning, no indication that the midmorning calm would be shattered in the elite, heavily guarded diplomatic enclave of the Pakistani capital, Islamabad. Outside the Egyptian Embassy, scores of Pakistanis waited to be called into the visa section, but few of them noticed a light tan pickup truck until its Egyptian driver crashed it into the embassy's iron gate. A deadly explosion followed, killing seventeen people—including the suicide bomber—and wounding sixty more.

Six days earlier, in the Saudi Arabian capital of Riyadh, five Americans had been killed, and some forty wounded, when a remarkably similar car bomb exploded outside the headquarters of a U.S. military training center for the Saudi National Guard. And a month after that, in a crowded market in Peshawar, there was yet another powerful car bomb, which killed thirty-six people and wounded about a hundred and twenty more. The car bombings in Pakistan followed threats from three militant Egyptian Islamist groups who demanded that the government of Pakistan stop extraditing those of their members—all of them veterans of the jihad—who had stayed on when the war came to an end and were using Peshawar as a base. The groups also demanded that the government of the United States, for its part, release Sheikh Omar. As for the attack in Saudi Arabia, it was almost certainly aimed at the Saudi dynasty as well as at the United States.

Five underground Islamist groups claimed credit for the bombings, including Egypt's Gama'a and al-Jihad and the Saudi Islamic Movement for Change—which also warned that there would be further attacks. All of the groups had participated in the jihad in Afghanistan.

Speaking of the bombings, a former U.S. diplomat specializing in Saudi Arabia told me at the time, "Whether the attacks were carried out by the same or allied Islamic militant groups is not the most important thing. What is far more troubling is that these attacks illustrate the changing nature of terrorism since the Cold War. There's been a marked decline in the fairly well-funded, ideologically organized groups like the Red Brigades. More and more we're seeing a proliferation of amorphous underground Islamic groups that we've never heard of before." He added that what was most significant was that larger numbers of people are prone to enter the new-style groups. "That, to me, is highly worrisome. Their operations are easy to do. They're basically low-tech. Sure, a certain amount of training is required—and then you go to a feed store and to a Radio Shack.

The common element in all these attacks—whether in Cairo or Riyadh, Islamabad or Algiers, Europe or New York—is the veterans of the Afghanistan war."

Washington's financial commitment to that war had been exceeded only by Saudi Arabia's. At the time the jihad was getting under way, there was no significant Islamist opposition movement in Saudi Arabia, and it apparently never occurred to the Saudi rulers, who feared the Soviets as much as Washington did, that the volunteers it sent might be converted by the jihad's ideology. Therein lies the greatest paradox of the bombing in Riyadh (and perhaps of an even more deadly, still-unsolved June 1996 bombing of a U.S. military housing complex in the Saudi city of Dhahran, in which 240 U.S. airmen were wounded and nineteen were killed). For both this explosion and the ones in Peshawar and Islamabad have now proven to be part of the negative fallout—or "blowback," in the parlance of intelligence—of the U.S.- and Saudi-orchestrated Afghan jihad.

The bombings—the first such terrorist attacks in Saudi history, and among the worst in Pakistan's—were the clearest warnings yet of an ominous escalation in the conflicts between the governments in Cairo and Riyadh and their Islamist foes. And the carnage in Islamabad—the fourth attack against the Egyptian government abroad in a span of months—indicated that Egypt's militant Islamic groups, facing an increasingly vengeful crackdown at home, were transferring their war to the international front. U.S. policy makers were stunned. In less than a week the vulnerabilities of three of Washington's pivotal regional allies had become clear.

Egypt, Saudi Arabia, and Pakistan had all served U.S. interests during the jihad in Afghanistan; none appears able to cope with its aftermath. Mubarak's anger was palpable when he told me, only a few months before the bombing of his embassy in Islamabad, that he laid the blame for Islamist terrorism squarely on Pakistan for, in his words, failing to "clean up" Peshawar and its environs. After the bombing, the bewilderment of Pakistan's Prime Minister at the time, Benazir Bhutto, was evident: once again she faulted the United States and the CIA, which she accused of continuing to finance Pakistan's radical Muslim clerics and fundamentalist groups. As for the rulers of Saudi Arabia—whose princes and foundations, ironically, remained the leading benefactors of many of the militant Islamic groups, in a shortsighted attempt to placate the Kingdom's own expanding fundamentalist constituency—they seemed shaken out of their placidity. And government officials in all three capitals began to wonder, as they redoubled their efforts against such attacks, whether the Islamists could still be contained.

People in the Peshawar bazaars and in the overcrowded refugee camps still remember Sheikh Omar from the jihad years. A short, rotund man, dressed in long gray clerical robes and a red fez-like cap with a wide white band, he was easily distinguishable by his blindness and by his full gray-white beard, which rested on his chest. It was in Peshawar that Sheikh Omar became involved with the U.S. and Pakistani intelligence officials who were orchestrating the war. The sixty or so CIA and Special Forces officers based there considered him a "valuable asset," according to one of them, and overlooked his anti-Western message and incitement to holy war because they wanted him to help unify the mujahideen groups.

Unifying the groups, which had been fighting among themselves for years, proved impossible even for Sheikh Omar, but he did succeed in coordinating some of their activities. As he did so, he favored the two most anti-Western and fundamentalist of them—one led by his friend from that 1985 trip, Gulbadin Hekmatyar, the other by a fellow Ph.D. from the University of al-Azhar, the stridently anti-American professor Abdurrab Rasul Sayyaf. A swashbuckling figure, often draped in blankets of homespun cloth, Sayyaf was a warlord of considerable controversy. He had studied in Mecca and had been a professor at Kabul University, but his power base inside Afghanistan was limited. Nevertheless, largely because he was an adherent of the puritanical Wahhabi school of Islam (the dominant school in Saudi Arabia), he was lavishly funded by Riyadh.

But Sheikh Omar's closest friend in Peshawar was a highly respected Palestinian cleric, Sheikh Abdullah Azzam, a man of erudition, refinement, and eloquence, who also had a Ph.D. from al-Azhar but was everything the blustering Sayyaf was not. Azzam favored long, flowing clerical robes, as well as the black-and-white kaffiyeh of the Palestinians, and, like Sheikh Omar, he had been a professor of Shariah law (at the University of Jordan) before joining the jihad. Azzam became the pivotal figure in the Arab world in popularizing the cause. The Service Office, which he led until November 1989, when he was killed by a still-unidentified assassin, was the largest recruitment center in Peshawar, perhaps in the world, for Arab volunteers. It became, in a sense, the nexus for the Pan-Islamic effort both inside and—after the Soviet occupation ended, in 1989—outside Afghanistan. (Hekmatyar, Sayyaf, and Azzam were favorites not only of the United States and Saudi Arabia but of Pakistan's then military ruler, General Mohammed Zia ul-Haq, through whose Inter-Service Intelligence organization, or ISI, the CIA channeled its weapons pipeline.)

Money flowed into the Service Office from the Muslim Brotherhood, to which Sheikh Azzam belonged. But the heaviest funding, which may have totaled hundreds of millions of dollars, came from Saudi Arabia. Some of the Saudi funding was overt, some difficult to trace; some of the money came directly from the government, some from official mosques, and some from individual Saudi princes and members of the Kingdom's financial and business elite. Prince Salman bin Abdul-Aziz, the governor of Riyadh, who headed a support committee that funded the Arab mujahideen, was a heavy contributor, as was the Grand Mufti, Sheikh Abdul-Aziz bin Baz, who chaired the immensely powerful Muslim World League, the main conduit for Saudi government funds to Islamic causes worldwide. As is true of much of Saudi Arabia's clandestine funding abroad, the League's funds were often distributed somewhat indiscriminately, and they still are. As the war progressed, the Service Office set up branches in Europe and the United States, and Sheikh Azzam picked trusted lieutenants to carry out his work abroad. East Coast efforts in the United States centered on the Alkifah Refugee Center, on Brooklyn's Atlantic Avenue. More than two hundred Arabs and Arab Americans were recruited and sent to the jihad.

As Sheikh Azzam recruited, Sheikh Omar preached, and he carried his message of jihad—using first-class airline tickets—across four continents: from the Pakistani refugee camps to the towns of Upper Egypt, into Saudi Arabian mosques, and to Islamic centers in Germany, England, Turkey, and the United States.

They cut vastly different figures, Sheikh Omar and Sheikh Az-zam, as they toured the Peshawar refugee camps and traveled together inside Afghanistan: one, a short, blind man wearing a red-and-white fez-like cap who, because of lifelong illness, looked much older than his years; the other, tall and strikingly attractive, in his Palestinian kaffiyeh and Afghan tribal robes. But both men—who produced hundreds of audiotapes and videocassettes popularizing the jihad—were exceedingly charismatic in their different ways.

As he traveled in and out of Peshawar to the battlefields, Sheikh Omar was often accompanied by one or another of his two eldest sons, who were fighting in the jihad with the army of Gulbadin Hekmatyar, and who are known in Peshawar by their noms de guerre, Abu Hamid and Abu Nasir. In 1988, as teenagers, they had come to the jihad from the Egyptian oasis town of Faiyum (where the sheikh's two wives and eight other children continue to live). When they kissed their father goodbye at Cairo Airport, Sheikh Omar's parting words to his sons had been: "If it's victory, I'll see you in Afghanistan; if it's martyrdom, I'll see you in Paradise."

Martyrdom has been a constant theme in Sheikh Omar's life. A Western diplomat who had heard him preach in Peshawar during the war years told me that the sheikh reminded him a bit of a biblical prophet whose message was simple and clear: The path to Paradise is found through martyrdom. "He would wave his arms, and his voice would rise as he challenged the crowds, telling them that they must be willing to suffer as the Prophet Muhammad did. He is, in every sense, a pre-Renaissance man."

Indeed, the more I learned about Sheikh Omar, the more biblical he appeared. As early as his student days at al-Azhar, he had seemingly been preoccupied by both jihad and martyrdom. In his Ph.D. dissertation—a two-thousand-page exposition of a Koranic verse entitled "Repentance," in which the Prophet Muhammad exhorts his followers to wage war on non-Muslim tribes—the sheikh describes "the violence and persecution" the Prophet suffered at the hands of the "infidels," concluding that "jihad was the only way to vanquish the enemies of Islam." Explaining in the introduction why he had chosen "Repentance," Sheikh Omar wrote: "It represents the foreign policy and military affairs of the Islamic state. . . . I've loved it since childhood." This is not unlike Sheikh Omar's message in *A Word of Truth*.

When I asked Dr. Kamal Abou el-Magd, a moderate Egyptian Islamist and an authority on the Koran, what "Repentance" meant to him, he replied, "It's a very ticklish process to attempt to reinterpret this verse, and it must be interpreted within the context of the rest of the Koran. If you take it out of context and interpret it literally, it would mean that you should be in a continuous state of war with the rest of the world."

Sheikh Omar's message of martyrdom and jihad was all the more powerful because he appeared to be living it himself.

One afternoon a few years ago, I called on Nawab Salim, who had accompanied Sheikh Omar into Afghanistan on that 1985 trip, and asked what, for him, formed the basis of Sheikh Omar's appeal. He sipped his tea for a moment, and then he replied, "Sheikh Omar is one of the greatest mujahids of our time. It says in the Koran that a blind man is exempt from jihad, but he's devoted his life to it, at great personal cost. He's helped transform the Gama'a into an international movement while, at the same time, the Egyptian Muslim Brotherhood is becoming more passive each day. It's become totally bourgeois—sitting in fake parliaments, participating in fake elections. Sheikh Omar is leading a *real* struggle. He symbolizes the struggle for Islam."

Since the early 1970s, Sheikh Omar had admonished young men in his native Egypt to accept conscription into the Army to learn military skills; since the early 1980s, he had urged them to embrace jihad. The American war in Afghanistan fused his two goals into one.

To the young militants who fought in the jihad, Sheikh Omar

—his fire and oratory well suited to his role as a twentieth-century Islamic warrior—became an icon.

Of the two thousand or so Egyptians who came to and went from Afghanistan over the years, many, like Khaled al-Islambouli's brother, Mohammed, and Mustafa Hamza, had been defendants on the periphery of the Sadat-assassination trials; others had been imprisoned in Tora with the sheikh; still others had fled Egypt in the 1980s precisely to avoid the trials. Nearly all of them are members of Gama'a or al-Jihad, whose military wings organized the attempted assassination of Mubarak and the assassination of Sadat.

Looking back on the war years now, those who met Sheikh Omar in Peshawar vividly recall his passionate sermons and his fiery temperament, but few felt they ever really came to know him well. For, not unlike Hosni Mubarak, the sheikh betrayed scant emotion and revealed little about himself. He had come to Peshawar in search of the Afghanistan dream, which, in a curious way, bonded him with the Egyptian President. For the preacher and the soldier—whose lives had been joined, in a sense, by Khaled al-Islambouli on the eighth anniversary of the 1973 October War—finally met, if only metaphorically, on the battlefields of Afghanistan. Both had come of age during the 1967 Six-Day War and been deeply affected by Egypt's devastating defeat: the sheikh, then a Ph.D. candidate at al-Azhar, had been radicalized; the President, then a mid-career fighter pilot, had been part of the nation's shame. Afghanistan, for both men, was part of exorcising that shame.

They embraced the jihad with equal avidity. Mubarak and his Army secured and conduited tons of weapons into the CIA's pipeline, while his religious establishment posted thousands of flyers in government-controlled colleges and mosques. The foot soldiers of Sheikh Omar were given government tickets and sent off to fight in the jihad.

For his part, Sheikh Omar continued to preach his message of jihad and martyrdom; of driving out the infidels; and of adhering to the laws of the Koran. He sometimes seemed to be preaching in riddles or code. His long clerical robes and his gray-white beard gave him a medieval countenance, and at times he recalled Henry II bemoaning Thomas à Becket: "Who will rid me of this turbulent priest?"

But despite the double-entendre that often masked his words, Sheikh Omar's constant was his reliance on the Koran.

Liaqat Baloch, the parliamentary speaker of Pakistan's fundamentalist party, the Jama'at-i-Islami, recalls meeting the sheikh in Islamabad in the autumn of 1988. Benazir Bhutto had just been elected the first woman prime minister of a Muslim country, and the Jama'at leaders were appalled. One evening, seeking advice, they called on Sheikh Omar. "He told us that a woman leader was totally contrary to the Koran, citing the applicable verse," Baloch told me afterward. When the sheikh had completed his recitation, he glanced around the room, where the highly embarrassed fundamentalist leaders were assembled on straight-backed chairs. "The only conclusion I can arrive at," he said, "is that there are no men left in Pakistan."

As he traveled in and out of Peshawar—over nearly five years—Sheikh Omar's stature continued to grow, which pleased the CIA and Special Forces officers who were based there. It also pleased Sheikh Omar, who for the first time had an international platform for his views. With an eye to the future, he shored up old friendships and made new ones along the way, cultivating men whose assistance would eventually lead to the formation of an international support network for his activities—an axis that now links Europe and the United States with the Sudan, Pakistan, and Afghanistan. For he always kept in mind his ultimate goal: the establishment in Egypt of a theocratic Islamic state.

The sheikh met frequently during those years, in London and Khartoum, with the Sudanese Islamist Dr. Hassan al-Turabi—from whose country U.S. diplomats were withdrawn in February 1996 because of fears of terrorist attacks. He wooed Pakistani generals, many of whom were, and are, committed Islamists, and all of whom were charmed by Sheikh Omar's extraordinary knowledge of the Koran. And he returned to Saudi Arabia, where he had previously lived, there proving adept at exploiting political divisions within the ruling establishment. He dined regularly with Saudi princes and members of the Kingdom's financial and business elite, including men like Osama bin Laden, a multimillionaire scion of one of Saudi Arabia's leading families, who eventually came to Peshawar as a mujahid himself and who, in the future, would underwrite many of Sheikh Omar's activities. The sheikh also cultivated Prince Salman, the governor of Riyadh, and the Grand Mufti, Sheikh Abdul-Aziz bin Baz.

Two of his most abiding friendships, however, turned out to be with his traveling companions on that 1985 trip. Gulbadin Hekmatyar was named Prime Minister of Afghanistan in 1992, three years after the Soviets withdrew, when the puppet Communist government in Kabul finally fell. The fighting continued, in the form of a fratricidal civil war in which Hekmatyar unleashed a deadly offensive against other factions of the mujahideen, using a formidable arsenal of arms—all of them supplied by the United States and Saudi Arabia. Ironically, Hekmatyar and the other former leaders of the Afghan government, who among them had stockpiled some five hundred "missing" Stinger antiaircraft missiles supplied by the CIA, have lost control of some 90 percent of the country to an even more fundamentalist Afghan student militia, the Taliban, which grew out of the chaos left by the CIA's war. With the strong backing of Saudi Arabia and Pakistan, it has managed to wrest control, not only of most of the country, but also of several Stingers, from the leaders of the jihad. The CIA attempted to buy the Stingers back, a retired Pakistani general from the ISI who had been deeply involved in the war told me one morning over coffee in Islamabad. It was a joint endeavor with the ISI called Operation Trojan Horse, but it was rather muddled and highly flawed, he said. "The CIA told us we could pay a hundred thousand dollars each, and seventy-five million dollars was set aside. It was ridiculous from its inception: You don't bargain for Stingers *below* the going black-market rate!" The ISI and the CIA were consistently outbid, and some of the missiles—which are capable of destroying aircraft at a range of three miles—were purchased by the revolutionary government in Iran; others appeared on display in the tiny sultanate of Qatar in a military parade. At least two of the Stingers were bought by Islamic fighters in Tajikistan, and another two were purchased by a militant separatist group in the Philippines called Abu Sayyaf, a group that grew out of the CIA's jihad.

Mohammed al-Islambouli, who at one time was a student of Sheikh Omar's at the Upper Egyptian University of Asyut, has since that trip in 1985 become a prominent figure in the external leadership of Gama'a. As a member of its military wing, he is primarily involved in procuring weapons for the organization, both in Pakistan and abroad. And although sentenced to death in absentia by the Egyptian government, he nevertheless continues to move with apparent ease among Europe, Peshawar, and the mountains of Afghanistan, all of which serve as organizational centers or training grounds for Egypt's militant Islamic groups.

Sheikh Omar came to Peshawar for the last time in May 1990 —via Saudi Arabia and the Sudan—and stayed for two months, visiting a number of the two dozen or so military training camps that hugged the frontier, preaching, and traveling with Islambouli and Hekmatyar inside Afghanistan. He was both more subdued, yet, on occasion, less guarded and more visibly angry than during previous trips, according to Senator Khurshed Ahmed, a member of Pakistan's Jama'at-i-Islami party. Six months earlier, in November 1989, Sheikh Abdullah Azzam had been killed by a powerful car bomb as he drove to Peshawar's Saba-e-Leil Mosque to lead Friday prayers. (A year and a half later, in March 1991, Mustafa Shalabi, Azzam's representative in the United States, who headed the Alkifah Refugee Center in Brooklyn, was found dead in his apartment with multiple stab wounds and a bullet through the head.) And although some Pakistani officials were quick to blame KHAD, the Afghan secret service, for Sheikh Azzam's death, the retired ISI general told me more recently that there had never been an investigation and that the government blamed KHAD for everything during the years of the jihad. Another casualty of that war may well have been Pakistan's military ruler, President Zia ul-Haq, who died along with twenty-nine others, including Arnold L. Raphel, the American Ambassador to Pakistan, in a still-unexplained August 1988 crash of his military transport plane.

There were more dinners and luncheons than usual for Sheikh Omar during this trip, Pakistanis and Afghans recall, including one particularly lavish lunch at the residence of the Saudi Arabian Ambassador in Islamabad. It was a large, gala affair, and among the guests were many of the American and Pakistani intelligence officials who had courted Sheikh Omar during the war years.

In July 1990, after visiting the grave of Sheikh Azzam, Sheikh Omar left Peshawar for the last time. He flew first to Saudi Arabia, then to the Sudan and onward to New York, traveling on what would be his last U.S. visa issued by an undercover agent of the CIA.

Many of his followers remained in Peshawar, however, and continued their work. Some forged links with other militant Islamist groups, including a cadre of demolitions and weapons experts from the Saudi Islamic Movement for Change, which claimed responsibility for the Riyadh car bomb. Others were instructors or trainees in the military training camps that hugged the border on both sides of the Pakistan-Afghan frontier. Still others went off in search of new jihads, in Tajikistan or Kashmir, or joined some three thousand veterans of the jihad who went as volunteers to Bosnia, where, easily distinguishable by their dark beards, they fought alongside the predominantly Muslim Bosnian Army for two years. Still others fought and went home—to Egypt, Algeria, the West Bank, and the Gaza Strip—where many are now engaged in open warfare with secular governments.

And from somewhere in Peshawar, probably along University Road or in a storefront mosque that no one will ever be able to find, Sheikh Omar's supporters continue to charge that his 1993 arrest was in violation of a pledge, given the year before by an American diplomat in Peshawar, to Islambouli and Hekmatyar.

Little is remembered about Muslih al-Shamrani in Peshawar's "Afghan Arab" hostels along University Road. He was short and squat, a Sunni Muslim who wore the broad beard and the white calf-length robe that are emblems of devout Islamic faith in his native Saudi Arabia. He had just turned twenty-eight in April 1996 when, in what by all accounts was a scripted confession on Saudi television, he confirmed his role—as did three of his childhood friends—in the car bombing in Riyadh that left five Americans dead. He then spoke with obvious—and unscripted—pride of how religious fervor had led him to a distant Muslim land to participate in the jihad in Afghanistan. He also named exiled Saudi dissidents whose writings had inspired him to plant the Riyadh bomb, including the elusive multimillionaire Osama bin Laden.

The following month, on May 31, Shamrani and his friends—all but one of them veterans of Afghanistan—were beheaded in a Riyadh public square. Their executions angered U.S. officials, not only because the Saudis did not allow American investigators to interrogate the four, but also because the beheadings had cut short an inquiry into the broader dimensions of the bomb: the organization behind it; the persons who funded it; and the more senior leaders who were almost certainly involved in it. The beheadings also followed threats of retaliation against the United States if they were carried out. Less than a month later, on June 25, 1996, a massive truck bomb ripped through the Khobar Towers U.S. military housing complex in Dhahran.

The United States knows little about the extremist movements in Saudi Arabia, one of the most reclusive and mysterious nations in the world, and investigators were still attempting, in the fall of 1998, to determine whether the two attacks were linked. Circumstantial evidence certainly suggests that they were, but there is one key difference between the two: the four men executed for the Riyadh car bomb were all members of the country's Sunni Muslim majority; the forty or so who have been in custody since October 1996 for the Dhahran attack are from the Shi'ite minority. The two groups are not known to have collaborated before, except when they fought together in the jihad.

According to Canadian investigators—who deported a Saudi Shi'ite dissident suspected of involvement in the Dhahran attack to the United States in the summer of 1997—that bombing was carried out by a previously unheard-of underground group called Saudi Hezbollah, which, they claimed, had ties to the much better-known

Iranian-trained and -financed Lebanese Hezbollah.* (Known for its expertise in explosives, the Lebanese group was responsible for two truck bombings in 1983 that devastated the U.S. Embassy and the Marine headquarters in Beirut; during those attacks, nearly three hundred Americans were killed.) The Canadian assertions, coupled with the fact that a detonator found at the scene of the Dhahran attack was similar to those used by the Lebanese group, raised new questions about whether there was an Iranian, or even a Syrian, link to the truck bomb—a view that the Saudi dynasty had privately and consistently held, although U.S. investigators remain unconvinced.

Washington had long been critical of the Saudi government for its lack of cooperation in either investigation into the bombings of U.S. military sites: it had not permitted U.S. officials to interview any suspects in Saudi jails, nor had it shared its own findings with the FBI. That criticism gave way to anger when, in the spring of 1998, the Saudi Minister of the Interior announced that his government had completed its investigation into the Khobar Towers bomb and that it had found no evidence of any foreign involvement in it. Startled U.S. Justice Department officials—whose own investigation into the bombing was far from complete at the time—learned that the Saudis had closed theirs when they read about it in the press.

Thus, as with the bombing in Riyadh, the Saudis had abruptly foreclosed any inquiry into the larger question of what, if any, links exist between the four attacks in Saudi Arabia and Pakistan, all of which involved from two hundred to some five thousand pounds of ammonium nitrate and fuel oil—the same highly combustible mixture used in the World Trade Center bombing in New York.

"The bombs in Saudi Arabia are of far greater interest to me,"

---

*The suspect, Hani Abdel-Rahim al-Sayegh, had appeared ready to cooperate with U.S. authorities in order to avoid extradition to Saudi Arabia. But when he reached Washington, he abrogated a plea-bargain agreement, insisting at the time that he was not even in Saudi Arabia when the bombing occurred. As of June 1998, he remained in custody in the United States, awaiting a ruling on whether or not he was to be deported to Riyadh.

the former U.S. diplomat specializing in Saudi Arabia told me. "The ones in Pakistan were more comprehensible, and highly predictable. Saudi Arabia was not. Never before has the Saudi Islamic opposition been so emboldened. In a sense, they ripped off the veil."

Thousands of Saudis had fought in the jihad. Largely funded and supported by their government, they came from good families, some immensely wealthy ones. I asked the diplomat what, in his view, made the Saudis different from other Islamists who came to the jihad.

"Their government sent them," he replied. "It was the patriotic thing to do. But when these guys got there, they met others and began to network; they found a whole new world out there. And despite their wealth, they were underemployed, frustrated, an accident waiting to happen—and it did. Also, unlike the others who went to Afghanistan as members of Islamic groups—Gama'a, al-Jihad, Hamas, and the like—there *were* no organized Saudi groups. That's what makes these guys very different: *they* set up the networks when they came home."

Other U.S. officials agree, and warn that despite the Saudi government's efforts to privately blame the usual regional suspects—Iran, Iraq, and Sudan—for the car bombings, the Islamist discontent in Saudi Arabia is real, and, like Egypt's, the movement is basically homegrown.

One of its most charismatic and powerful champions is Osama bin Laden. A tall and bearded, forty-year-old ascetic who dresses in gold-trimmed robes, he is the seventeenth of twenty sons of one of Saudi Arabia's wealthiest families. Reclusive, fervent, and devout, he was described to me by one U.S. intelligence official as "a religious fanatic with enormous wealth—a man with a vision, who knows precisely how he wants to convert that vision into reality." According to a 1996 State Department report, bin Laden is "one of the most significant financial sponsors of Islamic extremist activities in the world." The report also linked him to terrorist training camps in the Sudan, and in Afghanistan.

Bin Laden worked closely with Saudi intelligence and with Prince Salman in funding the jihad, and eventually came to Peshawar as a mujahid himself. There he befriended Gulbadin Hekmatyar and Sheikh Omar, and fought with the forces of Professor Abdurrab Rasul Sayyaf. He also established an organization called al-Qaida— "the Base"—which was involved in raising funds and in recruiting and training fighters for the jihad. (A decade later, al-Qaida's fighters would form part of a bin Laden network stretching across four continents.)

From 1991 until the spring of 1996, bin Laden divided his time between Khartoum and London, where he owns large and opulent estates, and he places his formidable wealth—a personal fortune estimated at more than $250 million, largely in foreign bank accounts—at the disposal of militant Islamic groups around the world. Whether he retains access to his family's fortune, which is based largely on construction and is thought to be worth some $5 billion, is a matter of dispute. The family has publicly renounced the activities of its renegade son, but there are many who believe that it remains a source of financial support. Bin Laden's relationship with some family members, including one of his brothers-in-law, a Saudi financier named Mohammed Jamal Khalifa, continues to be close.

Khalifa was a prime conduit for funding militant Islamic groups in the Philippines, Filipino officials assert. According to U.S. investigators, there is evidence that during the mid-1990s, when he was the head of the Islamic Relief Agency—a quasi-government Saudi charity—in the Philippines, Khalifa had contact with the man known as Ramzi Ahmed Yousef, the convicted mastermind of the World Trade Center bombing in New York. In the years preceding his extradition to the United States in February 1995, Yousef had largely divided his time among the Philippines, Afghanistan, and Peshawar—where he most often lived at the House of Martyrs (Bayt Ashuhada), a bin Laden–financed guest house. During that time, the paths of the two men must have crossed, since bin Laden, too, frequently traveled to all three places from his base in Khartoum.

Then, in May 1996, under pressure from the United States and Saudi Arabia, the Islamic government of the Sudan asked bin Laden to leave, and he returned to Afghanistan permanently—accompanied by two military transport planes carrying some of his wealth, hundreds of his "Afghan Arab" fighters, and his four wives. Much to the displeasure of the United States, within four months bin Laden had secretly returned to Khartoum, although his base of operation continues to be Afghanistan, where he now lives under the protection of that country's new, and Saudi-financed, fundamentalist leadership, the Taliban.

In 1994, at U.S. urging, the Saudi government had stripped bin Laden of his citizenship because of his "irresponsible behavior . . . and his refusal to obey instructions issued to him." When I asked a U.S. counterterrorism expert what this meant, he replied, "Osama was warned by Saudi intelligence: Do nothing against us and we'll leave you alone." Bin Laden ignored the warnings, and the Saudis began running intelligence operations against him and his entourage in Khartoum; during the Bush Administration—presumably with the knowledge of the United States—they had secretly dispatched hit teams with a contract on his life. When the U.S. military installations in Saudi Arabia were blown apart, the expert said, "Osama bin Laden was the first guy who came up on the radar screen in Riyadh."

The bombings, bin Laden would later say, marked "the beginning of war between Muslims and the United States." In a July 1996 interview with the London *Independent*, at his heavily fortified base camp, in a remote mountainous area of Afghanistan, he took no responsibility for either of the bombs, but he did indicate that he was familiar with both the circumstances and the motives of those involved, and he warned of further attacks, not only against U.S. forces but also against those of Britain and France.

In June 1998, U.S. forces in Saudi Arabia were placed on high alert as the result of a number of new fatwas issued by bin Laden to his followers, in which he called on them to kill Americans around the world. (The fatwas were issued in the name of a newly formalized, yet long-standing, alliance of a number of militant Islamist groups—including Egypt's Gama'a and al-Jihad—called the International Islamic Front for Jihad Against Crusaders and Jews.)

Washington took the warnings seriously: the National Security Advisor, Sandy Berger, described bin Laden as "perhaps the most dangerous non-state terrorist in the world." As alarming to U.S. officials as anything else was a recent assessment by the CIA that the high-tech bin Laden—who has a World Wide Web site and satellite centers in Europe and throughout the Persian Gulf—now commands a private army of at least three thousand men.

Smiling benignly into the camera lens of an ABC news team later that month, bin Laden told the network that he did not differentiate between American military forces and American civilians in targeting his prey. He then reiterated forcefully his determination to rid Saudi Arabia and the Gulf of U.S. military personnel. "You will leave in coffins," he said, from somewhere in the Afghan mountains, at one of his military training camps. (Two months later, in August 1998, when the U.S. embassies in Kenya and Tanzania were bombed—provoking retaliatory U.S. missile strikes on the Sudan and on alleged bin Laden training camps in Afghanistan—U.S. officials immediately charged that the bombings had been carried out by bin Laden and his shadowy Islamist underground.)

As he spoke to ABC News, the elusive Saudi multimillionaire was surrounded by scores of guards—Egyptians, Algerians, Jordanians, and Saudi Arabians—all of them veterans of the jihad who are now denounced by the kings and presidents of half the Arab world.

Although virtually unknown in the West, bin Laden is a towering figure to these Islamic militants. He had distinguished himself during the jihad on the battlefields of the erratic Afghan warlord Abdurrab Rasul Sayyaf, brandishing his AK-47 with the same consummate skill he would later employ to solicit hundreds of millions of dollars in funds from wealthy compatriots in Saudi Arabia and the Gulf to underwrite his continuing jihad.

One U.S. intelligence official told me that bin Laden's financial backing has reached from Egypt—where he has underwritten some of Sheikh Omar's activities and those of Gama'a and al-Jihad—to Algeria; from Yemen to Somalia, where he has targeted U.S. troops;

and from Paris to the Philippines. His Advice and Reformation Committee in London oversees the distribution of much of his wealth, which is based, in large part, on a financial empire of more than sixty companies, many of them in the West.

Ironically, or so it seems to me, it was one of bin Laden's family's construction firms that built the new and isolated desert headquarters of U.S. troops in Saudi Arabia—the Prince Sultan Air Base—when it was decided that the Americans were no longer secure in Saudi cities after the Riyadh and Dhahran bombs.

In talking about bin Laden, one senses that for the enigmatic Saudi businessman, the United States is to Saudi Arabia what the Soviet Union had been to Afghanistan: an infidel occupation force propping up a corrupt, repressive, and un-Islamic government. In 1990, when Saddam Hussein invaded Kuwait and the Saudi dynasty first permitted U.S. troops to be based on its soil, the House of Saud, in the eyes of bin Laden, lost its remaining legitimacy. The very presence of some five thousand American military women and men near Islam's holiest shrines—of Mecca and Medina—with more than twenty thousand others standing guard in the region nearby, was the final apostasy.

Perhaps not surprisingly—considering the fact that U.S. officials believe that bin Laden helped to fund at least one, and probably two, of the assassination attempts against the Egyptian President, including the attack in Addis Ababa—when I asked Hosni Mubarak about bin Laden, he winced. "He wants to take over the world," he said. "He's a megalomaniac." Mubarak then expressed his growing concern—bordering on outrage—about Peshawar and the veterans of the jihad.

He told me about a meeting he had had in Bonn in April 1993 with the Pakistani Prime Minister, Nawaz Sherif. "It was a tough meeting," he said. "And I couldn't believe my ears: this man was the leader of Pakistan and he told me, quite frankly, 'We cannot control Peshawar. We cannot prevent these people from running loose.' I asked him then if he wanted me to send the Egyptian Armed Forces to Peshawar to clean up the mess."

Mubarak had demanded that all of the Egyptian jihadis be extradited; Sherif demurred. Nevertheless, on Sherif's return to Pakistan, he reluctantly instructed his even more reluctant security men to "look into Peshawar." I asked a Western diplomat based there what had happened then.

"It was absolute chaos," he replied. "This town has become one huge storefront since the war: there are storefront presses, storefront arms dealers, storefront drug traffickers, storefront mosques. The government started to review all of the NGOs"—nongovernmental organizations—"and all the expatriate workers here. But when they got to the thirty-five or so marginal organizations of the Arabs, they couldn't find the offices, the buildings, the people! Earlier that year, they actually conducted raids, and they were only able to find some two hundred Arabs, even though they had issued identity cards to more than five hundred the previous month. They set a deadline when all of the Arabs without proper papers had to leave. I think we're on our sixth or seventh deadline now, and somewhat fewer than twenty have actually left."

He turned more serious, and then he went on: "It's an immense problem for Pakistan. The government doesn't want to deport these people and send them back to trial or to their execution. And where can you expel them to from Pakistan? They're clearly not going to take them to the Afghan border and set them loose."

It was only after the bombing of the Egyptian Embassy in Islamabad that Pakistani security forces fanned out across Pakistan and made more than three hundred arrests: of militant Pakistani clerics and fundamentalists; of some sixty Afghans; and of two dozen or so Arabs, including a Saudi national who had arrived in Peshawar during the jihad and was deported to Saudi Arabia in connection with his alleged involvement in the car bombing in Riyadh. The security forces also made arrests at the capital's International Islamic University, which Pakistan's Interior Minister called a "haven for Islamic terrorists." Ramzi Ahmed Yousef spent a considerable amount of time at the university before his extradition to the United States; Sheikh Omar lectured there; and Sheikh Azzam was once a tenured professor there. The university's primary benefactors have been the Saudis, who, according to Pakistani officials, used the university as a cover during the jihad for the funneling of fighters, money, and arms.

Driving toward the University of Dawa and al-Jihad, on the outskirts of Pubby, a dusty market town some thirty miles east of Peshawar, everything seemed normal—at least at first. On one side of the twisting dirt road, teenagers played soccer in a field; on the other, a solitary figure sat on a craggy rock, playing a flute as he watched his flock. Outside tea stalls, men sat cross-legged on rope charpoy beds, arguing and gesticulating and smoking opium pipes.

I was unprepared for the towering dun-colored walls and the barbed wire atop them. Soon I saw guard posts and what appeared to be machine-gun nests. Beyond them, hidden behind the walls, stood the sprawling Jalozai Refugee Camp and the University of Dawa and al-Jihad, which is set in the middle of it. Its entrance is lined with a dozen or so shops, where grenades and Kalashnikovs are stashed among the firewood and the vegetables and kebabs. The camp is the Pakistani home of the Islamic Alliance, a group of fundamentalists led by Professor Abdurrab Rasul Sayyaf, one of the most fanatic of the powerful Afghan warlords who led the jihad. It is also believed to have been the training ground of the mysterious stranger known to the world as Ramzi Ahmed Yousef, who was sentenced in January 1998, in New York, to life imprisonment for masterminding the bombing of the World Trade Center and planning to blow up American jumbo jets—as many as twelve of them in what would have been a spectacular two-day spree.

An elusive figure, Yousef's conflicting accounts of himself have bedeviled federal prosecutors and intelligence agencies on three continents.

I had gone to Pubby in the spring of 1995 because there was reason to believe that the key to the bombing of the World Trade Center could be found among the children of the jihad. I was traveling with an introduction from the retired Pakistani general who had been a member of the ISI and who retained influence among the mujahideen. Thus I was permitted past a cluster of students who had gathered around my car at the gate, vociferously insulting the driver and brandishing Kalashnikovs in his face. Two of the students said they would take me to the camp commander, Hajji Dost Muhammad, who was a "captain in the jihad" and a cousin of Abdurrab Rasul Sayyaf.

In front of a squat bungalow set in the middle of an open field about twenty minutes by jeep from the wall, efficient-looking young men with machine guns hanging from their shoulders and bandoliers of ammunition strung across their chests instructed me to cover my head and remove my shoes. Hajji Dost was busy, and I had to wait awhile, but in due course I was taken to meet him in Sayyaf's "operations room." Hajji Dost, who appeared to be in his late sixties, had a small, shriveled face and a waist-length white beard. He was wrapped in blankets and wore a brown Pashtun cap. He is a man of few words, and the few he spoke to me were in Pashto, but he was cordial, offering me tea and cakes to accompany our conversation, such as it was.

"I have never heard of Ramzi Yousef," Hajji Dost replied to my first question.

"What is the World Trade Center?" he asked. This last evoked giggles from my student escorts and members of his staff.

"Your university [which Sayyaf founded in 1985 during the jihad] has a reputation as a training ground for Islamic militants," I said.

He smiled, neither confirming nor denying anything, but seemed to nod his head.

Having despaired of finding out anything from Hajji Dost, I glanced out the window and saw, on a slight escarpment at the end of a dusty field, a group of men engaged in what appeared to be hand-to-hand combat; behind them, only slightly visible through rising dust, others practiced at a rifle range.

"Who subsidizes this university?" I asked Hajji Dost.

"Saudi Arabia," he said.

As we headed back to the car after my tea with Hajji Dost, I asked the young men with Kalashnikovs and bandoliers how they would describe their university.

"As an Islamic Sandhurst," one of them replied.

The analogy seemed right.

Ramzi Yousef, who lived under at least fourteen other aliases—and traveled on nearly as many passports over the years—is one of the soldiers spawned by the jihad, a thirty-year-old, anti-American militant who came of age on the Afghan battlefields. He made his first trip to the United States in September 1992, six months before a twelve-hundred-pound bomb exploded in the underground garage of the World Trade Center in New York. A thousand people were injured, six people died, and half a billion dollars in damage was done.

Yousef arrived at JFK Airport from Peshawar with a traveling companion, Ahmad Mohammed Ajaj, who had also fought in the jihad and is believed to have trained at the University of Dawa and al-Jihad. The two separated before leaving the first-class section of the Pakistan International Airlines plane, and when they arrived in the immigration lounge, Ajaj embarked on what investigators say was "a performance that was nothing short of incredible," and which was most likely aimed at deflecting attention from his companion—and most probably other passengers—as they entered the United States.

Ajaj, a bearded and swarthy Palestinian, presented a Swedish passport to the Immigration and Naturalization Service agent behind the desk. He was also carrying a Jordanian passport in his briefcase, along with a British one and another from Saudi Arabia. The four passports were all in different names. The INS agent looked at Ajaj and at the first passport with suspicion. The photograph on it seemed far too thick, and, with his fingernail, the agent peeled it off. Underneath was the photograph of another man.

Ajaj became agitated and began shouting. "My mother was Swedish. If you don't believe me, check your computer!" When inspectors opened his leather bags, they found, to their astonishment, videotapes of suicide car bombings, guides to planting land mines, and directions on how to forge documents and how to make large improvised bombs.

Meanwhile, at a second immigration desk nearby, the man calling himself Ramzi Yousef presented an Iraqi passport; he had no United States visa, but he did have a laminated identification card bearing his photograph from the Al-Bunyan Islamic Information Center in Tucson, Arizona. The card was issued under another name—Khurram Khan, which was also the name on Ajaj's Swedish passport—and the INS agent was not convinced. But Yousef, unlike Ajaj, did not create a scene, and smilingly asked for political asylum in the United States.

Immigration agents remember a lean, bearded man with piercing dark eyes and a beaklike nose. He was dressed in a silk *shalwar kameez*, the top of which had "enormously puffed" sleeves and flowed down over blousy Afghan pants. He raised his right hand and solemnly swore that he would be persecuted if he was not permitted to stay in the United States.

"What is your full true name?" the INS agent, Martha Morales, asked.

"Ramzi Ahmed Yousef," the bearded man replied—despite the fact that the airline ticket on which he entered the United States and the Iraqi passport on which he left Pakistan were in another name, Azan Muhammad. According to her testimony later in court, Morales suggested that Yousef be detained, but she was overruled by her superior. The immigration center was full, and the bearded man was told to appear before an INS judge for an asylum hearing in three months. He thanked Morales and disappeared into the streets of New York.

Ajaj was sent directly from JFK to jail, and he remained there until two days after the World Trade Center was bombed. He was later rearrested and tried, in 1994, along with three co-conspirators, for his role in the bombing. All four were convicted, and each was sentenced to 240 years' imprisonment.

According to Pakistani intelligence sources, the man known as Ramzi Ahmed Yousef is a Pakistani tribesman from the southwestern province of Balochistan. His real name is Abdul-Basit Mahmud Abdul-Karim. His father, Mohammed, had emigrated to Kuwait, where he worked as an engineer, and where Abdul-Basit was born to a Palestinian mother in the oil town of Fuhayhil in April 1968. The population of Fuhayhil was about 40 percent Palestinian when Abdul-Basit was growing up, and both he and at least one of his younger brothers speak Arabic with a distinctive Palestinian accent. When I asked a Palestinian friend from Fuhayhil to estimate which of the many political groups who had sought refuge there—including radical Palestinians, Iraqi Communists, and members of Egypt's Muslim Brotherhood—had the greatest impact on the city's large immigrant community, he replied, "The Palestinian Marxists and the Islamists—and both had international links."

Few people in Fuhayhil remember Abdul-Basit's father, Mohammed Mahmud Abdul-Karim, but according to those who know him in Balochistan he is not particularly religious or sophisticated politically. He is said to have only two passions—Baloch nationalism and an abiding hatred of Islam's minority Shi'ite sect. In the early 1980s, Mohammed was introduced to the puritanical Wahhabi school of Sunni Islam (the dominant school in Saudi Arabia) and to a fundamentalist group closely associated with it, known as the Salafis. According to their doctrine, Shi'ites are infidels. The most extreme members of the group believe that Shi'ites should not simply be shunned or converted; they should be killed.

These were the views that the young Abdul-Basit—later Ramzi Yousef—absorbed. He was a bright boy who did well in school, expecially in physics, chemistry, and math. He also had a proficiency in foreign languages. As a teenager, he was tall and handsome, with jet-black hair, and he began to grow a beard, not for religious reasons, as many of his schoolmates did, but because it made him appear older and more debonair. In October 1984, he received what officials now believe was the first of many Pakistani passports on which he would later travel across three continents—sometimes in disguise and sometimes not, but always first class. This first passport, however, was issued in his real name. He was only sixteen, and although he was already imbued with his father's anti-Shi'ite vitriol and his Palestinian classmates' revolutionary zeal, he had no reason to conceal his identity.

In the fall of 1987, Abdul-Basit enrolled in an electrical engineering course at the West Glamorgan Institute of Higher Education—now the Swansea Institute—in South Wales, and in 1989 he received a degree there. These two years, during which he perfected his English, gave him his only experience of living in the Western world, except for those months in the winter of 1992 that he spent in New York.

By the time Abdul-Basit completed his studies, his father, Mohammed Abdul-Karim, had moved back to Turbat, Balochistan, with his family. Balochistan had by then become, after Peshawar, the second staging area for the jihad. The CIA used the Baloch tribesmen as guides and scouts, drivers and trackers, and for logistical support. For years they had been traveling back and forth, without documents and without passports, across the highly porous borders that divide their traditional homelands in Pakistan, Iran, and Afghanistan—sometimes smuggling arms and drugs, sometimes blowing up rail lines and power plants in the Ayatollah Khomeini's Shi'ite Iran.

On his return to Pakistan in 1989, Abdul-Basit, along with his father, one of his uncles, and at least two of his brothers, journeyed to Peshawar as an eager recruit for the jihad. The family's links were primarily with the Islamic Alliance and Professor Abdurrab Rasul Sayyaf, who, like Abdul-Basit's father, was a Wahhabi and, as a consequence, was lavishly funded by Saudi Arabia. Of the twenty-five thousand or so non-Afghan Islamic militants who fought in the jihad, the largest single number—including Osama bin Laden—fought with Sayyaf. And it was with them that Abdul-Basit became a seasoned fighter and spent his formative years. He adopted the nom de guerre Ramzi, but some of his fellow fighters knew him as Rashed. His electrical engineering background served him well, and he became a skillful builder of astonishingly innovative bombs. According to U.S. investigators, his specialty was assembling bombs from innocuous-looking materials, nearly impossible to detect—a digital wristwatch, for example, modified into a timing device; a plastic contact-lens solution bottle filled with the liquid components for nitroglycerine. It was his techniques that made Abdul-Basit unique.

According to those who know him, he carries the scars of his bomb-making with flamboyance and style. He is described, variously, as being partly blind, or at least light-sensitive, in his right eye; as having burn marks on his feet; and as having fingers or fingernails that are disfigured or deformed—all by-products of the skills he would perfect during the jihad.

Long after the CIA and Special Forces officers who had been overseeing the war left Peshawar and went home, Abdul-Basit and his friends—using the House of Martyrs and the Khyber Plaza, a cream-colored apartment building on University Road, as their headquarters—continued their work.

Soon after Abdul-Basit walked out of JFK Airport in September 1992, he appeared in Brooklyn, in the primarily Arab neighborhood that runs along Atlantic Avenue. He told most people that his name was Rashed and said he was from Iraq, but not everyone in the neighborhood believed him. Certainly the Iraqis didn't. Not only was his accent Palestinian when he spoke Arabic (and Indian or Pakistani when he spoke English, they thought), but he didn't know anything about Baghdad. One of his landladies, an Iraqi, was suspicious of him from the start. She tried to find his passport, but his briefcase was usually hidden away, and it was always locked.

Abdul-Basit had a mission, U.S. investigators say: putting together a team of Islamic extremists from Brooklyn and Jersey City, all of whom were linked to the jihad, and turning their wildest fantasies of holy war into a nightmarish reality on American soil. Investigators believe that he was sent to the United States at someone's behest, and had not previously known any of the men who were recruited for the bombing. It may be that outraged supporters of the Egyptian El-Sayyid A. Nosair, who was charged with the 1990 murder of Rabbi Meir Kahane, acquitted, and then sentenced to seven to twenty-two years in prison on weapons charges relating to the crime, had something to do with it. (In 1996, Nosair was found guilty of the murder and sentenced to life imprisonment.)

"To these guys, Nosair was a saint," one investigator said to me, "and we think his sentencing is what crystallized it all. These guys wanted to do something to lash out. I doubt that they knew what, but they began casting their net about. One of them"—Mahmud Abouhalima, a Brooklyn taxi driver from Egypt who had fought in the jihad, is a member of the Gama'a, and was Sheikh Omar's chauffeur until the two had a falling-out—"traveled to the Middle East and to Pakistan. And there's a very good likelihood that it all came together in Peshawar in the spring of 1992."

It is perhaps not surprising that Abdul-Basit's first known stop in Brooklyn was the Alkifah Refugee Center, which had been set up from Peshawar by Sheikh Abdullah Azzam as part of the effort to internationalize the jihad. For Muslims in the United States, it became, in a sense, the nexus for the Pan-Islamic effort inside Afghanistan. It also may have been, one of Mubarak's top advisers said to me, a front organization for the CIA during the jihad: money, he said, had been laundered through it, weapons transferred, and Arab Americans recruited and trained. Over $2 million a year was sent from Alkifah to the Afghan battlefields.

Abdul-Basit also frequented the mosques in Brooklyn and Jersey City where Sheikh Omar preached his fiery message of jihad. And it was from among the followers of the sheikh, all of whom were active at Alkifah, that he recruited the lower-level members of his World Trade Center team: two Palestinians; Mahmud Abouhalima, the Egyptian taxi driver who may have cast the original net; and three or four others who were never brought to trial, either because they had left the country or because their lawyers plea-bargained out of court, or because they remain unknown.

From the start, the plot and the convicted plotters didn't seem to match. The plot was ambitious, but the execution was amateurish. There were bomb-making mistakes and premature explosions, and in January 1993 Mohammed Salameh—who was ultimately convicted of renting the Ryder van that carried the bomb into the Twin Towers garage—crashed his car, with Abdul-Basit in the passenger seat, which led to Abdul-Basit's hospitalization for over a week.

"It never would have happened without Ramzi Yousef," one U.S. investigator said to me. "He built it, he organized the whole thing."

And then he slipped away, leaving behind many unanswered questions. For at the trial of four of his convicted co-conspirators, early in 1994—a pattern that would be repeated three years later when he himself was tried—none of the central mysteries were addressed: Who ordered the bombing? What was the motive? Who financed it? Was Abdul-Basit summoned to Brooklyn, or was he sent?

Abdul-Basit flew out of New York on February 26, 1993, the day the bomb went off. The plane on which he traveled may even have flown over the World Trade Center and the clouds of acrid black smoke that punctuated the sky above New York's financial heart.

"Is he an evil genius or a streetwise kid from Balochistan who was very lucky?" I asked one U.S. investigator.

"I go for the evil genius theory," he replied. "The times he has tripped up—including when he was captured—were all by accident. He always got away with everything he was involved in. And, tempting as it must have been for him to see the apocalypse at the World Trade Center, he was on a plane that night. If he were just a street-smart kid, I'm not sure he would have had that kind of discipline."

Much about Abdul-Basit remains anomalous. Some of his accomplices were Islamic militants; some were secularists. Some were from the Arab world; some from the Philippines and Pakistan. Some were based in the United States, some abroad. Some of the groups joined together just long enough to carry out a single terrorist act and then dispersed. And although many of his causes have been Islamic, Abdul-Basit is not particularly Islamic himself. He rarely attended Friday prayers, a fellow fighter in Peshawar said, nor did he fast during Ramadan. He also seemed to particularly savor the more indulgent aspects of nightlife in Manila, where in the years preceding his 1995 arrest he spent a considerable amount of time, usually with the Filipino Abu Sayyaf group, some of whose members he had come to know well during the jihad, when they fought together with Professor Abdurrab Rasul Sayyaf.

Artfully embellishing a blend of bitter anti-Americanism and Palestinian militancy, Abdul-Basit found eager recruits for his newest jihad. And it was in Manila that he planned his most chilling retribution against the United States: to blow up as many as twelve U.S. commercial airliners departing from East Asian cities and flying over the Pacific Ocean in January 1995, killing several thousand people, many or most of them Americans. The plan was aborted, only two weeks before it was to have gone into effect, when Abdul-Basit and some friends from the Abu Sayyaf group mixed a witches' brew of chemicals in the kitchen sink of a rented Manila apartment and caused a minor explosion and fire. Abdul-Basit fled, but he left behind all of his carefully worked-out plans and his phone directory on a computer disk. Revelations from the disk included plans to assassinate Pope John Paul II on a visit to Manila and to carry out a kamikaze-style plane crash into the headquarters of the CIA. All of these outrages would have occurred, Abdul-Basit would later say, because of the support given Israel by the United States.

Shuttling between Manila and Afghanistan, and spending long periods of time in his native Pakistan, Abdul-Basit would be re-united there, in the 1990s, with a number of fighters he had known during the jihad—all of whom had fought, as had he, with the forces of Professor Abdurrab Rasul Sayyaf. During recent years, the fighters attached to Sayyaf have become increasingly active in Pakistan—particularly in the port city of Karachi, which is the country's financial and political heart and has come to resemble Beirut during its war. Thousands of people have been gunned down in its streets, either in religious or ethnic warfare or in turf battles between drug barons and racketeers or in an increasingly vengeful proxy war between Iran and Saudi Arabia. Abdul-Basit's principal alliance in Karachi was with the Saudi-financed SSP—the Sipah-e-Sahaba Pakistan—a militant group of Sunni supremacists with a huge stockpile of arms, its own training camps, and the shared legacy of the jihad. The SSP's ideology emphasizes the "termination" of Shi'ites, and for Abdul-Basit, according to one of his friends, this was one of the most attractive things about it. Another attraction, a Pakistani intelligence official told me, was that one of its underground commanders is Abdul-Basit's father, Mohammed Abdul-Karim.

The elder Abdul-Karim, who is now in his sixties, has in recent years moved between Pakistan and Iran, crossing the tribal border in Balochistan, whether as a saboteur or as a drug runner or as a combination of the two is still unclear. Abdul-Basit seems to have sometimes traveled with him, and has been credited—as Ramzi Yousef—in a newspaper in Pakistan with blowing up a Shi'ite shrine in the Iranian city of Meshed in June 1994. Some seventy people were wounded and at least twenty-four were killed.

Abdul-Basit's life as one of America's most-wanted men came to an end almost as suddenly as it began. His convicted co-conspirators in the World Trade Center bombing had implicated Ramzi Yousef at the time of their arrest, and the FBI, on several occasions, had laid elaborate plans to capture him in Pakistan, but each time he had been alerted in advance and had disappeared, either into Karachi's underground or across the border into Afghanistan. No one had ever seriously considered the possibility that someone from Abdul-Basit's circle of friends would betray him, but that is what happened in the end. Another member of Sayyaf's group, a South African Muslim graduate student named Ishtiaq Parker, turned him in.

On the evening of February 6, 1995, his last night of freedom, Abdul-Basit spent most of his time in his room at the Su Casa Guest House in Islamabad, tinting his hair and making at least two bombs. Had he looked out his window, he probably would have seen a dozen agents from the FBI, the State Department's Bureau of Diplomatic Security, and Pakistan's ISI. They were hoping that Abdul-Basit would lead them to his friends. Ultimately, he did. When he was not working on his hair or stuffing explosives into two toy cars, he was on the phone—a phone that was not equipped for long-distance dialing. Calls had to be placed through the hotel receptionist, and no sooner had Abdul-Basit's numbers been connected than one or another of the agents outside would dart into the lobby and jot the number down. Three of the calls were to Abdul-Basit's Peshawar neighborhood, University Town.

By the time I arrived in Peshawar, Abdul-Basit's arrest and the telephone calls had rocked the city's militant Islamic underground.

Arrest warrants had been issued for two of his brothers, Abdul-Muneim and Abdul-Karim, and for an uncle of his, whom police in Peshawar later identified as Zahid Sheikh, the regional manager of a Swiss-based charity, Mercy International. Surprisingly, no one made any mention of Abdul-Basit's father, Mohammed Abdul-Karim. He seemed to have vanished into the murky Karachi underground.

Concluding what is likely to be the final major trial in the World Trade Center case, Judge Kevin T. Duffy, in the early days of January 1998 in New York, sentenced the man known as Ramzi Ahmed Yousef to life imprisonment in solitary confinement without the possibility of parole. Two of his three co-conspirators—two Pakistanis and a Jordanian Palestinian—were sentenced to life as well, for their roles in the Trade Center bombing or the Manila airline conspiracy. The third, Wali Khan Amin Shah, a veteran of the jihad who has described himself as a key operational lieutenant to Osama bin Laden, the militant Saudi financier, was not sentenced at the time, for he had agreed to cooperate with the FBI. Federal investigators, who suspect that wealthy businessmen in Saudi Arabia and the Gulf helped finance some of Yousef's activities, were hopeful that Shah might be able to provide a link between Ramzi Yousef, Osama bin Laden, and the World Trade Center bomb.*

For, after three years in U.S. custody, Abdul-Basit remains a mystery. During his trials, he showed no remorse, and was defiant to the end. According to the testimony of a Secret Service agent, he boasted to U.S. investigators aboard the aircraft that returned him to the United States from Pakistan about what he had hoped to achieve with the Trade Center bomb: causing one of the Twin Towers to collapse into the other, killing up to 250,000 people—to let

---

*The question of whether bin Laden has been funneling money to militant Islamist groups in the United States is under investigation by a federal grand jury in New York, which, in the summer of 1998, handed down an indictment charging him with conspiring to kill Americans abroad. A subsequent indictment charged him with conspiracy in the bombings of the two U.S. embassies in Africa.

Americans know that they were "at war" and to punish the U.S. government for its support of Israel.

"You are not fit to uphold Islam," Judge Duffy told Abdul-Basit at his sentencing, after the judge had read aloud several passages from the Koran. "Death was truly your God, your master, your one and only religion," the judge said. "The only brave thing you possibly ever did was to fight in the war in Afghanistan."

During the year-long trials, in which Abdul-Basit refused to testify, he—unlike his co-defendants—sat alone in the courtroom in downtown Manhattan without family or friends. To the end, he never revealed his identity. Nor did he ever give U.S. investigators any indication of who sent him from Peshawar to New York in 1992 and who financed his operation once he was here. There had been tantalizing hints of ties to Iraq: Abdul-Basit's two Iraqi passports and, at one time, his claim to Iraqi nationality; the fact that another suspect in the bombing "fled" to Baghdad; and Saddam Hussein's history of funding covert networks. Saddam Hussein also had a motive for the bombing—revenge. The attack on the World Trade Center occurred on the second anniversary of his defeat in the Persian Gulf War.

Abdul-Basit is not an Iraqi, of course, and the other suspect's journey to Baghdad may not have been a "flight." Abdul-Rahman Yasin, one of Abdul-Basit's roommates in Brooklyn, who is charged with having helped to mix the chemicals used in the bomb, had cooperated with the FBI to the extent of giving agents a guided tour of the converted garage where the bomb was made, and even though he is now wanted by the FBI, the agency has never requested his extradition from Baghdad, where he lives quite openly in his family's home.

And what of the anniversary of the Persian Gulf War? The bombing of the World Trade Center was planned to occur considerably earlier, but with all the mishaps that ensnarled the motley group—including the crash of Salameh's car, which in itself delayed the bombing for at least two weeks—frustrated investigators now concede that they no longer see an anniversary link. And the Iraqi connection seems particularly dubious if one believes, as most investigators do, that the key to the bombing lies in Peshawar's militant Islamic underground and with the children of the jihad. Saddam Hussein, one of the Arab world's most secular leaders, conspicuously distanced himself from that war.

Since both the groups to which Abdul-Basit and his father have been linked—Sayyaf's Islamic Alliance and the SSP—fought in the jihad and received substantial financial backing from Saudi Arabia, I asked one ranking U.S. investigator if he considered it plausible that Saudi funding, even if it was indirect, had enabled Abdul-Basit to build the World Trade Center bomb. He paled slightly, and then replied, "If it was ever established that one of our major allies, for whom we've gone to war and sacrificed American lives—if a definitive link was ever made to such a government, I can only tell you there will be hell to pay."

In January 1996, Sheikh Omar Abdel-Rahman was sentenced in New York to life imprisonment for seditious conspiracy to wage a "war of urban terrorism against the United States," to assassinate Mubarak during a planned visit to New York, and to bomb various New York landmarks. The sheikh was never brought to trial for the World Trade Center bombing, although prosecutors contended that that blast was part of the conspiracy. Instead, he was tried under a rarely used law enacted after the Civil War: the prosecutors built their case around intent to wage a general campaign of terror against the U.S. government. It probably would have been impossible to have convicted him otherwise, one American investigator told me at the time. For three years of investigation had failed to establish a link between the sheikh and the enigmatic stranger who had arrived from Peshawar to build the World Trade Center bomb—other than the fact that Abdul-Basit had recruited followers of the sheikh and that both men had served American interests during the jihad.

Some months after his conviction, Sheikh Omar's lawyers appealed, and subsequent to that, they brought suit against the U.S. government over the conditions under which the sheikh is being detained. Since the spring of 1997, the spiritual mentor of Gama'a has been virtually in solitary confinement to prevent him from communicating with his followers. Among the specific complaints filed by the sheikh's legal team was that prison officials had taken away his special Arabic Braille compass and watch. The blind cleric consequently did not know the time of day, or the direction of Mecca that he must face to pray.

"I am not a conspirator," Sheikh Omar had told me in the days before his trial began. "And it makes absolutely no sense that I would conspire to blow up a city in which I chose to live. I'll tell you who the real conspirator is: the American government, and especially Janet Reno. She should be ashamed of herself. She knows full well that when Senator Alfonse D'Amato went to see her, forty-eight hours—*forty-eight hours*—before she detained me" (in the summer of 1993), "and asked her to indict me, she responded that she didn't even have enough evidence to *arrest* me, let alone indict me."

The sheikh threw up his hands. He was seated on a metal chair at a Formica table, in a small visitors room at the Metropolitan Correctional Center in lower Manhattan. Flanked by William Kunstler, one of his lawyers, and by Ahmad Sattar, my interpreter, he was dressed in a green prison shirt and a pair of matching trousers. He wore a plain white crocheted prayer cap on his head, and his eyes were covered by the heavy black glasses he normally wears. His greeting to me had been cordial, but he had made it clear that he would discuss neither the wiretaps of a secret FBI informant, which were at the core of the government's case against him, nor any other evidence to be presented at his trial.

The sheikh sipped a Diet Coke and went on to say that in the days before he was indicted, in August 1993, his immigration lawyer had been negotiating with the U.S. Attorney's office: if the sheikh was released from prison, where he was being detained on an immigration technicality, and permitted to leave for Afghanistan, he would drop his appeal for political asylum and for the return of his green card, which had allowed him to remain in the United States. But when the Egyptian government learned of the negotiations, the sheikh said, officials in Cairo "applied pressure on Washington, and Miss Reno simply acquiesced."

Since I didn't know when, or if, I would see Sheik Omar again, I asked him what, for him, had been the most important thing about the jihad in Afghanistan. Friends of his had told me that it had been cathartic for him. "When the Afghans rose and declared a jihad—and jihad had been dead for the longest time—I can't tell you how proud I was," he said. "It was no longer just in the Koran. It was there on the battlefield. And what a sense of pride I felt when the mujahideen drove the Soviets out of Afghanistan." He smiled.

When Sheikh Omar arrived in this country, his sponsor had been Mustafa Shalabi, who headed Sheikh Azzam's jihad effort in the United States from the Alkifah Refugee Center on Brooklyn's Atlantic Avenue. But the two men had had a falling-out after Shalabi was accused, by officials of Brooklyn's al-Farouq Mosque, of having embezzled some $2 million that had been raised for the Arab volunteers who were fighting in Afghanistan. (In March 1991, Shalabi's body was found in his Brooklyn apartment, a killing that remains unsolved.) I asked Sheikh Omar if he had denounced Shalabi as a bad Muslim. He grew noticeably tense and said, "No, I did not."

"Were notices posted in mosques? Was a fatwa issued?"

"No," he replied. "There was nothing at all." He did not want to say anything more about Mustafa Shalabi, so I quickly moved to safer ground.

"What radicalized you?" I asked.

The question seemed to relax him a bit. "I guess it began with the injustice around me in Egypt during Nasser's regime, including the regime's attempts to prevent me from getting my Ph.D. Then the periods of detention, the imprisonments"—largely from 1981 through 1984, when he was charged with having conspired to overthrow the government and with having issued the fatwa that resulted in the assassination of Anwar Sadat.

I asked Sheikh Omar if he had been tortured during those prison years.

"In many ways," he replied. "At least ten different methods were used on me, among them being hung from the ceiling by my ankles, being beaten with sticks, and receiving electric shocks. And there were other things that, in the presence of a lady, I would not like to discuss. What is important is that both judges [in the assassination and the conspiracy trials] were able to prove that this torture occurred, and the judge in the conspiracy case actually condemned the Egyptian government for the torture I'd been through."

He thought for a moment, and then he said, "Yet, in spite of all this—and all these Egyptian court documents are with the U.S. Immigration Service now—the U.S. government still does not believe that I will be persecuted if I return to Egypt, or that I deserve political asylum in the United States."*

For a moment, no one at the table said anything more.

I hadn't been at all certain what to expect when I visited Sheikh Omar in prison this time. I had been told that his moods had fluctuated dramatically in the months leading up to his trial, a result both of the proceedings and of the fact that, even though he was not unfamiliar with imprisonment—having spent some seven years in Egyptian prisons or under house arrest—he had never been held in solitary confinement before, or been in a place where he did not speak the language or where the FBI had strictly forbidden prison officials to permit him any sweets. (The sheikh, who is a diabetic, continues to have a potentially deadly passion for chocolate, which makes him exceedingly ill, though this does not prevent him from eating it anyhow.)

But as our conversation progressed, he proved to be as puckish as he had always been.

Since I was not permitted to ask him anything about his New York conspiracy trial, I asked Sheikh Omar if there was a connection between the jihad in Afghanistan and what was happening now in Egypt and Algeria, where militant Islamists had intensified their

---

*Among the documents in the possession of the INS are a 1988 Cairo court decision ordering the state to pay Sheikh Omar 17,000 Egyptian pounds for his prison duress, largely caused by the torture he had been subjected to. In 1991, in Case No. 105-10386/10505, an appeals court doubled that amount, to the equivalent of $10,600. That court decision, along with testimony given at both of the sheikh's trials, is also in the possession of the U.S. government.

campaigns to wrest control of those countries' Army-backed regimes.

"Absolutely," he replied without hesitation. "These are most definitely linked." He leaned back in his chair and began rocking a bit, his gray-white beard resting on his chest.

Before leaving, I asked Sheikh Omar how he felt now that, having worked alongside the governments of Egypt, Saudi Arabia, and the United States in Afghanistan, he was facing charges in the United States that could imprison him for life. Many of his followers in Egypt and Saudi Arabia who had fought in the jihad were being tried and imprisoned, and a number had been hanged in Egypt, solely for participating in that war.

"We have an expression in Arabic," he replied. " 'Everybody sings for those whom he loves.' In effect, it means that everyone is singing for something different. And that is exactly what happened in Afghanistan. Do you think we were naïve enough to believe that the U.S. government was helping the Afghans because it believed in their cause—to raise the flag of jihad for Islam? That they were helping a people, a country, to free themselves? Absolutely not. The Americans were there to punish the Soviet Union, and when they were sure that the Soviet Union had suffered and was about to collapse, they stopped everything—all the aid, all the equipment—just like that." He snapped his fingers, and his voice began to rise. "They didn't *care* that there was still a Communist government in power in Afghanistan. They simply turned their backs and walked away. And the Saudis, oh, the Saudis, and the Egyptians—they did precisely the same. It took three more years for the mujahideen to oust the Najibullah regime. Thousands of lives were lost; crops and livelihoods were destroyed. But not one life mattered to the Saudis, the Egyptians, or the United States."

He placed his hands on the table around which we sat, as though steadying himself, and then he said, "You've got to understand that the Egyptians and the Saudis were also using the war to try to get rid of their own problems at home. They were sending young men into battle as cannon fodder, without training, without any understanding of what war was. They were saying, 'Let's get rid of our headaches, and send them off to the jihad to be killed.' "

He fell silent, as if he were considering whether or not to go on. Then he said: "So what the American government and the Egyptians and the Saudis are doing now is not surprising. In fact, we were expecting it. But what bothers me, and makes me feel bitter toward the whole thing, is when a person who was willing to sacrifice himself and spill his blood for truth and freedom and was called a freedom fighter then, when the war is over he is labeled a terrorist."

THE APOSTATE

D<small>R.</small> N<small>ASR</small> H<small>AMED</small> A<small>BU</small> Z<small>EID</small> <small>IS A BALDING, MIDDLE-AGED</small> professor of substantial girth—a private, timid man. He is fastidious neither about his appearance nor about his health, and is largely unassuming in all manner of things except his scholarship. "Professorial" is the epithet typically ascribed to him by his Egyptian friends. His life was well-ordered, if a bit predictable. He had spent most of the last twenty-five years, first as a student, then as a professor of Islamic studies, at Cairo University, to which he commuted each day in a battered Volkswagen from his small one-bedroom apartment in the suburbs, an hour away. He had married a fellow professor, Ebtehal Younes, somewhat late in life—in April 1992, at the age of forty-nine. Fifteen years his junior, she is slim and attractive, fiery and outspoken; the widely traveled daughter of an Egyptian diplomat; a French and Spanish literature professor; a writer; and, if only by force of circumstance, a combative feminist. The couple lived quietly in his cluttered apartment, which was bursting with books, furniture, rugs and china, and family photographs. On the refrigerator door, a drawing of Don Quixote stared down; directly across from it, a Koranic inscription from his childhood in a Nile Delta village hung somewhat haphazardly on the wall.

Over the years, Abu Zeid's scholarly studies on Islam and the Koran—in which he argues, not unlike many nineteenth-century rationalist Islamic thinkers, that Islam's holy texts should be interpreted in the historical and linguistic context of their time, and that their interpretation should heed social change—had been published in twelve books, professorial treatises largely unread outside the academic world. A political liberal, though of a less-than-passionate sort, Abu Zeid had read Aristotle, Averroës, Kant, Marx, and Engels, but as an Islamic scholar he had spent nearly his entire life studying the Koran, which he had memorized as a child while attending religious schools. Everything about him seemed unremarkable.

Outside academic circles he was virtually unknown, until his trial.

It all began in 1993—three trials in ever-higher courts, culminating, before the appeals process began, in August 1996 before the prestigious Court of Cassation, Egypt's equivalent of the Supreme Court.

As was his habit, Abu Zeid had risen early; it was May 1993, he told me later, and he remembers nothing of any particular significance that was *supposed* to happen that day. He sat and perused the papers while sipping his usual morning cup of tea, and then he was stopped—"dumbstruck, incredulous," he said—as he first read of what amounted to a blasphemy case against him, which was featured prominently in the pro-Islamist press. "I simply couldn't believe it; none of us could," he said. "One of my friends went to the court to inquire. He came back dumbfounded, and he said, 'It's true. You've got to get a lawyer.' "

A few weeks later, in the Giza Primary Court—a civilian court on the west bank of the Nile, not far from Cairo University and in the shadow of a thirteenth-century mosque—the trial of Nasr Abu Zeid began. There he was forced to defend his innocence against a sweeping indictment that neither he nor his lawyers were fully able to comprehend. It appeared to be contrary to all Egyptian laws and legal precedent. There he was confronted by accusers whom he did not know and who had never read his books, but who nevertheless charged that, in their opinion, he was an apostate who had abandoned his faith in Islam. There he was accosted by the memory of an acrimonious decade-long academic dispute with a shrewd, polemic foe—Dr. Abdel-Sabour Shahin, his chief accuser—who had demanded, and was still demanding, that he be banished from the university and that his books be burned. And, from there, he became a virtual prisoner in his tiny suburban flat as government-supplied armed guards took up positions along the perimeter of the block, their automatic assault weapons drawn.

For far from the courtroom and the trial, across Cairo during Friday prayers, both government-appointed and "popular" sheikhs had begun calling for Abu Zeid's death. "Apostate!" his enemies shouted, backed by the powerful government institution of al-Azhar, whose clerics, nearly every day of the trial, shuffled in and out of the judges' chambers in their prayer caps and long robes, walking silently in single file, as if performing a secret military drill. "Repent! Repent! Repent!" Abu Zeid told me that the words kept ringing in his head.

Yet, for him, as he waited for the verdict to come, the single most haunting aspect of his trial was that since Egypt has no apostasy law, he was being tried under family law, where matters of inheritance, the welfare of children, and divorce are adjudicated according to Shariah law. One tenet of traditional Islam is that a Muslim woman may not marry outside her faith. That meant that if his writings were deemed by the court to be blasphemous, his marriage would be dissolved.

In effect, Nasr Abu Zeid was being sued for divorce, not by his wife, who has remained loyal to him, but by a group of Islamist lawyers acting on her behalf—initially without her knowledge and later without her consent. (The lawyers argued that since Ebtehal was a Muslim woman, it was their Islamic duty to defend her, even against her will.) The lawyers—nearly all of whom were Islamist disciples of Abdel-Sabour Shahin's—were headed by a flamboyant sheikh and former member of parliament, Youssef al-Badry, who between 1992 and early 1993 had been the imam of a Paterson, New Jersey, mosque. They based their case on an obscure and rarely used ninth-century principle of Shariah law called *hisbah*. (According to this principle, which translates loosely as "accountability," any Muslim may sue before a court if he believes that Islam is being harmed, even if he himself is not personally involved.)

Abu Zeid's lawyers argued that since 1955, when Shariah courts were abolished, *hisbah* had ceased to exist in Egyptian law, this in spite of a highly controversial and largely untested 1980 constitutional amendment—a concession to the Islamists by the government of Anwar Sadat—that made Shariah law "the principal source" of Egyptian law. The defense was confident of victory. It had been decades, at the very least, since *hisbah* was last invoked in an Egyptian court; some of the defense lawyers admitted that prior to the trial they had not even heard of *hisbah*. And indeed their position was upheld by the lower court in January 1994. Abu Zeid's reprieve, however, did not last long.

Shahin and al-Badry's team appealed the case, and in June 1995, Abu Zeid's worst fears were realized. In an unprecedented ruling, the Cairo Court of Appeals found that Nasr Abu Zeid, by propagating the view that certain Koranic references to angels, devils, genies, and the throne of God were to be taken not literally, but as metaphors, had denied that the Koran was the word of God; and that by challenging certain basic tenets of Shariah law—in particular, the half measure granted to women, as compared with men, both in the weight of court evidence and in the rights of inheritance—Abu Zeid had, in effect, called on Muslims to abandon their religious laws. Neatly circumventing the fact that the court had no jurisdiction to declare anyone an apostate, since there was no apostasy law, its three judges found that Abu Zeid's writings in and of themselves proved him to be an apostate. They declared, in effect, that he had convicted *himself*. Therefore, the court pronounced, he had lost the right to be married to a Muslim woman, and it ordered Abu Zeid to divorce Ebtehal.

In August 1996—despite the fact that Abu Zeid and Ebtehal were, and are, happily married—Egypt's highest court upheld this absurdity. In a ruling unparalleled in the Islamic world, the Court of Cassation upheld the verdict of the Court of Appeals. Then, going further than any Islamic religious court has ever done, and well beyond its writ as a court of form, not substance, five of the most senior civilian judges in Egypt ruled that although the Constitution enshrined freedom of belief, there was a difference between belief that was spoken and belief in the mind. In his writings—which are now banned at Cairo University—Abu Zeid had crossed that line.

For forty days after the first judgment against them, Abu Zeid and Ebtehal stayed at home; they were not permitted to go outside by their security guards. Then, one day, Abu Zeid insisted that he be permitted to go to Cairo University to chair a defense committee for a student's dissertation. It was the first and the last time.

"I was surrounded by two police cars en route," he told me when we met. "A bodyguard was in my car. When we arrived at the university, the whole campus was sealed off. Police dogs were in every corner. I felt like I was entering my grave, not my university. There were electronic detectors at the gates, and everyone who entered was checked. I can't tell you how terrible I felt." He realized that day that he would never be able to return to Cairo University.

He also well understood the risks of having provoked Egypt's powerful religious establishment. Six days after the Court of Appeals ruling, a group of scholars from al-Azhar called on the government to carry out the "legal punishment for apostasy" in order to force Abu Zeid to repent. That punishment, according to the orthodox school of Shariah law, is death.

Seemingly overnight, a little-known and little-traveled professor—who had left Egypt only twice in his life—had become the newest victim of religious intolerance, threatened not only with death by Islamic militants but with helplessness on the part of an embattled secular government that failed to stir. Abu Zeid and Ebtehal fled to Leiden University, in the Netherlands, fearing for their lives.

By May 1998, Islamist lawyers had filed some eighty lawsuits against the Egyptian government, against artists and intellectuals, academics and journalists, in their efforts to implement Shariah law. More alarming than the fact of the lawsuits themselves are the verdicts: in case after case, filed in secular courts, the Islamists have largely won. They have succeeded in banning films, censoring school textbooks, and reversing a government ban on female circumcision, a ban they claimed was un-Islamic. And although its ruling was later overturned on appeal, a Cairo civilian court agreed. Everyone—the

government, secular lawyers and judges, and even moderate Islamists—was stunned.

The Egyptian courts appeared to have been transformed into the
newest battleground between the Islamists and the state, and everyone to whom I spoke during the summer of 1997 agreed that this
almost certainly would not have occurred had there been no Abu
Zeid trials. The three closely followed proceedings were a turning
point. This was not only because of the legal precedents they set or
the possibility that even more writers, thinkers, filmmakers, and cabinet ministers could now be tried, transforming the Egyptian courts
into a venue for a modern Islamic Inquisition—a possibility that has
rattled Hosni Mubarak's already rattled Army-backed regime. But
perhaps more alarming than anything else is the fact that Abu Zeid's
trials were neither initiated nor orchestrated by the Peshawar and
Afghan-based militant Islamist underground but by "moderate" Islamists within the Egyptian government, including a key presidential
adviser on Islam, and by government-appointed sheikhs at the state-
run University of al-Azhar.

Increasingly, the country's already powerless writers, directors,
playwrights, and poets found themselves caught between the Islamists, on the one hand, and the government, on the other—especially
the official sheikhs of al-Azhar, whose provocative and strident pronouncements, as they attempted to guide artistic thought, were proving as outrageous as the demands of many militants. It was a more
subtle battle than that being fought between the armies of Hosni
Mubarak and Sheikh Omar Abdel-Rahman, but like it, it was a
battle with no front lines, in which anyone could be targeted at any
time.

Yet the government of Mubarak—which has already endowed
al-Azhar with greater authority than it has possessed at any other
time during this century—seemed ever more eager to acquiesce to
the sheikhs, as it continued to veer between suppression of the Islamists and its highly orchestrated, and highly shortsighted, campaign to make itself appear more Islamic than the Islamic activists.

Thousands—according to most estimates, more than twenty
thousand—Islamists, some of them far from militant, moldered in

jail, where at least thirty had died; the sweep of arrests had widened to include nearly a thousand respected professionals from the Muslim Brotherhood, as well as most of the founders and many of the supporters of the newly formed—and banned—Wasat Party, a group of younger professionals who had broken away from the Brotherhood. (The party is a novelty, since its members include not only Islamists but also leftists and Christian Copts.) They had all been arrested in the run-up to the 1995 parliamentary elections, which they had hoped to contest—elections that human rights organizations condemned as "fraudulent, undemocratic, and grossly unfair"—a sentiment presumably shared by the Egyptian courts, which nullified more than 50 percent of the electoral results. Special in-camera military courts (which Amnesty International has also called "grossly unfair" and against which there is no appeal) had sentenced nearly a hundred men to the gallows, and nearly all of them had been hanged. According to the Islamists' lawyers, all had confessed to militant activity under torture, which is now an integral part of official policy.

But as ruthless as the Mubarak regime is in dealing with militant Islam, it has continued to condone Islamist influence in those places where perhaps it has the greatest impact on society. The regime's inability, or unwillingness, to come to grips with the immense challenges that the Islamists posed; its refusal to open the political arena to voices other than its own; its disregard of basic civilities, most strikingly of human rights—all had coalesced to create an ambience in which an Abu Zeid trial was not only possible, it was almost inevitable.

Not only were Egypt's increasingly beleaguered intellectuals shocked by the trials, even some orthodox Islamists were alarmed. Writing in the semiofficial daily *al-Ahram*, Fahmy Huweidi, a conservative Islamist commentator, expressed his dismay. "That the plaintiff, an obscure Islamist lawyer, should carry an intellectual issue into a family court is symptomatic," he wrote, "of a breakdown in Egyptian society. Nobody debates anymore. Consequently only two channels are left: judges and guns."

Until the fall of 1997, the guns had fallen largely silent, thanks to the government's brutal crackdown against its militant Islamist foes. Only in the mountains and in a handful of towns in Middle and Upper Egypt did the insurgency go on. But Egypt's Islamist militancy, though outmaneuvered and repressed, has a way of reappearing, often in new mutations and forms, and there was every sign that it was now reinventing itself in yet another guise. For although its military cells had been undeniably weakened over the previous year, religious conservatives continued to infiltrate the schools and universities, the bureaucracy, the news media, and the arts in much the same manner as they had infiltrated the Egyptian courts, to which secularists had turned with greater frequency to protect liberal values and thought. That trust was badly shaken as a result of the Abu Zeid trials. For more than any legal battle in recent memory, they had been a litmus test for the Islamists, intent on installing Islamic law, and for secular Cairenes, ever more fearful of losing basic freedoms of expression and belief.

One morning, I called on two writers who had received death threats from the Islamists, and found both of them hidden away— one inside his shuttered apartment, the other in his office, with thick curtains drawn. In both cases, outside their doors, standing at attention, were heavily armed guards. Both men had earned the displeasure of the sheikhs of al-Azhar.

And neither had received even token support, they told me, from the Mubarak regime, whose retreat from secular politics and culture continued apace.

One cannot escape the impression that the old multicultural, cosmopolitan, secular Egypt is slipping away. As recently as twenty years ago, during my student days, Egypt's great men of letters were ensconced on the remarkable sixth floor of the building that houses Cairo's leading newspaper, *al-Ahram*, where, since the days of Nasser, they had held court, providing the most viable secular alternative to the teachings of al-Azhar. The venerable eighty-year-old playwright Tewfik al-Hakim sat in a usually sunny corner office, wearing his trademark black beret. Naguib Mahfouz was in the office just next door, and down the hall were other literary lions: the short-story writer Youssef Idris and the eminent literary critic Louis Awad. But when I stopped in on a recent afternoon, there were few reminders of that literary scene. And there were still fewer reminders, in the pages of *al-Ahram* itself, of the paper's once distinguished history. It no longer produced thoughtful analysis, investigative journalism, or astute political commentary, as it once had done. As I sat with the leftist commentator Mohamed Sid-Ahmed in *al-Ahram*'s cafeteria over lunch, he told me that Egyptian intellectuals now read the paper "mainly to see who died."

Pressures from the Islamists and pressures from the regime, which in the spring of 1998 embarked on the most severe crackdown on press freedom in Egypt in years, have all coalesced to guarantee a largely government-sanctioned official press. This—combined with corruption and poverty, and with an acute disappointment in the mediocrity of public life in a nation caught between its present and its past—has begun to take its toll on Cairo's—and, by extension, Egypt's—once vibrant cultural and intellectual life. A university professor now earns less than a household servant—about three hundred dollars a month. Egypt produced better and freer cinema in the 1930s than it does now. And in a country that three-quarters of a century ago published thousands of books and some two hundred newspapers and journals, a mere 375 books were published last year. It was as if this ancient city, which has been so many different cities, had returned to an age, in the words of the retired ambassador Tahseen Basheer, of "Mamluk mentality"—a period both oppressive and bureaucratic, and of gradual intellectual decay—the time of the military oligarchs who ruled Egypt from the thirteenth to the sixteenth century. The Egypt of Mubarak and his generals had produced no peers to rival the great men of letters who had come of age during the Revolution of 1919 and the Liberal Age. Instead, the ruling triad of king, army, and church, draped in its own Mamlukian shroud, had ceded—and continued to cede—ever more significant ground to the voices, and the nonsecular forces, of political Islam.

It was as if Egypt was still struggling to identify itself.

As I wandered around Cairo late one afternoon, drinking tea in the Khan el-Khalili Bazaar, clambering through Imbaba's dark and

narrow lanes, and browsing in a number of fairly new and outrageously overpriced Zamalek boutiques, the layers of the country's
past now seemed more often jumbled than distinct. There was the
Mohammed Ali layer. In a sense, Egypt still has the feel of the colonial outpost that the Albanian soldier of fortune and his heirs were
determined to bring into the modern world in the nineteenth century. Their policies had produced a Westernized intellectual elite,
the Suez Canal, European-style bungalows with sweeping gardens,
and an elegant opera house. But the people who mattered most now
rarely spoke English or French. They knew only the language of the
Koran, Arabic.

There was also the layer of Nasser and the young army officers
who staged the Revolution of 1952: faint voices now, increasingly
unmoored from the Pan-Arabism, Marxism, and socialism of those
days, and from the moment of promise the Free Officers held out
before their revolutionary experiment of the 1950s and 1960s ran
badly aground.

And there was also the Islamic layer, not yet fully defined, yet
always at one's elbow here—mosques, minarets, calls to prayer—as
omnipotent as the sandstorms blown by the desert's wind. And this
was the layer with which the ruling oligarchy was now dancing a
progressively more difficult minuet.

Ultimately I made my way to the banks of the Nile and to the
tea shop that overhung it where I had spent so many mornings with
Miss Pennypecker twenty years before. The sun was just beginning
to set, and I watched the feluccas as they glided by, their lateen sails
reaching for heaven, as they have done since Cleopatra's time. Just
beyond them, on the other side of the Nile, I spotted the red-and-
yellow sign of McDonald's, which rose from a grassy knoll, behind
a sea of women who were promenading, dressed in *hijabs* and long,
flowing Islamic robes.

Cruise ships were once again sailing down the Nile, accompanied by security guards who stood slightly disheveled in small patrol
boats. Their faces were partly hidden by visored helmets, and it was
impossible to know who they were.

The campaign by Islamic militants to cripple Egypt's economy through attacks on tourism had cost the government $4 billion, and had decimated the industry until its revival for the first time in 1996. There was uncertainty, however, over how long that revival would last. For the powerful sheikhs of al-Azhar had already succeeded in banning liquor in private clubs, and their more militant youthful counterparts had killed eighteen Greek tourists that April near Cairo's ancient Pyramids. Yet, in spite of such attacks, an Egyptian journalist told me one afternoon that her primary concern was not the Islamist underground but the continuing Islamist revolution by stealth. She used to count the number of women on state-controlled television who were veiled; now she counted the number who were not veiled. One could say that the Islamists had already succeeded in imposing their own dress code.

A professor at the American University of Cairo remarked to me that his greatest concern was the growing number of plainclothes policemen, casually dressed in designer jeans but with guns displayed conspicuously in the back pockets of their pants, who are stationed on university campuses and in "popular" neighborhoods, where they cordon off, seemingly at whim, entire blocks. He told me that they reminded him of the Haitian Tontons Macoutes.

But it was the precedents set in the Abu Zeid trials that caused the most concern, in the summer of 1997, for Egyptian intellectuals. For perhaps the ultimate irony of the trials is that they need never have occurred had an academic dispute between two rivals been resolved inside Cairo University, where it belonged. The Egyptian courts had been used in the Abu Zeid trials, and their reputation irrevocably harmed.

Abu Zeid had first been singled out by the Islamists in December 1992, when his promotion to full professor at the government-supported Cairo University was denied, on the basis of a report by three academic experts. Two of them had praised his Koranic research, but were nevertheless swayed by the third, a charismatic and influential cleric named Abdel-Sabour Shahin, who vehemently opposed everything that Abu Zeid espoused.

A professor of Arabic linguistics at Cairo University's College of

Dar al-Uloum, Shahin is a rigid, doctrinal watchdog of orthodox Islam, which considers the Koran, as transmitted by the Prophet Muhammad, to be the literal word of God. For a number of years, he had loudly disputed Abu Zeid's iconoclastic and probing interpretations of Islam's holy texts, which, Shahin contended, bordered on heresy.

It seemed to matter little to Shahin that Abu Zeid was not alone in his views; Cairo has a school of liberal interpreters of the Koran. But none of them had directly challenged Shahin as Abu Zeid had. Debate followed acrimonious debate between the two men, at the university, at symposia on Islamic thought, and at open public seminars. When Abu Zeid's promotion was denied, he fought back, urging his fellow professors to appeal to the Minister of Education— more than fifty did. More than five hundred of his students marched in protest on his behalf, gathered signatures, and appealed to Hosni Mubarak to intervene and review Shahin's report, charging that it had little to do with academic matters, but was political. Shahin, not surprisingly, was furious. Then Abu Zeid presented his case to the Egyptian press, and Shahin's fury turned to rage—for Abu Zeid renewed his attacks on Egypt's Islamic investment firms, many of whose accounts were secretive at best, haphazard at worst. When they had collapsed in 1988, hundreds of thousands of middle-class Egyptians lost their entire savings in the greatest financial scandal in Islamic history. Shahin was particularly enraged by Abu Zeid's innuendo in these new attacks, since it was well-known that Shahin had served as a legal consultant to the largest firm.

The dispute between the two men evolved. It was no longer only academic and religious, but also highly personal. And Shahin proved to be a man with far more pulpits from which to argue his case than the usually timid and scholarly Abu Zeid had.

An imam of the airwaves, Shahin was sometimes called the "Sheikh of Takfir" for his self-appointed role in targeting "nonbelievers" for what he perceived to be their disrespect, or disregard, of the Koran. It was only in recent years, however, that the graying cleric had ventured into literary criticism of the most chilling sort. Along with other like-minded, government-appointed sheikhs,

Shahin had worked deftly behind the scenes, launching investigations into the alleged heresy of writers and poets, actresses and actors, academics and journalists, acting as both inquisitor and judge.

Significantly, his religious anathemas were dispensed with the tacit approval of the Mubarak government—a government that Shahin served as a key presidential adviser on Islam. In the early 1980s, he was given a weekly program of his own on government-controlled TV and biweekly broadcasts on government-controlled radio. An avuncular but insistent advocate of Islamic piety, he was thus able to speak directly to rural villagers and the urban poor, who customarily gather around communal television sets and radios in the coffeehouses and in the souks. His renown became such that even celebrities visited his office, seeking religious counseling. A fiery speaker whose views carried great weight, I was told, he presided over Friday prayers at the prestigious Amr Ibn al-As Mosque. Yet, most significantly, for over a decade—from 1986 until the summer of 1996—Shahin was one of Mubarak's key advisers on Islam, as the chairman of the Religious Committee of the ruling National Democratic Party, and, as a consequence, he had the President's ear. In a sense, Abdel-Sabour Shahin is a creation of the Mubarak regime.

Cairo's lavishly appointed seventh-century Amr Ibn al-As Mosque is the oldest mosque in Egypt, and one of the oldest in the Islamic world. It was from its prayer hall, in April 1993, that Shahin first publicly accused Abu Zeid of apostasy. Nearly half a million worshippers were present, Shahin told me later, and the word quickly spread through the mosque network and through the pro-Islamist press. The following week, at Friday prayers across Egypt, Abu Zeid was declared a heretic.

It happened even in his home village near Tanta, where he had memorized the Koran along with a childhood friend who was now the imam at the local mosque. After prayers, Abu Zeid's brother approached the imam and asked, "How can you call Nasr a heretic? Have you read any of his books?"

"No," the imam replied. "But Abdel-Sabour Shahin says he's an apostate, and Abdel-Sabour Shahin doesn't lie."

Not surprisingly, no one from Mubarak's regime or its religious establishment censored Shahin, nor did they protest the following month when Shahin and his disciples filed court papers to have the apostate's marriage dissolved.

The siege of Egypt's secularists was taking many different forms.

Abu Zeid had been deeply shaken in June 1992, six months before his own ordeal began, when his friend the writer Farag Foda was shot to death outside his Cairo home after he had been accused of apostasy. It was the first assassination of an Egyptian intellectual, and, for many of them, it marked the beginning of the siege.

In retrospect, it is difficult to say which of the trials—that of Abu Zeid or that of Foda's accused assassins from the Gama'a, both of which opened in the summer of 1993—had the greater impact. In effect, they fed each other, and all the Egyptians to whom I spoke agreed that, at both trials, the sheikhs of al-Azhar had perceptibly raised the stakes.

Stunning both Western diplomats and Egypt's growingly be-leaguered secularists, not only had Sheikh Mohammed al-Ghazali of al-Azhar, testifying for the defense in the Foda trial, effectively endorsed the extrajudicial killing of apostates or of anyone who opposed the implementation of Shariah law, but the sheikh was testifying in his role as one of Egypt's leading moderate scholars of Islam—a scholar who, not unlike Abdul-Sabour Shahin, was frequently consulted by the Mubarak regime. He represented the regime abroad, at international conferences and seminars, while at home—not unlike Shahin—he was given widespread exposure on government-controlled radio and government-controlled TV to, in effect, combat the message of the Islamic militants.

But for a growing number of secularists, sheikhs like al-Ghazali and Shahin had come to represent a dangerous convergence between Egypt's radical and moderate Islamist political trends. In their view, the separation between the militants whom the government had been suppressing and the clerics whom it had been condoning was less than absolute.

One Friday morning I went with a friend of mine, an Islamist lawyer who was now living underground, to the University of al-Azhar, where we hoped to meet with one of the twenty or so sheikhs who had provided religious counsel behind the scenes during the Abu Zeid trials.

As we approached the gates of the university, I watched a group of men, bearded and dressed in long, flowing white robes and white crocheted prayer caps, transform a small adjacent square as they spread out straw mats for midday prayers. The few women in evidence were shrouded in black abayas, covered from head to toe, anonymous forms gliding in and out of storefront shops. All around us, the new Cairo continued to define itself: crumbling buildings, torn-up sidewalks, sewage on the street. And the more the city crumbled and the more its population swelled, the more sharply defined was the line dividing its less-Islamic haves and its more-Islamic have-nots. Here was the center of a new, different Egypt, no longer the Egypt of a Westernized intellectual elite or of European-style bungalows with sweeping lawns. But it was also not a downtrodden Egypt that I was seeing at al-Azhar. For the theocratic ambitions of its clerics have gained power and momentum over recent years, not only from the tolerance exhibited by Mubarak's government but also through lavish funding from Saudi Arabia.

Every day, thousands of new recruits joined the Islamist movement—young people who could not find apartments, who could not marry or find jobs, the intellectual and retired ambassador Hussein Amin had told me a few years ago. When I called on him last summer, I asked him if this was still true.

"Their revolution by stealth continues, of course," he replied. "They are taking over—the bureaucracy, the trade unions, the universities, and the courts. They're also taking over writers and journalists, via money primarily from Saudi Arabia but also from the Gulf. If you write for an Egyptian newspaper, you get the equivalent of eight dollars a piece; if you write for a Saudi paper, you get two hundred dollars a piece. Saudi Arabia doesn't have enough intellectuals to fill one newspaper, so you will find more and more Egyptians writing for the Saudis, and toeing the Saudi line."

I asked the ambassador what, for him, was the most frightening aspect of the Abu Zeid trials.

He answered without hesitation: "That Islamist thinking has

penetrated the highest levels of the Egyptian judiciary." He then added that what alarmed him equally was to find that the majority of Egyptians, even among the educated, were truly against Abu Zeid. "Many intellectuals who are not really religious and may very well be atheists," he said, "now tend to believe that Islam may be the only way to combat Western influence in our lives."

I thought of what Ambassador Amin had said as we entered the campus of al-Azhar, making our way through its courtyard, past its stunning tenth-century mosque with its towering minarets, from which muezzins, five times a day, call the faithful to prayer. For it was from here, in a sense, in the classrooms and the mosques of the world's oldest university, that Egypt's—and, by extension, the larger Arab world's—most crucial battle was being fought. And it was a battle not only between political Islam and an authoritarian state, or between the inheritors of Lieutenant Khaled al-Islambouli's and Anwar Sadat's legacies. It was a battle over Islamist versus secular thought, a battle whose outcome will clearly shape the future of North Africa and the Middle East.

Al-Azhar had long been a prime recruiting ground for the Muslim Brotherhood, and its graduates had, in turn, reexported the Brotherhood's brand of militant Islam throughout the Muslim world. What is far more worrisome, however, to Egyptian secularists is the Brotherhood's recent success—thanks largely to Saudi funding—in recruiting prominent sheikhs from within al-Azhar itself. The sheikhs have then, in turn, infiltrated the Egyptian courts in their efforts to implement Shariah law.

Slowly, almost imperceptibly, over the years, Egypt's Islamist revolution by stealth has burrowed its way into the very heart of the institutions of the Arab world's largest and most important state. And it seems to me that the far greater threat to the old multicultural and secular Egypt of my student days, and to the interests of the United States, lies not in the battle now being fought in Upper and Middle Egypt between the armies of Hosni Mubarak and Sheikh Omar Abdel-Rahman—a battle that has claimed some two thousand lives in the last five years—but rather in the probability that the other Islamist revolution, the revolution by stealth, will succeed.

Secular Cairenes, who have increasingly been left behind in the growing polarization of political life, have abdicated the middle ground. And many intellectuals, Hussein Amin among them, have come to believe that an Islamic state in Egypt now seems inevitable. And, in the event that that occurs, unlike with Shi'ite Iran, whose revolution failed to export itself, its impact on the Muslim world—and on the oil-rich Middle East—will be profound. For even among scholars who normally shun domino theories of history, there is a growing concern that if Egypt "goes Islamic," so could much of the Arab world.

As I glanced around the campus of al-Azhar, richly endowed by Saudi funds, I puzzled over the role of the House of Saud, whose princes and foundations and wealthy businessmen—including a number of friends of the Afghan-based Osama bin Laden—remain the leading benefactors of many of the world's militant Islamist groups. Saudi Arabia's role, both official and private, in Egypt's Islamist revolution, if not duplicitous, is certainly a curious one. It continues to be based partly on the Kingdom's geopolitical concerns and its antipathy toward the Shi'ite ayatollahs who preside over Iran. It is also partly an attempt to buy protection for its beleaguered regime by placating its own expanding fundamentalist constituency—a notion forcefully belied by the 1995 and 1996 bombings in Dhahran and Riyadh of U.S. military facilities. But perhaps as important as anything else, the Saudi role, in every sense, sprang from the legacy of the jihad in Afghanistan.

A veteran Western ambassador told me one afternoon that "the Saudi hand" was being seen increasingly, not only at al-Azhar—in Egypt's film industry, its publishing houses, and its mosques—but also in the courts, and that there were some within the Mubarak government who attributed the Abu Zeid verdicts to Saudi payoffs. "That's only the informed rumor, there's no concrete evidence, of course," the ambassador said. "But there are a growing number of Egyptian judges who want to maintain their purity in Saudi eyes; who want to work in Saudi Arabia or the Gulf. And because of that, Saudi control over the courts need not be so blatant as bribes." He then explained how it works: "An Egyptian judge is promised work in the Kingdom—where he'll make three times the money that he makes here—if he keeps his skirts clean. And there's also a whole section of judges who are dominated by al-Azhar. It's cyclical: Saudi money pours into al-Azhar for studies of Shariah law, and, in turn, al-Azhar graduates then sit on the Egyptian bench, totally disdainful of secular law. There are judges who actually begin court proceedings by expressing their deep-felt sorrow that they have to apply man-made laws, rather than God-given laws."

"Did this happen in the trial of Abu Zeid?" I asked.

"No." He smiled. "Because in the case of Abu Zeid, they applied God's law."

Youssef Chahine, the eccentric genius who is Egypt's most accomplished filmmaker, arguably the best in the Arab world, looked out the window of his tenth-floor apartment in Zamalek, and down into the street and said, "The atmosphere is pretty electrified; it's becoming pretty vicious down there."

A tall, slightly disheveled man of seventy with a wry sense of humor, a French education, and a Hollywood background, Chahine—who received the lifetime-achievement award at the Cannes Film Festival last year—has been the enfant terrible of Egyptian cinema for more than forty years. Still, he told me, he has never known "anything quite like this." His voice began to rise. "How dare they? I do not think *anyone* has the right to monopolize God, or his message, whether it be in the Bible, the Torah, or the Koran. And where's the international community? There are *hundreds* of us who have been declared blasphemers, apostates, heretics—Salman Rushdie, Taslima Nasreen [the Bangladeshi writer], Tahar Djaout [a writer and editor assassinated in Algeria]—and no one in the international community seems to give a damn."

Ala'a Hamad, a balding, middle-aged tax inspector who dabbled in writing in his spare time, might seem an unlikely candidate for Islamist censure. Over the last few years, he had written two novels, *A Distance in a Man's Mind* and *The Bed*, which, he told me one morning when I called on him, were meant to be no more than harmless fantasies. But they, too, were judged blasphemous by a committee of clerics from al-Azhar, and he was sentenced, by a special state security court, to eight years in prison—an unprecedented term. He was free pending an appeal when we met in 1996, but because of the publicity surrounding his trial, this little-known writer—who had sold only eighty-nine copies of his books before they were banned—had been hounded from his job and threatened with death by Islamic militants.

By the summer of 1997, Hamad had been sent to prison for one year of hard labor. And Youssef Chahine was being threatened with legal action once again by the sheikhs of al-Azhar for his latest film, an allegorical treatment of the persecution of the twelfth-century Islamic scholar Ibn Rushd, known in the West as Averroës.

And although that September another court reversed yet another book banning by al-Azhar—of the most recent work of Sayed al-Qemni, a historian of Islam—the ruling was of only scant comfort to secularists. For, by then, the most serious accusations to be brought against an Egyptian intellectual since those involving Abu Zeid had been leveled against his mentor, Dr. Hasan Hanafi, a professor of philosophy at Cairo University who is widely respected in academic circles abroad. The Scholars Front Association of al-Azhar accused Hanafi, who is sixty-three, of having "denied Koranic verses on miracles" and of having "contradicted the clear teachings of the Koran." The clerics not only were demanding his expulsion from Cairo University but also were holding out the possibility of another trial based on the principle of *hisbah*—this in spite of a somewhat clumsy government attempt to restrict its use through two new laws passed shortly before the final verdict in Abu Zeid's trials—laws that were simply ignored by the Court of Cassation.

Egypt's courts are now being used even against their own. The retired judge Said al-Ashmawy, one of Egypt's most prominent Islamic scholars, has been threatened on several occasions with death for apostasy. His transgression? He opposed the further implementation of Shariah law and questioned in his writings whether Islam offered a firm foundation upon which to build a state. He now lives a secluded life in an apartment whose thick draperies are always drawn; for his protection, outside the door or downstairs in the lobby, connected by walkie-talkie, are three armed guards.

"The Grand Sheikh of al-Azhar"—Gad al-Haq Ali Gad al-Haq —"spent years, and millions and millions of petrodollars, trying to build an independent fiefdom—a theocratic authority, like the Vatican," Ashmawy told me one morning when I called on him. "Shortly before he died, a year or so ago, he issued a fatwa that all non-Muslims were infidels. This is absolutely preposterous, and was a call to war." Ashmawy shook his head sadly. "And the government did absolutely nothing to censure him."

"Daily fatwas, underwritten by Saudi Arabia, pour out of al-Azhar, charging that *we* are heretics. And this is *illegal*." His voice began to rise. "The fatwa committee is illegal itself: it is simply a domestic committee of al-Azhar. And where on earth, in all this bedlam, is our government? It has prevented me, and other enlightened Islamic scholars, from appearing on television to defend our views. The Egyptian government is blocking all my avenues from the front, while al-Azhar and the militants are hitting me from the back."

Whenever our conversation turned to Abu Zeid, Judge Ashmawy became visibly agitated. "The Court of Cassation simply refused to apply the law, and this is rebellion!" he declared. "The court is supposed to uphold the law, not ignore it!" He thought for a moment, and then he said, "But, for me, the most frightening thing about the Abu Zeid precedent is that the courts have no jurisdiction to judge whether a person is a believer or not—they can judge only concrete issues, not ideas. But in Abu Zeid's trial, it was ideas that were on trial. This is the first time that the courts have ruled someone an apostate in modern history. We're returning to the Inquisition. With this decision, we have gone backward five hundred years."

Dr. Abdel-Sabour Shahin, Nasr Abu Zeid's chief accuser, agreed to meet me one autumn morning in his office at Cairo University's College of Dar al-Uloum, a dusty complex of dun-colored buildings and untended lawns. The college is actually more akin to the University of al-Azhar, where many of its professors taught, than it is to Cairo University: it admits only Muslim students, and its curriculum concentrates on studies of Islam. Every male student I noticed on the college grounds wore a full Islamic beard, and every female student an Islamic veil.

I went in search of Shahin, and was stopped a number of times by not altogether friendly students who questioned me on why I was there. Shahin had fallen from official grace in mid-1996, partly as a result of the government's belated concern about the ominous precedents set by the Abu Zeid trials. In an exceptional display of independence from its "moderate" sheikhs, the government had barred him from preaching at the Amr Ibn al-As Mosque and had forced him to relinquish his political posts. It was immediately clear to me, however, that Shahin retained a faithful following.

I found him surrounded by a group of students who seemed enraptured by his every word. There was an erudition about him that I had not expected to find—an erudition that evaporated the moment he mentioned Abu Zeid. But it was his appearance that I found most startling: he looked far less like a sheikh than I had expected, and more closely resembled a diplomat. He was dressed in a smart blue blazer and gray flannels, and was impeccably groomed, exuding an air of sartorial elegance. His hand-painted silk tie was set off by a matching handkerchief.

His voice was full of energy, and a torrent of words spilled out: "French is really my native tongue," he said as he motioned to me to sit down. Once his students had left the room, he confided, "My students think I'm capable of anything. They even think I'm capable of interpreting their dreams. Of course, I know Koranic interpretation very well." He lowered his voice. "And whatever anyone tells you, I'm still a sheikh at many 'popular' mosques. The government forced me out of Amr Ibn al-As Mosque, but I continue to preach each Friday; I move about from mosque to mosque. And, of course, I'm always welcome by the sheikhs of al-Azhar.

"But the government has not only taken away my mosque, it has canceled my television program, banned me from the official press. The music has stopped; the party is over." He paused and shook his head. Then he leaned toward me across his desk. "But what is of far greater importance to me than the government is the fact that when I walk in the streets people come up to me and kiss my hand and head." He clearly relished the attention. He is not considered to be a modest man.

"Why did you bring the case against Nasr Abu Zeid?" I asked.

His face hardened and his smile disappeared as he leaned toward me even closer across his desk.

"Because he's a Marxist and an atheist!"

"But all he did was to interpret the Koran slightly differently than you . . ." I began.

"Slightly differently!" he interrupted, and began to shout. "Nasr Abu Zeid is not speaking of *ijtihad*"—the contemporary interpretation of Islam's holy texts—"in areas where *ijtihad* is possible. He is saying that the Koran is *human*, that it is not godly in inspiration, that it is not the revelation of God."

For a few moments, neither of us said anything more. I glanced out into the hallway and watched a group of students, all of them women veiled in the enveloping *niqab*, pass by. Just beyond them, loitering in a corner, were six or so security men, their handguns displayed prominently in the back pockets of their pants. Dr. Rifaat Said, a prominent leftist writer and politician who is also a member of parliament, had told me earlier that the security services had recently discovered, much to the government's dismay, that Islamic militants had been using Dar al-Uloum to see the degree to which they could infiltrate an institution of higher learning, and that nearly all the Arabic language professors were now members of the Muslim Brotherhood. Some of them operated above ground. Others did not.

"None of this need have happened," Shahin went on, returning to the subject of Abu Zeid's trials. His speech was once again measured, his voice highly controlled. "Nasr Abu Zeid rushed to judgment. Had he accepted my critique of his academic work, had he rectified his studies and corrected his mistakes, this matter never would have gone beyond Cairo University. But he went to the newspapers, and all the Marxist journalists stood by his side. They shouted against Islam, and insulted it; they shouted against me, and insulted me personally."

"Is that why you forced Abu Zeid to divorce his wife?" I asked.

"His marriage means nothing to me," Shahin replied. "It was never an object for us in this case. Let Abu Zeid and his wife live happily ever after, like a king and queen, in the Netherlands, as long as he never sets foot inside Cairo University again!"

He studied me from across his desk, looking slightly bemused.

"You don't seriously believe that I *care* about Abu Zeid's marriage," he said. "I want Nasr Abu Zeid *out* of Cairo University. How can an apostate teach the Koran?" He began to shout again. "How can a criminal teach the word of God? We were *forced* to adjudicate this case. There would have been no need to go to the courts if Nasr Abu Zeid had accepted my original promotion report."

"Abu Zeid is now being threatened with death," I said.

"Yes," Shahin replied without emotion. "The prescribed penalty for apostasy is execution."

He thought for a moment, and then went on: "But an apostate has to be given a chance to repent. Let Nasr Abu Zeid come before the Court of Cassation that condemned him and answer its indictment, point by point. Let him renounce his ideas. Let him publicly burn his books. Let him repent. And that is absolutely mandatory. *He must repent!* Otherwise"—he tilted his head and smiled—"let Nasr Abu Zeid stay in his Netherlands paradise, and may his body be saved from any assault. As for his soul, let that decision be by and for God."

When I arranged to meet with Abu Zeid on a November afternoon in Amsterdam, I wasn't at all certain what to expect. Would he be a shy, cautious scholar or a defiant defender of his views? When we met in the tearoom of my hotel, he proved to be both, gliding, seemingly without effort, in and out of both roles. Dressed in a dark blue suit, a white shirt, and a dark tie, he discarded a heavy down jacket, which seemed uncomfortable on his short, heavily rounded frame. He carried a brown attaché case, worn and battered with age, which somehow seemed to symbolize the wanderings of a man exiled far from home who had become a scapegoat for reasons that still eluded him. His most prominent features were penetrating dark brown eyes and an equally dark Islamic beard, flecked with gray, which he had grown since his trials. I told him what Abdel-Sabour Shahin's final words to me had been, and asked whether or not he would repent.

"Repent what?" he answered. "This is insane! I feel humiliated, because I always have to say 'I am a Muslim.' This is an insult to my beliefs and to my dignity. I have devoted my entire life to Islamic thought, and no one—I dare them—can find one word in any of my writings that shows me to be an apostate, an atheist. If the courts thought that it was within their jurisdiction to rule on my beliefs, then they should have read all twelve of my books; but all they read were the papers submitted by the lawyers of those who want to silence me."

I asked Abu Zeid about Ebtehal, who had declined to meet with me. "In a sense, it's even more difficult for her," he replied. "They treated her as though she were a teenager, an incomplete human being who had no rationality of her own. They treated her as though she were a toy to be taken out of my hands. They used Ebtehal to punish me. She's a very strong person, very independent, but she's hurt. She's also considerably younger than I am and is just beginning her career, and she's risking it all; she cannot renew her sabbatical from Cairo University because she's on sabbatical with me. I told her, 'You go back. Don't give it all up for me.' And she refused, most emphatically." He thought for a moment, and then he said, "After the verdict, when Ebtehal told the Egyptian press that she would never leave me, Shahin said that was only because it was not easy for her to find another husband. And then he said that she need not worry: he would find another husband for her, and even provide her with a dowry from money from the mosque. The son of a bitch!"

Abu Zeid fell silent. Then he turned to me and asked, "Why me? Why take me to court? It's only pen and paper. I'm not part of a political party; I'm not going to enforce my interpretations. Why are they so *afraid* of my ideas?"

A moderate Islamist lawyer in Cairo had told me earlier that the Egyptian courts had been used in Abu Zeid's trials to settle what was essentially a university dispute. So I asked Abu Zeid if he agreed with that view.

"Absolutely," he responded, and went on to say that the denial

of his professorship at Cairo University could only be explained in
the context of 1992 and 1993. "Terrorist attacks were extremely
severe at the time: tourists were being threatened; Farag Foda was
assassinated; so was the speaker of parliament; bombs were going
off every month. We know that the Minister of the Interior, [General
Abdel-Halim] Musa, held a series of secret negotiations in prison
with the leaders of the underground groups. He set up a committee of mediators, whose members included Sheikh al-Ghazali and
Abdel-Sabour Shahin. The terrorists laid down a number of conditions to stop their attacks, which were threatening the Egyptian
economy. And in that sense I was one of those sacrificed for following an enlightened brand of Islamic thought, for the government
found at least one of the answers in the university. Why should the
university promote a professor whom Shahin had already declared
a *kafir* [nonbeliever] in the mosque? The students might cause trouble, and more trouble was one thing that the government was not
in need of. So everyone thought: Abu Zeid can be promoted later
when things calm down. But you see, this was never enough for
Shahin. He wanted me censured; he wanted me expelled from Cairo
University. So they found the *hisbah* loophole in family law, which
was the only way to have a court look at the issue of apostasy. They
used it as a tool—and they used the courts—to demand my separation from Ebtehal."*

Abu Zeid paused for a moment, and his eyes studied the room.
Then he turned back to me and said, "Silencing is at the heart of
my case, and what happened to me is far more dangerous for Egypt
than many things that the underground militants have done, like
shooting at a busload of tourists and missing, then escaping into the
sugarcane fields. For my verdict was meant to control thought. Like
the assassination of Farag Foda, it's intellectual terrorism of the
worst sort."

---

*Following a two-year campaign by Abu Zeid's students and his fellow pro-
fessors, Cairo University, in May 1995, reversed its earlier decision based on Shahin's report, and awarded Abu Zeid his full professorship. Two weeks later—at
Shahin's behest—the Court of Appeals declared his writings to be blasphemous.

I asked him how he felt when he heard the verdicts of the courts. "There's got to be a word larger than shock," he replied. "It was actually far worse the first time, with the Court of Appeals' verdict [in June 1995]. Ebtehal and I were at home when the news came. We looked at each other, and didn't say a word. I had been working the entire day at my desk and hadn't shaved. I don't remember even moving, but obviously I did. I went to the bathroom, showered and shaved. Friends arrived; the government reinforced my security guard."

Within hours of the verdict, a fax arrived at foreign news organizations via Switzerland from al-Jihad, whose military wing had assassinated Anwar Sadat. "Al-Jihad's message was simple," Abu Zeid recounted. "It said that it was an Islamic duty that I be killed."

Abu Zeid stopped our conversation for a moment as we watched two young and bearded Islamist-looking men walk toward our table; they seemed to pause. Then they moved on to the table behind us and sat down.

"What, for you, was the most egregious thing about your trials?" I asked.

"Everything about them was egregious," he replied. "They were totally contrary to all of our laws, and there are so many things which, even now, I don't understand. There are many different circuits within Egyptian courts, and my case before the Court of Appeals was suddenly transferred to another circuit, which was a surprise, even to my lawyers. We could never find out who transferred it to this particular judge"—Farouq Abdel-Aleem—"whose reputation as an Islamic extremist is well known."

Shortly before he heard the case, Abdel-Aleem—who, after receiving a judicial appointment in Saudi Arabia, had abandoned his judicial robes and appears in court instead dressed in traditional Islamic attire, including a white crocheted prayer cap—had published an astonishing article for a judge, in which he decried Egyptian law because it was not in conformity with Shariah law.

Abu Zeid studied the young men behind us, and then he went on: "I genuinely believe that, in a larger sense, it wasn't me who was on trial. The Islamists raised this suit to put the political regime on the spot. When their case was won, they called on the government to kill me as a heretic. And if the government refuses, then they can say that the government is un-Islamic."

I asked Abu Zeid how he would compare what had happened to him with what had happened to others around the world—the case of Anglo-Indian writer Salman Rushdie being the best known —who had been sentenced to death by Islamic extremists. "Looking at it as an outsider, I would say that my case is more serious in its grounding than Salman Rushdie's is. He had a fatwa issued against him, but a fatwa can be refuted by another fatwa; it's merely a religious opinion. A court judgment, though, is a notice of truth. It's far more final." He paused, and then said, "And another big difference is that Rushdie did not have his country taken away from him."

The Abu Zeids have not divorced. In December 1996, an administrative court suspended the divorce proceedings permanently. Its ruling, however, did not overturn the Court of Cassation's verdict, and the apostasy conviction was left untouched. Abu Zeid's lawyers are now challenging the constitutionality of the verdict, and are also attempting to prove "gross judicial error" on the part of the court—a courageous and unprecedented move. The validity of the constitutional challenge, which some human rights lawyers consider to be pro forma at most, was nonetheless accepted in the last days of May 1998 by a lower court, and was referred for consideration to the Constitutional Court.

When I asked Abu Zeid how he felt now, on that afternoon in Amsterdam, he responded without hesitation. "Angry," he said. "I don't know if I'll ever feel the same toward my country again, and I'm very, very Egyptian. I lived in the United States for two years, and I longed every moment to go back. But now I've told Ebtehal that if I die somewhere else, please don't take my body back to Egypt for burial, even though this is a dream of every Egyptian: to be buried on his soil."

He looked out the window, where rain was pelting the sidewalk and the winter sky had become dark. After a few moments, he turned toward me and said, "When we first came here, it had been so long since I'd worked that I was terrified about my brain. I was afraid to start working. I thought there would be damage to my brain over all of this. Then one day I went to the library and I started reading a translation of the Koran. I read until after dark. After two days, I was energized. I was able to read. I felt reborn. For if something had affected my brain, I knew: Then they've got me! But"— he smiled—"I can still think; I can still work; I can still write. And as long as I have these powers, they'll never be able to get me— including you, Abdel-Sabour Shahin."

THE TURNING POINT

SAID AHMED GASSEM NOTICED THEM FIRST: SIX YOUNG MEN of dark complexion, medium height, and medium build, dressed in black shirts and trousers resembling police uniforms and carrying black vinyl bags. A few of them wore red headbands, curious for Egyptians, he mused to himself. But as a guard at the magnificent thirty-four-hundred-year-old Temple of Hatshepsut—just across the Nile from the Upper Egyptian city of Luxor in the Valley of the Kings, the site of hundreds of royal tombs, including that of the boy-king Tutankhamen—Gassem had seen all manner of dress. But red headbands, he would later say, were normally only worn by foreign tourists, most frequently the Japanese. It was 8:45 in the morning of November 17, 1997, and hundreds of tourists were already wandering through the massive temple and its three courtyards; others scampered out of buses in a nearby parking lot; still others bargained and bartered with merchants in a dozen or so curio shops.

The best time to see the temple of the only woman who reigned over Pharaonic Egypt, fourteen hundred years before Christ was born, has always been at dawn, when it is bathed in early light: a pink-violet hue sweeps across its colonnades and the sheer limestone cliffs into which it is built, and somehow magically seems to loft the temple even higher above the silent and empty desert that lies just beyond.

As the six men walked by him toward Hatshepsut's

tomb, Gassem held out his hand and asked for their tickets. He believes it is a miracle that it was not the last thing he ever did. The last of the six opened his black shirt-jacket and said, "Here's my ticket." He pulled out an AK-47 machine gun, and shot Gassem and three of his friends. Four of the young men then split away and raced up the temple's ramp. The gunman who shot Gassem stayed behind with one of his companions, near the spot where Gassem lay, at the entrance to the first platform of Hatshepsut's three-tiered masterpiece. They pulled cans of Coca-Cola out of their vinyl bags; one lit a cigarette, and they chatted with each other as they waited for the police counterattack, which never came.

Meanwhile the four other young men—perhaps assisted by still others already hidden among the temple's colonnades—opened fire with ruthless efficiency. It was a well-planned attack. They ran through the temple's first courtyard, then up its ramp in pairs. Methodically, twisting from side to side, they sprayed bullets from AK-47s into the milling tourists at point-blank range. Mothers were separated from their children; people began to scream; four Japanese couples on their honeymoons died in each other's arms as they attempted to find shelter behind the Birth Colonnade. The carnage was the bloodiest terrorist attack in Egypt's modern history, and the most shattering since Anwar Sadat was killed, sixteen years before, by his soldiers at a military parade.

Sixty-two people—all but four of them foreign tourists—died.

The gunmen met no resistance, for only two policemen (both of whom were shot) stood guard at Hatshepsut's sanctuary that day, despite the fact that, as one of Egypt's most popular tourist sites, its potential as an obvious target of the militant Islamist underground should have been recognized. For forty-five minutes, uninterrupted, the killers hunted their quarry down. They shot them where they lay or where they crouched. Many had sought safety in and around the Birth Colonnade, a small sheltered space at the back of a vast terrace, where ancient murals depict the procreation and birth of the Pharaonic queen, who ruled Egypt for some twenty years in the late fifteenth century B.C. But safety was an illusion. The colonnade offered no route of escape. Blood soaked its sandy floor, and bits of human flesh spattered the walls, including pieces of scalp with hair attached. A bloody handprint was silhouetted on a sandstone pillar. A gold earring lay beneath it in the dust.

After the gunmen finally moved on and silence fell over Hatshepsut's burial ground, the bodies of Swiss, Japanese, British, and German tourists, one by one, were carried out: men, women, and children; young and old; retired couples and a six-year-old.

It was the sheer savagery of the attack that no one was able to comprehend. Some of the victims had been mutilated with long knives; some of their throats were slit. Ahmed Youssef Aly, a Luxor-based journalist, said that during a visit to the Luxor morgue that night, he saw the body of a Swiss man whose nose had been cut off, and that of a Japanese woman missing an ear. He watched a doctor as he removed a bloody pamphlet stuffed inside the eviscerated corpse of an old, bespectacled Japanese man. The message on the pamphlet was simple, he said—"No to tourists in Egypt"—and it was signed "Omar Abdel-Rahman's Squadron of Havoc and Destruction—the Gama'a al-Islamiya, the Islamic Group."

When I revisited the temple, two months after the massacre, the surrounding desert, in a strange and haunting way, had begun to reclaim the site. Dust and sand danced in its nearly empty, sprawling courtyards, and the late afternoon January sun streamed through its limestone columns, some of which were still flecked with blood. The penumbra of the unbroken rhythm of Egyptian time was there. Its silence was broken only by the desert's wind. Statues of two of Egypt's wise men, each holding a key of life, stood guard, as they have done for thousands of years, at the entrance to Hatshepsut's burial chamber, her cocoon to her immortality.

There were probably as many security guards at the temple as there were tourists that afternoon, some two dozen or so in all. The tourists, nearly all of them Egyptians, had come on the first day of Eid, the festival that follows the holy month of Ramadan, one of the most sacred on the Islamic calendar. There was also a scattering of Russians who had come by bus from the Red Sea resort of Hurghada, but, they told me, they were not staying in Luxor after dark.

The six young gunmen, who had seemed so ordinary when they

arrived, had left the temple slowly, without panic, shopkeepers in the bazaar told me that afternoon. "They swaggered, and they laughed, and they shouted out: 'We killed all the tourists! *Allahu akbar!*' "

As the gunmen inserted new clips into their AK-47s and finished their work—shooting an occasional tourist in the bazaar or in the adjacent parking lot—Hagag al-Nahas was driving his tour bus back toward the main entrance of the temple complex. Around 8:30 that morning, fifteen minutes before the killing began, he had dropped off a group of thirty Swiss tourists, and he had returned to pick them up. All but eight had died in the massacre. But Nahas did not know that anything was wrong until the attackers, at gunpoint, waved down his bus and ordered him to "go to another place" where they could "shoot more people," Nahas later recalled. He drove around in circles, through mud-brick villages, around souvenir shops, and toward other ancient tombs, praying silently to himself that the police would come. He drove for perhaps thirty minutes in ever-widening circles, but to no avail. No police arrived at the temple complex until an hour after the massacre came to an end.

Nahas then remembered that there was a police checkpoint, which was normally manned by two or three guards, near the access road to the Valley of the Queens, a half mile or so from Hatshepsut's burial ground. He raced toward it down a desert road. When he reached the checkpoint, Nahas slammed on his brakes, and the gunmen rushed out of the bus, one of them clubbing him in the chest with his rifle butt. An exchange of gunfire with the police ensued. One of the gunmen was wounded (as were two of the three guards). Before his companions fled on foot into the nearby desert hills, one of them killed him with a bullet through his head.

The last time the five remaining gunmen dressed in black were seen alive, by scores of angry villagers from the nearby hamlet of Gourna who had followed Nahas's bus—some on motorbikes and scooters, others on donkeys and mules—they were running through the hills, indistinguishable forms that became smaller and smaller as they were engulfed by the desert's towering limestone walls.

What followed next remains one of the central mysteries of the massacre: there is still no credible information on how the gunmen were killed. Mubarak's government was quick to announce that they were shot by the police, following a protracted gun battle in the Valley of the Queens. But according to the results of a still secret security investigation, this seems impossible, for the handful of security officials who initially pursued them (according to the villagers, there was only one—the surviving police officer from the checkpoint where Nahas stopped his bus) did not possess weapons with a range sufficient to have hit the men in black, who died in a circle inside a deep cave.

According to Egyptian press reports, the five men were killed by the villagers who had chased them riding donkeys and mules. But the villagers told me that this was impossible: apart from staves and rocks and knives, *they* had no weapons at all.

The gunmen almost certainly died from self-inflicted wounds. But did they kill each other? Or did they commit ritualist suicide? Or, as the Gama'a later claimed, were more than six attackers involved? (The group said there were fifteen.) And, if so, did an unknown assailant from the Islamist underground kill the five young men, who had arrived at Hatshepsut's burial ground in a blue Peugeot taxi, drank American Coca-Cola, and smoked American cigarettes?

There were more questions than answers that late January afternoon as I wandered around the temple bazaar and sat with a group of villagers from Gourna in a tiny tea shop. Two of the bazaar shopkeepers, outside whose tiny stalls the massacre began, swore to me that the assailants who shot the policemen a few feet from their shops were dressed in faded blue denim jackets and jeans, not in black. When the massacre came to an end, the two young men in denim were not seen again.

The villagers and the shopkeepers also claimed that the gunmen in black all had walkie-talkies, into which at least two of them spoke as they sauntered through the bazaar on their way to the parking lot where they hijacked Nahas's bus.

"But who were they? Why did they do it?" I asked.

After much conversation, and considerable debate, one of the village elders turned to me and said that during the temple carnage, from time to time, commands were shouted out in Arabic, by someone with a distinctive Cairo accent. Yet five of the six gunmen in black (the sixth had not been identified as of the fall of 1998) were all from villages and towns in Upper Egypt, not far from Luxor and the Valley of the Kings, the burial ground of the Pharaohs of the last glorious period of Egyptian history.

Until very recently, Hosni Mubarak was convinced that his regime was breaking the back of its six-year Islamist insurgency. In a sense, perhaps it is.

All of the underground's original leaders are now in prison, in exile, or dead. Chains of command have been broken, and highly disciplined organizations—like Gama'a and al-Jihad—have yielded to far more loosely knit underground groups of cells. The Gama'a al-Islamiya had clearly been driven back to the Upper Egyptian villages and towns where the movement took root: a region of desperate poverty; blood feuds and vendettas; harsh desert and mountains; and closed societies. It is a region not unlike Imbaba, the Cairo slum, from which successive Egyptian governments have withdrawn, and where militant Islamists have retreated even further underground.

It is increasingly difficult to know who they are, for so much of the movement now wears a mask. The conspicuously ordinary-looking young men in black who killed at Hatshepsut's temple, seemingly without remorse, and the men who gave them orders— the same men who had organized the attempted assassination of Mubarak in Addis Ababa—were not so unlike the only female Pharaoh to rule over ancient Egypt, at whose burial ground they had sent their message to the world. Hatshepsut had concealed herself behind a false beard so that she could reign. And the majority of the gunmen, as their mentors in Afghanistan had been a generation before, were high achievers and popular students at the University of Asyut's most demanding and most prestigious faculties.

Yet theirs was a terror on a truly Algerian scale—in Algeria, more than seventy thousand people have died, many of them slaughtered, in that country's increasingly vengeful war between its security forces and its various branches of militant Islam. That war began, like Egypt's, in 1992, after Algeria's military regime canceled elections when it became clear that the Islamists would almost certainly win. Egypt is not Algeria. But it appeared to be catching up.

Mubarak's government was quick to argue that the barbarity of the Luxor attack was evidence of the militant Islamists' desperation and their lack of strength. The fallacy in this argument is that Egypt's Islamist militancy has always come in waves, and the decline of one generation has always produced the beginning of a new—and more violent—one.

The children of the jihad who stayed behind when that war came to an end, men like the bespectacled Egyptian engineer Mustafa Hamza; the soft-spoken accountant Rifai Taha; al-Jihad's leader, the medical doctor Ayman al-Zawahiri—all of whom were defendants on the periphery of the Sadat assassination trials—and Osama bin Laden, the Saudi multimillionaire who is one of their primary financiers, made it abundantly clear in the Valley of the Kings that they now had a far more dangerous agenda than previously seen.

Yet, for me, one of the most frightening aspects of the Luxor massacre is that the commander of the cell that carried it out, Medhat Abdel-Rahman, a thirty-two-year-old high-school graduate and a veteran of the jihad, had no difficulty in recruiting young men from Upper Egypt's most prestigious schools, who were considerably better educated and from more prominent families than he was.

In Upper Egypt's villages and towns, often tiny, obscure places hugging the banks of the Nile, the dynamics of the terror and counterterror in which Mubarak's security forces and the militant Islamist underground are engaged had acquired a momentum of its own. In one respect, it is less and less ideological and political, more and more a blood feud. And, in the process, traditional leadership is being increasingly defied and traditional loyalties are becoming more and more blurred.

As I watched Hosni Mubarak in Luxor the day after the massacre, his rage barely concealed, it occurred to me that he genuinely didn't seem to know what his security forces were doing in Upper Egypt, even though their atrocities were being committed in his name. Sheikh Omar Abdel-Rahman, in solitary confinement in a U.S. prison, seemed equally unaware of how far the Gama'a, which he had largely spawned, had spiraled dangerously beyond his control. Both the soldier and the preacher, who had left their own Nile Delta villages and followed in each other's footsteps for so many years, now appeared equally isolated, and equally marginalized, from the battle that their armies were fighting in their names.

Four months before the Luxor massacre, shouting across a Cairo courtroom from his security cage, an Islamist defendant made an announcement as unprecedented as it was startling: the jailed leaders of Egypt's militant Islamist groups had declared a unilateral and unconditional cease-fire. Mubarak's regime ignored the message, delivered in early July.

The leaders, six of the founding members of Gama'a (joined later by two others from al-Jihad), are all serving life terms for their roles in the assassination of Sadat. Among them was the former military intelligence officer Colonel Abbud al-Zumur, the military leader of al-Jihad. Within weeks, the cease-fire initiative was endorsed by Sheikh Omar. Two of the three arms of the other holy trinity had supported the call. The leaders had grown weary of their military fight against the state, which, after government successes over the previous two years, they knew they could never win. They had been flushed out of Cairo. Some twenty thousand Islamists were in jail. The casualty balance had shifted in favor of the security forces over the militants, two to one. Their impressive social structures of hospitals, orphanages, and schools were being dismantled by the regime, and their mosques were being closed. Their call for a cease-fire was, in the words of the London-based, Arabic-language newspaper *al-Quds al-Arabi*, "one of the most important developments on the Arab scene" in recent years. Nevertheless, the six exiled members of Gama'a's Executive Council repudiated it. The movement, whose leaders are scattered over three continents, was now clearly split.

In any case, there was no positive government response: no talks;

no releases of prisoners being held without charge whom the courts had ordered released; no improvements in prison conditions; no speeding up of the judicial process or the referral of Islamists to civilian, rather than military, courts. Instead, the government derided the cease-fire call, and its raids continued across Upper Egypt's villages and towns, as did its arrests. Increasing numbers of Islamists, in "encounters" with Mubarak's security forces, were being shot dead.

The man most intimately involved in brokering the cease-fire call is a large, lumbering Islamist lawyer, Montasir al-Zayyat. I had known Montasir since 1993, when I first began writing about Sheikh Omar, whom he represents in Cairo. And when he himself was not in prison, I had spent many long nights in his four-room suite of offices on the fifth floor of a dilapidated building in downtown Cairo. By the time I met him, he was already the unofficial spokesman of Gama'a, which he had joined as a law student at Cairo University in the 1970s when it was formed. Over the years, perhaps more than anyone else, Montasir became my eyes and ears into the closed world of the militant Islamist underground.

Consequently, before coming to Upper Egypt, I sought him out. Only a few weeks earlier, he had "retired" from Gama'a, disheartened by his failure to effect the cease-fire and appalled by the Luxor massacre. In the process, he had relinquished his role as a key defense attorney representing accused militants before the military courts.

As I sat in his now empty office, waiting for him to arrive, my mind wandered back to how different the office had been only a few months before, when, on any given evening, dozens of veiled women would gather in its waiting rooms, spilling out into its hall, seeking information on husbands, fathers, and sons. They were the wives, daughters, and mothers of Egypt's "disappeared ones."

I remember one evening in particular, a year or so ago, when the women arrived, four of them together on that night. They ranged in age from thirty to sixty, perhaps, and all of them were concealed behind flowing black abayas, their faces framed by waist-length black *niqab* veils. A thin, reedy man was with them, an older man, with a wizened face and white stubble on his chin. As they joined me in the waiting room, he carefully inserted a hearing aid.

I hadn't gone in search of the women; I had simply stumbled onto their stories that night.

They were all from Imbaba, they were all illiterate, and they hadn't known each other before, until they met in a local police station looking for their sons. Saad had been eighteen; Hussein, twenty-three; and Ahmed, thirty-five, when the State Security Investigation (SSI) officers came and took their sons away.

"They were collecting all the young people in the neighborhood," Saad's mother began. "They came, as they always did, in the evening, just after dark. My son tried to hide, and he succeeded for over a week, but they kept coming back. Finally, when they couldn't find him, they took me, his father, and his two young brothers, who were ten and twelve, instead. They took us to a police station in Imbaba, and they beat the young boys severely, continuously, for nine days: they poured boiling water on them and gave them electric shocks. My sons kept telling them that they didn't know where Saad was. I sat in the next room, and I heard their screams, but what could I do? Then they brought me into the room on the fourth day, and they tied my elder son to a chair, and connected an electric wire to his ankle. They gave him electric shocks and whipped him simultaneously until he fell unconscious." She looked around the office, and then she said, "He was only twelve."

On the evening of the ninth day, Saad, a medical student, turned himself in. He was never charged with any crime, nor was he ever brought to trial. More than a year had passed, and his mother still didn't know why he was arrested, or where he was.

We sat in silence for a few minutes, and then the old man, who was Saad's father, turned to me and said, "Logically, we should have been left alone when Saad turned himself in, but the SSI continued to come at night from time to time. They wanted to see who was visiting us; they wouldn't leave us alone. Sometimes they came at one o'clock in the morning, or three o'clock, or four, pounding on the door. One night when they came, they took away the door!"

"Why?" I asked.

"They do it all the time," he replied. "They've taken away many doors. It's a way of pressuring the landlord, to pressure us, to prevent our boys from going to the mosque."

He began rocking back and forth in his chair, a thin, tiny man, dressed in a brown galabiya, with a scarf around his neck, seemingly overwhelmed by the four considerably larger women dressed in black who surrounded him.

After a few minutes, he went on: "I remember one night in particular, when they broke into the apartment from the balcony, with their guns drawn. It was like seeing men fall into my apartment, with machine guns, from the sky."

Other women came and went from the office as we continued to talk. Most of their faces were lined, and they were all dressed in black. They had been raised to marry and bring up their own families; it was around their families that their lives revolved. And then, in a moment, everything came to an end. An estimated seven to eight thousand Egyptian mothers had lost their sons.

A large woman sitting next to me on a rickety couch, whose name was Um Mohammed, told me that she had divorced her husband when she discovered that he was a police informant. The other women fell silent as she began to talk.

The screams of her twenty-eight-year-old daughter, Amal Farouq, had kept her awake every night for months, she said. The nightmare was always the same since Amal's arrest by the SSI, which had held her hostage in a damp, dark room as they attempted to collect evidence against her husband, Ahmed, Um Mohammed's favorite son-in-law. The government's new strategy of targeting women in its increasingly ugly war, even some of its officials admit, is an exceedingly unpleasant one, but it is meant to break the spirit of male militants.

Amal was arrested only hours after Ahmed (who is now serving a twenty-five-year prison term for his alleged role in an assassination attempt against the Minister of Information) was captured by the police. The SSI wanted Amal to tell them about Ahmed's friends and to denounce him on government-controlled television as a terrorist.

Amal refused. Then slowly, over a period of days, the beatings began, and became progressively worse.

"They tore off her veil and blindfolded her," Um Mohammed said. "Then they stripped her down to her underwear and hung her from a hook in the ceiling by her hands. They taunted her; whipped her with cable wire; kicked her in the stomach; and, with razors, they sliced open her back. There were at least seven men in the room, Amal said, and some of them chanted, as they beat her, how much they would enjoy raping her."

From the next room, Amal heard Ahmed screaming in pain. "You bastards! I don't know anything. Leave her alone!"

Amal was held, incommunicado, for ten days.

On the morning of the last day, an officer named Mahmoud Hosny took her into a tiny room and stripped her naked. As she lay shivering on the floor, attempting to conceal herself, he promised her her freedom and a large sum of money if she signed a confession implicating Ahmed as a terrorist. When Amal refused, Hosny called another man into the room and told him, "The bitch is all yours. Rape her!"

When the man began to undress, Amal started to scream: "All right, I'll sign whatever you want." That evening, she was released without being charged.

Weeks later, Amal applied for permission to attend Ahmed's trial, in a military court, and to testify that her "confession" against her husband had been made under torture. For "security reasons," the government refused.

Montasir al-Zayyat subsequently filed a complaint on Amal's behalf, with the Ministry of the Interior, against Mahmoud Hosny and the other men involved. The authorities responded by taking Amal into custody again.

A secretary interrupted my thoughts about the women in black to tell me that Montasir had arrived. He seemed to walk with a heavier step than he had the last time we met, and his jet-black beard was flecked with gray. His eyes were red and puffy; disillusionment wrapped itself around his large frame. He greeted me warmly, although he did not shake my hand (he never did). It was considered to be Islamically incorrect. Yet I always found it curious, and I still do, that neither Montasir nor, for that matter, anyone I have ever met from Gama'a asked me to remove my shoes in their presence or to veil, which the more mainstream and moderate leaders of the Muslim Brotherhood always did.

As we settled into Montasir's office, I asked him why, at the age of forty-six, he had retired.

"I'm tired," he replied simply. "I'm frustrated with all of them: with my brothers in the leadership of Gama'a abroad; with the government; with the institutions of civil society. The Gama'a leadership in Egypt—in prisons all over this country—has, for some time, been discussing the need for a new strategy: a strategy of nonviolence, of pursuing political ends by peaceful means, of becoming part of the national debate. Violence has not achieved its goals for the past sixteen years, and the expatriate leaders have got to understand how firmly in control the state is. But they have rejected two cease-fire offers out of hand. As for the government, we had been led to believe that once the cease-fire was declared, it would take certain initiatives; but it did nothing, and simply belittled it. And the civil institutions: what did they do? The syndicates? The unions? The human rights organizations? The political parties, even the Muslim Brotherhood? Not one of them exerted any influence in an effort to stop the violence which is tearing this country apart. Only *al-Ahram* held a seminar, in which I was a participant, to debate the cease-fire call, but, to date, it has published nothing at all."

He stopped for a moment and stroked his beard. "Luxor was the last straw. Is it Islam to kill children and women and slit open their stomachs? I've always warned against the Algerianization of the struggle in Egypt. I've always feared its consequences, and I'm afraid it could recur. There is an increasing sense of hatred among those on the run, both those inside the country and the leaders abroad who are responsible for military operations now. They see their situation as one of limited choice: either they're captured and brought to trial or they're killed by the police. This, coupled with torture inside prison . . ." He said nothing more.

Montasir himself had been severely tortured prior to the Sadat assassination trials, in which he was one of the three hundred accused of organizing al-Jihad and of conspiring to overthrow the government. (He was acquitted of the charges.) It was in prison that Montasir first met Sheikh Omar. Then a young lawyer, he was on the verge of a nervous breakdown, he told me afterward, having been tortured for twelve hours without stop. Sheikh Omar found him battered in the corner of their cell. Kneeling down, the sheikh whispered, "Rely on God; don't be defeated." It was a line spoken by Muhammad in the Koran.

"They don't seem to understand the cult of pain they're creating," Montasir said to me now.

I asked him about the women, women like Amal Farouq, and four others who had recently stood trial before a military court, the first time in the history of Egypt that women had been tried for "terrorist activities" relating to political Islam. (Three of the four, including a grandmother, were sentenced to prison for up to fifteen years, convicted of smuggling weapons under their abayas; harboring terrorists; and carrying messages between leaders inside prison and their followers outside.) It was at their trial that the cease-fire call was made.

"It will backfire," Montasir replied. "The Islamist groups have a special sensitivity when it comes to women. The humiliation of a mother, a sister, or a wife is, for them, a red line that should not be crossed."

Before meeting Montasir, I had called on Dr. Sa'ad el-Din Ibrahim, my former professor of sociology at AUC, who had been studying the Islamist movement for more than twenty years, and I asked him what, in his view, had prompted the Luxor massacre. Desperation? Escalation? The government's derisive dismissal of the cease-fire call?

"All of the above," he had replied, "plus the fractionalization within the Gama'a itself: the split between the moderates—the elders of the movement, so to speak, now in their late thirties and forties in prison here—and the hard-liners, the leaders abroad and their young followers in the underground. The hard-liners, who condemned the cease-fire call and vowed to fight to the finish, seem to have concluded that the only way to prevent a dialogue and the cessation of hostilities between the Gama'a and the regime was to commit such a dramatic act that the government would be so outraged it would reject any peace overtures. Basically the hard-liners were saying three things: we still exist; we reject the cease-fire call; and this is a regime which doesn't understand the language of dialogue."

I now asked Montasir if he agreed with this view.

"I'm not totally pessimistic that the cease-fire initiative is dead," he replied, and then he told me that even though it had been rejected by Gama'a's de facto leadership in Afghanistan, he had, since Luxor, been in touch with Rifai Taha, the soft-spoken accountant who is the emir, or prince, of Gama'a's external leadership.

"He promised me that he would issue a call to stop all armed actions, without conditions, for six months, in order to give us a chance to continue our informal consultations with the government."

I was startled. "What consultations?" I asked.

For the only time during our conversation, Montasir responded, "No comment."

(I learned later, however, that the "consultations"—as they are judiciously called, as opposed to official talks—had been ongoing for a number of months and, as a consequence, Montasir and Salah Hashim, an engineer and one of the founders of Gama'a, not only had been permitted unlimited prison visits to negotiate with the group's internal leadership but had been given exit visas to travel abroad and had met in London and the Netherlands with the external leaders, including Taha.)

Montasir had last spoken to Taha in January; a month had passed, and the Afghan-based leaders had issued no cease-fire call. But he remained hopeful that Taha, his former roommate, would ultimately respond. "The door is still open," Montasir said. "I think there's still hope."

Some of the Gama'a leaders in Europe had already begun to challenge Taha's obdurateness and that of his military chief, Mustafa Hamza, neither of whom had been in Egypt for more than ten years. Once they left to fight in Afghanistan, they never came back.

Before leaving, I asked Montasir how he would explain a statement, issued in Taha's and Hamza's names, in which they claimed that the Luxor massacre had begun as an attempt to take hostages to barter for the release of Sheikh Omar and of other imprisoned leaders of Gama'a. The methodical nature of the killings suggested precisely the opposite.

He tilted his face as he rested his chin on his hand, reflecting for a moment. Then he said, "My understanding is that the original orders were to stage an operation, to take hostages, during the performance of [Verdi's opera] *Aida* the previous month." (At a gala moonlight performance, hosted by Mubarak at Hatshepsut's burial ground, hundreds of VIPs were in attendance, guarded by three thousand security men.)

"But," Montasir continued, "the operation failed because of the tight security. After that, I just don't know. My deduction is that they improvised and killed the tourists instead." He paused, as if he were considering his next words carefully, and then he said, "Those who carried out the Luxor attack did it as vengeance, as a vendetta for the death of their teacher, the engineer Samir Abdel-Mati, who is believed to have died under torture. He was arrested in 1996, and the last time he was seen alive, he was being tortured in a police station in Luxor by the SSI. His family came to me and they asked me to find him, and I inquired at the Ministry of the Interior, and I was told that he had been released. But he was never seen again. So we can only assume that he is dead."

"Who was he?" I asked.

"An engineer by training; a teacher of the Koran. A soldier in the Armed Forces, in air defense, based at Luxor Airport"—the same airport into which a young Hosni Mubarak had flown his planes to prevent their destruction during the June 1967 Arab-Israeli war.

As I left Montasir and climbed down the rickety stairs of his office building and walked out onto the street, it struck me that the engineer Samir Abdel-Mati was both a soldier and a priest.

Mahmud Ahmed Abdel-Karim was a bright young man: twenty-three years old; a medical student at the University of Asyut; a high achiever; and an *ibn balad*, or son of the soil, from Upper Egypt's governorate of Qena—the last "dangerous" area along the five-hundred-mile road that connects Cairo and Luxor and is the battle-ground of the armies of Hosni Mubarak and Sheikh Omar Abdel-Rahman. What was perhaps most frightening about Abdel-Karim was that he was so *ordinary*, according to his classmates and his friends. He had no known political interests; he went to the mosque and had a beard, but he was never suspected of any involve-ment in the militant Islamist underground. In fact, he was never even interrogated by the police, as thousands of other bearded young men from Asyut and Qena had been over the years. The only thing that seemed to matter to him was that, on the basis of merit and intellect, he had made it into the University of Asyut and left Qena behind. As with so many other students from tiny, obscure places of similar social background, Abdel-Karim's sense of entitlement was deep.

The university he had entered three years earlier is Upper Egypt's oldest and largest, and its most prestigious. Hidden behind towering stucco walls in the dreary cement-making and food-processing city of Asyut, the university had also been, for the past twenty years, a nerve center of the militant Islamist groups. When I revisited it in early 1998, I discovered that it still is.

As I wandered around its well-endowed campus, across lawns green and lush, my mind traveled back to my own student days, when it had been transformed by Anwar Sadat in his campaign to undermine the left. For it was here at the University of Asyut—two hundred miles south of Cairo on the west bank of the Nile—that today's militant Islamist movement was born. Sheikh Omar had been a professor here in the 1970s, when the Gama'a al-Islamiya was formed. Rifai Taha, Mustafa Hamza, and Mohammed al-Islam-bouli, to name a few, had all been pupils of the sheikh's, early student leaders of the Gama'a, and—not unlike Mahmud Abdel-Karim—high achievers in the university's most demanding faculties. It was from the University of Asyut, more than any other place, that Gama'a's political inheritance sprang.

I had come here in an attempt to find out about Mahmud Abdel-Karim and two of his high-school friends—Essmat Erian, a twenty-four-year-old student of veterinary science, and Saed Mohammed Shawaki, twenty-three, who took courses at the university as a student of agriculture at a nearby institute. On the morning of November 17, 1997, they had donned black shirts and trousers and stuffed their vinyl bags with knives and ammunition and machine-gun clips. Then they drove along the Nile, for thirty minutes or so, from their hometown of Qift—midway between the provincial capital of Qena and Luxor—to Hatshepsut's burial ground. Their reasons for so doing died with them inside a desert cave.

Interviews with their friends and associates yielded mostly disbelief.

When I had asked Sa'ad el-Din Ibrahim what he thought: Why was it always Upper Egypt? Why the University of Asyut? He answered without hesitation, "Pain. It's an open wound." He thought for a moment, and then he said that what mystified him the most was that Abdel-Karim and his friends did not fit the profile of a typical militant, driven by economic desperation or by a sense of being marginalized. They were not part of the floating population of university graduates who were unemployed or underemployed; who had thought that they had made it by entering the most prestigious schools, then discovered, when they completed their studies, that they had not. Abdel-Karim and the other young men in black were still moving forward, not yet rejected by society.

"It makes me wonder," a Western diplomat in Cairo had said to me. "What is the dynamic of the Gama'a? We just don't know. How does it recruit? What is its appeal? What the Luxor massacre suggests to me is that even people who were not known to be part of a militant group may be sufficiently impassioned to risk their lives in order to carry out a dramatic statement. And that is frightening."

I thought of what the diplomat and Sa'ad el-Din had said as I left Asyut in a battered local taxi for what is normally a four-hour drive through Upper Egypt to Luxor and the Valley of the Kings. I had hoped to stop along the way in the villages and towns, but it was not to be. I was permitted by the police to travel the road only if I agreed to be accompanied by twelve armed guards, who had somewhat haphazardly piled themselves into two security cars, one in front of me, one behind. I was furious. But from the moment I arrived from Cairo at Asyut's airport, they had surrounded me. Someone had obviously alerted them that I was on the plane. I never discovered who.

As we skirted the desert, traveling down the west bank of the Nile, I followed our route on a map. Nearly every town and village we drove through—or avoided, according to the demands of my guards—had been the site of a massacre, or a shoot-out, or an atrocity over recent years, in the ongoing battle that neither the security forces nor the militant Islamist underground deserves to win.

Christian Copts had been massacred inside churches by Islamic militants; militants had been massacred by the security forces inside mosques. Women not unlike Amal Farouq had been arrested and tortured in an effort to force their husbands to turn themselves in. Hundreds, perhaps a thousand, people had disappeared. Hostage-taking, in which fifty people are arrested in order to find one, had become the norm. Entire villages had been cordoned off for days or weeks at a time. Sugarcane fields had been put to the torch to prevent militants on the run from finding a place to hide.

Only a few months earlier, the government had abolished rent controls on farmland, which had been the centerpiece of Nasser's sweeping land reforms. It also permitted landlords to revoke tenancies, which previously could be held in perpetuity and passed on through inheritance from father to son. A peasant uprising had been predicted, but it had not happened—yet. As I glanced out the window of my taxi, it was easy to see why land remains at the heart of Egypt's politics and its economy: it is wealth, pride, reputation, everything. And by the time the new law is fully put in place, one acre in five of the country's farms and fields under cultivation is expected to be affected. The livelihoods of nearly a million tenant farmers—who along with their families account for nearly 10 percent of the country's population—will be put at risk.

Violent protests had already broken out across Upper Egypt, as well as in the north: state-run farm cooperatives had been set to the torch; roads had been blockaded; and train traffic had been halted as farmers set fires on the tracks. By the end of 1997, over two dozen

farmers had been killed—some in protests, others in police custody—and over one thousand arrested when they refused to relinquish their land. According to Abdel-Mawla Ismail of the Land
Center for Human Rights, a Cairo-based pro-tenant organization,
the ultimate beneficiary of the controversial legislation could be the
Islamic militants, for when a rural Egyptian is cast from his land
and unable to find a job, he might easily join the ranks of the government's most violent foes. Of equal significance is the fact that in
their shared opposition to the new law, the Marxists and the Nasserites have bonded with the Islamists once more.

We continued along the highway, the farmland and desert yield-
ing to mud-walled villages and towns, then to urban sprawl: a grid
of sandpaper-hued apartment blocks, Stalinesque in design. Garbage
littered the rutted streets, and the January mud absorbed or was
overwhelmed by billowing clouds of dust. Apart from the electrical
wires and poles on either side of the road, there were few signs that
the area had been touched by the twentieth century.

The *saidis*, or southerners, the people of Upper Egypt who in-
habit that thin green ribbon of land hugging the Nile, stretching
from Cairo south to Aswan, are Egypt's poorest, its least educated,
and its most uncontrolled. Tough and hardheaded, they live according to well-established traditions of vendettas, lawlessness, and
blood feuds. Like Imbaba, the Cairo slum, Upper Egypt—where
nearly a third of the country's population lives—is an area that successive governments have simply ignored. It offers few jobs and
fewer services, and moves to the rhythms of life that were established
five thousand years ago during Pharaonic times.

I watched buffalo, lumbering and black, raise the Nile's price-
less water by turning a crude wooden lift, as they have done for
thousands of years. Blindfolded, they moved in endless circles, as
though in a trance. A hunched old man pulled a hand plow across
a parched field. An arms dealer roared by him—at least, my driver
said he was an arms dealer—in an air-conditioned Mercedes-Benz.
Students plastered anti-American slogans and pictures of Saddam
Hussein on baked-mud walls. Women returned from the fields carrying bundles of sticks, or produce, or urns of water on their heads.

By the time we reached the governorate of Qena, where Mahmud Abdel-Karim and his friends were born, I was not at all surprised, having revisited, or at least sped through, Upper Egypt's villages and towns, that they continue to provide fertile ground for the recruitment of ardent young men into the militant Islamist underground.

We stopped, for the ninth or tenth time on our trip, in Qena, as my guards argued among themselves about who would accompany me on the remainder of my journey south. And as I tired of sitting in the dreary parking lot of the even more dreary police station in the middle of town, I left my taxi and wandered through an open-air bazaar just across the road. Pony-drawn carts and camels clogged its parking lot. The faces of the merchants and the shoppers were hardened and wizened by the sun, and I wondered who belonged to Gama'a. In one fashion or another, probably all of them did.

For Qena, by all accounts, is the most forgotten governorate in Egypt's south—a brooding and melancholy place, in the midst of the desert, where families live in extended units, frequently ringed by rifle sights; where landlords are often brutal and peasants are serfs; where women are in purdah, and men work the fields, transporting to nearby markets their wheat, potatoes, and sugarcane on the backs of camels and mules.

I was not the first foreign traveler to have passed through the town. Flaubert had come in the 1850s to see a nearby temple, but had, instead, sought out a brothel. But he had abstained, he later wrote, in order to "preserve the sweet sadness of the scene and engrave it deeply on my memory." Florence Nightingale had also come, and she did visit the temple, but she later wrote that "Dendera is a vulgar, upstart temple, covered with acres of bas-reliefs which one has no desire to examine." I wondered what Qena's villagers of that century thought as they peered at the foreigners from behind their protective mud walls.

Yet it was something else that Miss Nightingale wrote, after she'd trekked through the temple's grounds, that fascinated me the most. For it was as appropriate then as it is now: "The power of the Egyptian priesthood was evidently given them by the spirit of the people, to whom religion was everything." It was not far from Dendera's temple, in one of Qena's storefront mosques, that Abdel-Karim and his friends met their teacher, Samir Abdel-Mati, the soldier-priest.

With my security escort again intact, we commenced speeding along the desert road, and I tried to recall all of the random musings I had heard about the three gunmen in black. They, of course, had shared a teacher of the Koran, and had been friends since their high-school days. They all came from lower-middle-class families. In 1993, following a perfunctory military trial, one of their classmates had been hanged. Their village, as a result of his arrest, had been placed under curfew for several months, and scores of its residents —old men, women, and children—had been arrested, in what is euphemistically called "collective punishment."

Bestawi Abdel-Meguid, an automatic rifle in his hand, had been caught at the scene of a 1992 ambush in Qena of a German tour bus. But no one from Qift was willing to say, when the security investigators arrived, whether or not he had been a friend of the three young gunmen dressed in black. Five of the German tourists had been slightly wounded, and panic spread. Eight months later, in July 1993, Abdel-Meguid, then eighteen, was one of seven young men—nearly all of them from Qena—whom the hangman strung up one at a time, starting just after dawn. It was the largest mass execution in Egyptian memory. When Lieutenant Khaled al-Islambouli assassinated Anwar Sadat at a military parade, raising fears of an Iranian-style revolution on the Nile, only five defendants were executed. They had murdered a head of state. Abdel-Meguid and his six friends hadn't actually killed anyone.

This was Qena, where Abdel-Karim and his friends, and thousands of others like them across the governorate, spent their formative years.

It is impossible to know what else they may have seen or done, for Qena is not a place that welcomes outsiders or foreigners. It has a reputation for a strict code of honor, which requires that revenge be exacted for a wrong. It also has the feel of a small, sparse place, with three or four small, sad parks, where there is nowhere to hide.

And since 1993, on and off for five years, Qena—like much of Up-per Egypt—along with its surrounding mud-walled villages and towns, has been a place under siege. Troops lumber down its narrow dirt roads in U.S.-supplied armored personnel carriers; its few public buildings are guarded by tin-hatted police-soldiers, who are heavily armed and protected from the world of Qena behind piles of sand-bags.

"What makes Qena different," Virginia Sherry of Human Rights Watch remarked, "is that the atmosphere of repression is so thick you can cut it with a knife. Entire villages have been cordoned off in security sweeps; rows of homes, really little more than mud huts, have been razed. Sugarcane fields have been burned, acres and acres of them. Farmers, of course, have been given no compensation; live-lihoods have been destroyed." She thought for a moment, and then she said, "The closest comparison that comes to mind is the scorched-earth policy of Vietnam."

I thought of what she said as we left the Qena border behind and continued down the desert road toward the Valley of the Kings and Luxor. Had Abdel-Karim and his friends been recruited at the University of Asyut by their cell leader, Medhat Abdel-Rahman, who had recently returned from Afghanistan? Or, rather, did the quiet young men from Qift already belong to an unknown Islamist splin-ter group that they had joined, during their high-school days, some-where in the barren hills near the Valley of the Kings?

The lights of Luxor twinkled on the horizon, and my security escort turned around and left. I looked out the window of the taxi, at the darkened desert on either side of the car, and I realized that no one will probably ever know.

But it also struck me, with equal certainty, that there were thousands of others, in Upper Egypt's mud-walled villages and towns, tiny places lining the banks of the Nile, who one day may vent their anger on a scale as vicious as that of the Luxor massacre.

I wondered if Abdel-Karim and the five other young men in black, who had arrived at Hatshepsut's burial ground in a blue Peu-geot taxi, with Coca-Cola in their bags, had known Abdel-Harith Madani, the young Cairo lawyer who had been tortured to death by the SSI. I imagine that they probably did, for his village of al-Mataana was not far from Qift. Abdel-Harith had been the first to leave al-Mataana for faraway Cairo, where he obtained a law degree. Many young men from the area had looked up to him as an example to emulate. And when his body was returned to al-Mataana by the SSI and buried in an unmarked grave, many were convinced that their options were even more limited than they thought they had been.

Those who directed and carried out the Luxor massacre achieved their short-term goals: Egypt's economy is damaged; Mubarak's government is damaged. Tourism was over for the season, and perhaps for many seasons to come. Luxor and the Valley of the Kings were empty now.

Nearly all of the city's 275 cruise boats had been tied up for months. They littered the banks of the Nile as far as the eye could see; their hulls painted yellow, blue, and white, they looked like seashells forgotten along a deserted beach. Five-star hotels were operating at occupancy rates of only 5 to 10 percent. Directly, or indirectly, over half of Luxor's inhabitants—and an estimated ten million Egyptians nationwide—had been involved in the tourist trade.

For tourism was not only Egypt's number one source of foreign currency; it had been expected to bring in a desperately needed $3 billion in 1998. Its plummeting fortunes could shave as much as a full percentage point off what was expected to be an annual economic growth rate of 5 percent. Thanks largely to intervention by the International Monetary Fund, Egypt's moribund economy had finally begun to turn around and was in its best shape in years. All of that, of course, was before the Luxor massacre. And it was also before an attack two months earlier, with guns and gasoline bombs, on a tour bus in front of Cairo's Egyptian Museum, in which nine German tourists were killed; and before yet another attack, eight months earlier, in which eighteen mostly elderly Greek tourists were shot dead, also in Cairo, near the ancient Pyramids.

But it was Luxor that was the turning point—not only in damaging the Egyptian economy but in traumatizing Hosni Mubarak's increasingly beleaguered Army-backed regime. For the massacre at Hatshepsut's burial ground raised new concerns, both in Washington and in other capitals around the world, about where Egypt is heading, about its future stability, and about its very identity. For the sheer survival of the Gama'a erodes Egypt's efforts to portray itself as the strongest, most dominant power in the Arab world, as Washington's most stable Middle Eastern ally, at the very time that the United States most needs its support to push the ossified Israeli-Palestinian peace process along.

Yet it is precisely those qualities that have made Mubarak's regime so attractive to the United States that have, over the years, made it suspect in the eyes of its own people, who see the U.S. role in the Middle East as a far too complacent one, and one in which Washington continues to show an astonishing lack of balance in its dealings with Israel and the Arab world. In the view of many Egyptians, the United States has taken the Arabs for granted and has assumed that their governments can control their populations. Luxor—coupled with daily anti-American and pro–Saddam Hussein demonstrations in Cairo in early 1998, when Washington was once again threatening to bomb Baghdad—clearly showed that Mubarak cannot.

It also often seems, to a growing number of Egyptians, Islamists and non-Islamists alike, that the United States raises questions about Egypt's abominable record on human rights only when it is displeased with Mubarak's failure to acquiesce to one of Washington's larger strategic priorities.

The Luxor massacre was a fitting final stop for my own journey through Egypt's world of militant Islam. I had first come to Cairo in the 1970s, when the present movement—of Gama'a and al-Jihad—was born; when the older militant movement, the Muslim Brotherhood, began to transform itself into the moderate voice of Egypt's political Islam. The events of 1979—the peace treaty between Egypt and Israel, the Ayatollah's victory in Iran, and the Soviet invasion of Afghanistan—forever changed the tapestry of the Middle East. And without the events of 1979 it would have been nearly impossible for a Luxor massacre to have occurred. For, as those events shaped everything else, so they shaped the world of Egypt's militant Islam. Opposition to the Camp David peace treaty bonded the Islamists and the Marxists for the first time, and that bonding considerably broadened the Islamists' secular base. The Ayatollah Khomeini's triumph in Iran emboldened the Islamists even more. And their foreign bank accounts began to swell as a result of unprecedented funding from Saudi Arabia and the Gulf, which began—as did their military training on some of the world's most sophisticated arms and their establishment of support networks scattered around the globe—during the jihad in Afghanistan.

Ironically, it was the very strength of the Islamists in the mid-1990s, moderate and militant alike, that forced them ever further underground, since it was their strength that precipitated the government crackdown. For in a closed political system like Mubarak's Egypt and much of the Middle East, which boasts the longest-serving rulers in the world—proof against any accounting or retribution for the frivolities and the crimes they have inflicted on their own people—there was no room for dissent. Thus, as the power of the Islamists grew and led to their gaining control of the trade unions, the syndicates, the student unions, and the schools through free and fair elections—and, through infiltration, the judiciary, the bureaucracy, and the arts—Mubarak's autocratic regime grew alarmed. Thus the repression, the arrests, the torture, and the trials. In such circumstances, terror is bound to gravitate toward its most extreme pole.

And that is why Luxor, again, was a turning point: not only because it portended a far more lethal agenda than any previously seen, or that it showed, in embarrassing clarity, how marginalized traditional leaders, including Mubarak, had become. But perhaps as important as anything else, its aftermath unveiled, in starker detail than at any previous time, the growing schisms within Mubarak's security establishment, most particularly between his army and his police. Army officers were outraged that the massacre was permitted to occur as the police, in spite of all their new and vastly expensive U.S.-supplied high-tech equipment and training, sat languidly on the

east bank of the Nile protecting their own generals, who were ensconced in large new villas, with large new cars. The security forces
in Upper Egypt had come to represent a force safeguarding not the
people or the tourists but the security apparatus of which they were
a part. They had been lavished with money and power, and had
been given a license to kill in their battle with the Islamist underground. Each of them had become a little Pharaoh. And Luxor was
a colossal failure on their part, a failure on the same scale as the
humiliating defeat of Egypt's Armed Forces by Israel during the
1967 Six-Day War. For what made the massacre—and the 1967
defeat—so painful to many Egyptians was not just its scale, or its
horror, but the fact that nobody expected it.

A year or so before the Luxor massacre, one Islamic militant
had told me that there was an operational scenario to commit such
an outrageous act that it would provoke the Army, which remains
Mubarak's only real constituency, to intervene on national security
grounds and unseat his regime. So one afternoon before coming to
Upper Egypt, as I sat with Dr. Sa'ad el-Din Ibrahim in his office at
the Ibn Khaldoun research center, high in the Mokattam Hills overlooking the suburbs of Cairo, I asked him if this seemed a plausible
explanation for the massacre.

He smiled and replied, "That is exactly what Mubarak
thought." He then went on to say that, for only the second time
since the Free Officers seized power in 1952, Mubarak had dispatched an active-duty army major general to Luxor, with the rank
normally accorded to a governor. He had also appointed three other
army generals to key positions in the south. "So the Islamists got
something close to what they wanted," he went on. "Not the way
they wanted it. But Mubarak brought in the Army precisely to pre-
empt your scenario. He's throwing the ball back to them; in a sense,
he's forcing their hand."

I couldn't help but wonder what the Army thought about the
ongoing guerrilla war now being played out in Upper Egypt between
the security forces and the Islamic militants. As recently as October
1996, during a monthlong battle in the Sohag mountain range, the
Army had declined to provide support to the security forces, which

suffered scores of casualties, a Western ambassador told me at the time. It was only after Mubarak personally intervened that a reluctant Army leadership agreed to dispatch its helicopters to evacuate the police.

Only twice in Egypt's modern history—in 1977 during the food riots and then again in 1986 during the riots by police recruits—had the Egyptian Army been brought into the streets in order to safeguard the country's presidency. Deploying, or even involving, the Army in his battle against the Islamist underground was something that Mubarak had avoided assiduously over the years. But now, with his appointments in the south, the Army had been brought in again. It was on a different and a smaller scale, but on a very significant scale.

As we continued chatting, Sa'ad el-Din smiled again. "You know," he told me, "on the surface it appears that it's Mubarak who's changing the Minister of the Interior [who had been forced to resign after the Luxor massacre.] But, in fact, it's the Islamists, not him. All three of our previous Ministers of the Interior who have been changed have been changed only because of something the Islamists did."

It was the blood feud between the Islamist underground and the security forces that produced Luxor, but it is what produced the blood feud that ultimately counts for more. And that has much less to do with Islam than it does with the social, economic, and political inequities that provided the Islamist groups with the impact they otherwise would not have had. For the movement, since its inception so many years ago, is at root, I remain convinced, a socioeconomic phenomenon—even secular, in a sense. And November's explosion of terror in Luxor can be seen as an indictment of the one-dimensional way in which Hosni Mubarak's government has responded to it.

Growing numbers of Egyptian intellectuals, among them Sa'ad el-Din Ibrahim, are convinced that the only way to stop the cycle of violence—and the fear of a repeat performance is great—is through dialogue and a power-sharing arrangement in which Mubarak's regime begins to work with the nonviolent Islamist groups. Only then will it be able to fully isolate, both politically and operationally, the underground militants. The Muslim Brotherhood, in their view—and mine—must be legalized, and the sincerity of Gama'a's cease-fire call must be tested by the regime. Luxor may have made this more difficult, but it has also made it more imperative.

"The Islamists are at the gate, knocking frantically, for inclusion, inclusion in the decision-making process, and the government must let them in," Sa'ad el-Din said. "There are parallels in sixteenth-century Europe; we, as Muslims, are simply four centuries behind. The Egyptian state has got to get its act together; it is a strong state—we're not a banana republic—and the state will prevail. But since 1974, with the mutiny at the Military Academy and the beginning of [the extremist Muslim sect] the Gama'a al-Takfir wal-Hijra, we have seen the same pattern: the government is taken by surprise by a military attack, it reacts, and it prevails. Then, for a year or two, there is relative calm, but it is only a temporary calm, because the state has never tackled the root causes of the revolt. Let the gates be opened: let Egypt's Islamists become the Christian Democrats of Germany. It has happened in Jordan, in Turkey, in Yemen, and in Lebanon. When the Muslim Brotherhood, following the elections of 1984 and 1987"—even though it was not permitted to stand as the Brotherhood, but contested seats instead in alliance with parties that are avowedly socialist or avowedly centrist—"led the parliamentary opposition, it performed very well and also very moderately. It is high time that this regime allowed it to participate in the political process, the economic process. It must be brought into the mainstream of Egyptian life." He thought for a moment, and then he said, "For if it is not, this war will go on, and like our own Army's defeat in 1967 and its victory in 1973, there is now a new dimension involved in the underground: they're stronger; they're more sophisticated; and they have more firepower than they used to have. They have *got* to be isolated, by opening the gates and bringing the moderates in."

But part of the problem is that Mubarak himself sees no political differences among the Islamists. "Mubarak has a mind-set against these groups, and he lumps them all together, insisting that they all come from the same tent," a Western ambassador explained. "He is totally unprepared to make a distinction between the militants and the moderates. The Egyptians tell us that if they hold free elections, the Islamic militants will win. They tell us that if they sell off the state industries and throw people out of work, there will be riots and the Islamists will gain even more support. And they tell us that if they devalue the currency, their economy will collapse and the Islamists will win again. And"—he paused for a moment—"all of this is true."

Mohamed Sid-Ahmed, the leftist commentator, remarked to me one afternoon that Mubarak, in his view, is more afraid of the moderate Islamists than of the militants. "He sees them as a Trojan horse," Sid-Ahmed said, "and his government knows that they are the best-placed party in Egypt to become the majority party if our elections were ever free and fair and if the moderate Islamists were not treated differently from the rest. When I last saw Mubarak at the Book Fair, and he wanted to hear my paradoxical views, I told him that instead of clamping down on the Islamists, he should have a constructive dialogue. He became quite harsh, and he said to me, 'I will not accept religious parties!' And I replied that as a leftist I, too, was against religious parties in principle, but that they presented assets as well as liabilities. If we have the Muslim Brotherhood, let the Copts have their own party. The two sides will work out an institutional arrangement, you'll see. Mubarak thought for a moment and then he said, 'I will not repeat the experience of Algeria here!' He just didn't seem to grasp the fact that the events in Algeria occurred precisely because its Islamists were shut out of the political process." After a pause he went on: "If there is to be change, it will only come through the pressure, or the wisdom, of the Egyptian Army. And only twice in the last half century has there been Army intervention in arriving at a political conclusion: the first was by Gamal Abdel Nasser, a socialist; the second by Lieutenant Khaled al-Islambouli, an Islamist."

There were many Egyptians who believed that the time had come for their Army—the country's most prestigious institution—to express itself politically, since Mubarak refused to share power with anyone else. His regime had become increasingly torpid, and although his military appointments in Upper Egypt, following the Luxor massacre, had slightly broadened its base, for many this was not enough. The main problem with this scenario, however, was that nobody knew for certain where the Egyptian Army stood. Certainly the military, including the officer corps, had become more conservative in its makeup over recent years, but aside from knowing that, we all had a tendency to read tea leaves: How many generals made the hajj, or pilgrimage to Mecca? How many of their wives were veiled? For Egypt's generals were disinclined to discuss their views with academics or intellectuals or Western diplomats; and they most certainly were disinclined to discuss them with the press.

It was therefore with some trepidation that I called on Major General Selmy Sleem, the newly appointed president of the Supreme Council of Luxor, in effect its governor.

Luxor, a few years ago, had become an autonomous city; hence the confusion in the title of the position that he held. He was technically the mayor, but the post was comparable to that of a governor, and it held cabinet rank. It also would have been considered an affront to have named the seventh-ranking officer in the Egyptian Armed Forces to a mayoralty post. So it was decided that General Sleem would be the president of the Supreme Council of Luxor. Since his arrival, two months earlier, his office staff had printed up three different sets of business cards.

General Sleem, who is in his late fifties, is a career military man who served most recently as the commander of the Central Military Zone, which is headquartered in Cairo. As an active-duty general, he was highly regarded in his job, and was considered to be a soldier's soldier, one of the best generals in the Egyptian Army. A tall and well-proportioned man, he walked with a general's gait as he strode across his office to greet me and shake my hand. He then invited me to sit on an overstuffed sofa, next to the companion armchair on which he sat.

Only a few weeks earlier, the police had opened fire on the villagers of Gourna—the same villagers who, at the risk of their lives, had pursued the gunmen in black into the Valley of the Queens—

in order to enforce a government order to demolish "illegal" houses near archaeological sites. The melee, on January 17, was two months to the day after the Luxor massacre. Now the villagers themselves were being treated as terrorists by the police. Four were killed and twenty-nine were wounded as they attempted to protect their homes by throwing stones at the security men. The police had been nowhere near Hatshepsut's burial ground; now they appeared eager to overreact. General Sleem was furious. He was quoted in the Egyptian press as saying that the heavy-handed police action was not authorized, and he intimated that it was meant to embarrass him. The friction between Mubarak's police and his army appeared to be on the rise.

So I asked the general how bad the relationship between the two services was.

He responded without answering: "I think I have said quite enough on that subject." And then he smiled.

"But you certainly must concede that the Luxor massacre was a colossal failure on the part of the police—" I began.

He interrupted. "You said it, I didn't."

He then went on to say that his appointment, two weeks after the massacre, had been a surprise to him, and that he was given only twenty-four hours to retire from the Army, in which he had served for thirty-five years and for which he had traveled around the world, having trained at the most prestigious schools, including the War College in Carlisle, Pennsylvania. His son, a police officer, was "teaching" him police work, he said.

"Governors of Luxor have always been civilians, retired police officers, or retired army generals," I said. "You were an active-duty officer. Does your appointment portend a more significant role for the Army in the decision-making process? In taking control of law and order in Upper Egypt?"

He thought for a moment, and then he smiled. "Ask the President."

"But if you were making decisions, what would you do?" I persisted.

He replied, "The massacre, the inhumanity of it, could have happened anywhere, under different names, and whether these groups are religious or not, they're outside the law. It happened here this time; it has happened in the United States. And we have got to unite against terrorism, and against those people who are helping these groups, whether it be financial support or giving them safe havens and hideouts. The leaders in England, in Peshawar and Afghanistan, in the Sudan and the United States, have got to be stopped."

"So you consider this to be a law-and-order problem?" I asked.

"Absolutely not. The government has ignored Upper Egypt for years. This is not just a law-and-order problem. It's complex. It's economic and social."

I was astonished. This is what my Egyptian friends and I thought, but it was totally contrary to the official pronouncements of the Mubarak government.

"No incident, no problem, has only one reason," General Sleem went on. "It's a number of factors coming together, and it's the root causes that have got to be addressed. Something that's always been curious to me is that it's always the south; not just in Egypt, but in the United States, in Italy and Spain. There's always the difference between the north and the south. The north lives in its richness; the south in its poverty. But in Egypt the divide is considerably worse."

He called for tea and coffee, but drank none himself, explaining that he was fasting, since it was Ramadan.

Before leaving, I asked General Sleem, as a military man, what he thought about Gama'a's cease-fire call, which the government had alternately derided and ignored. "Should it have been taken more seriously? Was there a need to negotiate?"

"Whatever I thought before, I don't now," he replied. "Not after Luxor. Luxor was a watershed. Violence destroys, it doesn't build. And Luxor was a totally new thing. We have not seen this kind of violence since [the High Priest of] Amon"—whose usurpation of the Pharaonic throne led to the division of Upper and Lower Egypt in 1085 B.C. General Sleem fell silent, and then he went on: "Negotiations can only take place now with those who give up their fanatic ideology. Whoever supports violence and the gun cannot get involved in negotiations. So what I am saying is, as a first step, let them renounce violence; let them lay down their arms. And then let them come to the negotiating table. In a democracy there are many different opinions, many gradations of thought. A democracy does not mean that you impose your own opinion on others. You talk; you negotiate. And the Egyptian people hate this violence. We have got to negotiate."

Nearly everyone I met in Upper Egypt offered a sad story or issued an appeal: Find my son. Find my father. Give me back my land. I heard the stories over and over again. For it is the people of Upper Egypt, more than any others in this ancient land, who every day are torn between official repression and Islamist militancy. It is difficult to determine which side they fear more, but I suspect, having listened to their stories, that it is the security forces, who came here from the north: an army of occupation, in their view, whose officers and men neither spoke their language nor understood their concerns.

Their faces remain clear in my mind, as my own journey through their world comes to an end. I remember the old woman in Gourna, dressed in a black abaya, her bony face framed by a white scarf, who asked me, almost rhetorically, as we sat in Gourna's tiny tea shop that late January afternoon: "Which side is worse? The militants killed tourism and deprived my son of his income from a tourist shop in the bazaar. The security forces burned my husband's land. We had less than an acre, but it's all we had. Why didn't they just pull up the sugarcane crop? Or cut it down? Why burn it and destroy the land? The land lies fallow now. For at least two seasons, nothing will grow."

I also remember the face of a young man, a high-school student, perhaps sixteen, who one day may don a black shirt and trousers and travel to another temple, or to an airport, or to a tourist site. He reminded me of another young man I'd met, in a military courtroom in Cairo, soon after this last phase of my own journey began. He was also sixteen, and was dressed in a white robe and clutched a Koran in his hand as he stood inside a security cage. He had been charged in the same case as Bestawi Abdel-Meguid—the attack against the German tour bus in Qena, six years ago. "Don't ask me what I did. Ask me why I did it," he'd said to me then. A few months later, he was hanged.

When I look back on all the faces now, and recall all the stories I've heard, I realize that the six young gunmen in black who went to Hatshepsut's burial ground are the third generation of the revolt that began during my student days. They had been too young to have been involved in the assassination of Sadat; too young to have fought in Afghanistan. I wondered how long the war would go on, and whether or not it would also involve their sons.

But when I look back on my most recent journey, through Upper Egypt's villages and towns, it is a place called Abu Shusha that I remember the most. It is a sad and forgotten place, perhaps fifteen minutes or so from the Qena border, hugging the Sohag mountain range. I had arrived there with my security escort just after dusk. Ramadan had ended, and *iftar*, the evening meal breaking the fast, had just begun. As we pulled into the Abu Shusha checkpoint, my security cars sped off. The security men patrolling the area didn't know I was coming; their radio equipment was down; and they had no orders. I was not permitted to leave without "proper protection," and thus I remained for two hours and twenty minutes in the middle of nowhere—a place of harsh openness, of sand, rock, and wind. Aside from the checkpoint, there was nothing else around except a fruit-and-vegetable stand a few yards away and, across the road, a small whitewashed mosque.

I had heard so much about the abuses of the security men that I did not relish spending the evening with them. In my boredom, I counted them; there were thirty-two. They came in all shapes and sizes—some in the uniforms of the regular police; some in battle gear (special forces, I thought); still others were in civilian clothes, mostly form-fitting black jeans; most of them wore Reeboks and exceedingly dark Ray-Ban sunglasses, even though the desert night was already exceedingly dark. They all bonded together in their arrogance.

Their walkie-talkies were U.S.-supplied, as were their jeeps and a squat blue vehicle with gun emplacements on either side. I couldn't tell if it was meant to be facing the highway or the mosque.

The Qena police refused to cross the border to pick me up, one of the officers said, and my police escort, which had abandoned me, had gone home for *iftar*. It became one of the longest evenings of my life. I was being held, for all intents and purposes, in "protective custody."

As I waited, vigilantes came in from the desert and the mountain just beyond and returned their weapons to the men in jeans. I had heard that the security forces were arming such groups, as had human rights organizations in Cairo, but they had not been able to confirm the existence of these armed bands, who roamed the mountains and deserts taking the law into their own hands. Now they passed by me, one by one: old men with rifles; young men with whips and staves; others with pistols. They would return in the morning to get the weapons back.

I looked across the road at the desert, silent and empty now. Lights twinkling in the distance spoke of a village beyond. The only sounds were those of the wind and the chants of a muezzin calling the faithful to evening prayers from the tiny mosque.

The security men strutted back and forth, stopping carts, wagons, and trucks that were transporting fruits and vegetables, including the small crop of sugarcane left in Upper Egypt, to markets in faraway Cairo. They nearly dismantled the vehicles, unnecessarily, I thought, including one of an old man who was driving an open-backed truck. "Take it out," one of the security men demanded. The old man, hunched and bent, removed his sugarcane stalks one by one and laid them on the road. His small frame moved rhythmically up and down. The mosque emptied, and twenty or so men, all dressed in galabiyas, with white crocheted prayer caps on their heads, stood across the road from me, their arms folded across their chests, and we all continued to watch the bent old man.

"Faster, faster," the security man in black jeans roared.

The old man struggled, and he slipped.

The security man kicked him. "Faster, I said."

I lost my temper. "Stop it!" I screamed.

The security man in the black jeans and Ray-Bans turned to me and laughed.

I had disliked him from the beginning, and I wondered if all the security men who had come south were as imperially Pharaonic as he was.

He had insisted earlier, when we first arrived, that I join him in his barracks. I had refused, and told him that I would prefer sitting in my taxi, or standing along the road, which I continued to do as the night passed.

How ironic, I thought. I had been welcomed into so many Egyptian homes, into so many mosques. So many people had shared their stories, and their lives, with me. And here I was, standing alone on a desert road on the last journey I would make, in a place called Abu Shusha, which I never wanted to visit again.

I thought of all the people who had helped me along the way on this journey of mine. Miss Pennypecker, of course, had died, but there were no traces of her grave. Nadine had disappeared, probably somewhere here in Upper Egypt—happily married with children, I hope—manning a machine-gun nest. Abdel-Nebi Khalifa, the "Afghan Arab" whom I had hoped to meet in Kasr al-Ayni Hospital, had also disappeared. And all of the prisoners whom Ali Ismail had told me about—along with thousands of others—remained in jail.

I looked across the highway at the men from the mosque, who stood in a neat row, staring at me as I stood alone. Then one of them, a wizened old man with white stubble on his chin, walked across the road and handed me an orange.

"Masallem"—"Go with God"—he said.

The desert wind had become harsh, and it was bitterly cold. The security men behind me sat around electric heaters powered by a generator, supplied by the United States. I listened to the desert; even its silence had a voice. And then I saw two little boys leave the fruit-and-vegetable stand next door, lugging a wooden chair. They pulled it along the highway until they reached the spot where I stood. The older one, who was perhaps six, looked up at me and said, "Sit, madame. Please sit."